Imagining Xerxes

Bloomsbury Studies in Classical Reception

Bloomsbury Studies in Classical Reception presents scholarly monographs offering new and innovative research and debate to students and scholars in the reception of Classical Studies. Each volume will explore the appropriation, reconceptualization and recontextualization of various aspects of the Graeco-Roman world and its culture, looking at the impact of the ancient world on modernity. Research will also cover reception within antiquity, the theory and practice of translation, and reception theory.

Also available in the Series:

Ancient Magic and the Supernatural in the Modern Visual and Performing Arts, edited by Filippo Carlà and Irene Berti

Greek and Roman Classics in the British Struggle for Social Change, edited by Henry Stead and Edith Hall

Ovid's Myth of Pygmalion on Screen, Paula James

Victorian Classical Burlesques, Laura Monrós-Gaspar

Imagining Xerxes: Ancient Perspectives on a Persian King

Emma Bridges

Bloomsbury Academic
An imprint of Bloomsbury Publishing Plc

B L O O M S B U R Y
LONDON • NEW DELHI • NEW YORK • SYDNEY

Bloomsbury Academic

An imprint of Bloomsbury Publishing Plc

50 Bedford Square   1385 Broadway
London   New York
WC1B 3DP   NY 10018
UK   USA

www.bloomsbury.com

BLOOMSBURY and the Diana logo are trademarks of Bloomsbury Publishing Plc

Hardback edition published 2015
This paperback edition published 2015

British Library Cataloguing-in-Publication Data
A catalogue record for this book is available from the British Library.

ISBN: HB: 978-1-47251-427-1
PB: 978-1-47426-072-5
ePDF: 978-1-47251-137-9
ePub: 978-1-47251-132-4

Library of Congress Cataloging-in-Publication Data
Bridges, Emma.
Imagining Xerxes : ancient perspectives on a Persian king / Emma Bridges.
pages cm. – (Bloomsbury studies in classical reception)
Includes bibliographical references and index.
ISBN 978-1-4725-1427-1 (hardback) ePDF – ISBN 978-1-4725-1137-9 (ePDF) –
ISBN 978-1-4725-1132-4 (ePub) 1. Xerxes I, King of Persia, 519 B.C.-465 B.C.
or 464 B.C. 2. Greece–History–Persian Wars, 500-449 B.C.–Historiography.
3. Iran–Kings and rulers–Biography. I. Title.
DS283.B75 2014
935'.705092–dc23
2014020188

Series: Bloomsbury Studies in Classical Reception

Typeset by Newgen Knowledge Works (P) Ltd., Chennai, India
Printed and bound in Great Britain

For my parents, with love and thanks

Contents

List of Illustrations and Photographs

Illustrations

Photographs

Note on Translations, Illustrations and Abbreviations

Translations are my own, unless otherwise stated. Translations of Persian inscriptions in Chapter 3 are from A. Kuhrt, *The Persian Empire: A Corpus of Sources from the Achaemenid Period* (Routledge: London and New York 2007), and are reproduced by kind permission of the publisher.

Chapter frontispieces were illustrated by Asa Taulbut. Plates 1 and 3 are original drawings created by the artist; others are based on the images referred to in the captions. Photographs in Chapter 3 (Figures 1 and 2) are reproduced courtesy of the Oriental Institute of the University of Chicago.

Abbreviations of the names of ancient authors and texts follow those used in the *Oxford Classical Dictionary*. Standard abbreviations are used for modern texts. Persian inscriptions discussed in Chapter 3 are referred to by the abbreviations used in Kent (1953) and Kuhrt (2007).

Acknowledgements

This book started life as a doctoral thesis written at the University of Durham and funded with the support of a Durham University Research Studentship and the Ralph Lindsay Scholarship. My doctoral supervisors, Edith Hall and Peter Rhodes, have continued to show their unfailing generosity in sharing their time and their wisdom, as well as in providing moral support and advice. I am especially grateful that both accepted and supported my decision to prioritize family life over academic pursuits for a time during the decade since the completion of the thesis, and yet unquestioningly resumed their roles as mentors when I was ready to take up the challenge of writing this volume. Edith's gentle yet firm encouragement inspired my decision to resume research; for this, and much else, it is no exaggeration to say that I will be forever in her debt. Both she and Peter offered comments on a complete draft of the finished work; as ever, I have benefited enormously from their combined expertise and their differing yet complementary approaches to the study of the ancient world.

The final version of the book has also been shaped along the way by the input of several other individuals and institutions. My examiners, Chris Pelling and Peter Heslin, offered invaluable insights which led me to think about the material in new ways; Chris has since then been a continuing source of support, and provided incisive comments upon Chapters 2 and 6. At the proposal stage Bloomsbury's anonymous referees offered detailed feedback and pertinent suggestions which enabled me to refine my thinking, and as the manuscript neared completion I was most grateful for the attention to detail exercised by a meticulous peer reviewer, who saved me from numerous errors. Charlotte Loveridge at Bloomsbury was a patient and enthusiastic supporter of the project from the outset, and Anna MacDiarmid provided invaluable assistance as the work went into production. As a part-time Associate Lecturer at the Open University, I have been fortunate to be able to indulge my love of things classical while still devoting time to raising a young family under sometimes challenging circumstances; the enthusiasm of my student cohorts continues to inspire me and to enrich my appreciation and understanding of the ancient world. Meanwhile I have also benefited greatly from the expertise and good humour of the staff at the British Library Document Supply Centre at Boston Spa;

without this invaluable facility in Yorkshire the pursuit of my research would undoubtedly have been far more difficult and drawn-out. In the final stages of the writing process Asa Taulbut offered up his time and his remarkable talent to produce the illustrations at very short notice; I valued greatly the opportunity to share ideas with him as well as his capacity to create beautiful visual representations of those ideas.

Several others also deserve credit for their role in developing more broadly my own ability and self-confidence as a classical scholar. The roots of my enthusiasm for the classical world were first planted by Ken Parham of Durham Sixth Form Centre and later nurtured at Brasenose College, Oxford, by Ed Bispham, Llewelyn Morgan, the late Leighton Reynolds, and Greg Woolf. I am indebted to each of them for their encouragement and their faith in me, and can only hope that the present work proves that faith to have been justified.

That this volume has eventually come to fruition is due in no small part to the love and understanding of my family, whose presence is my anchor. My husband David has wholeheartedly supported the project; along with our children, Charlotte and Joseph, he has patiently endured my preoccupation with Xerxes for the past year. My parents, Margaret and Terry Clough, provided the foundation upon which all that I have achieved has been built. As always, they have been an unfailing source of support – both emotional and practical – throughout this process yet, with their customary kindness and modesty, expect nothing in return. It is to them that this book is gratefully dedicated.

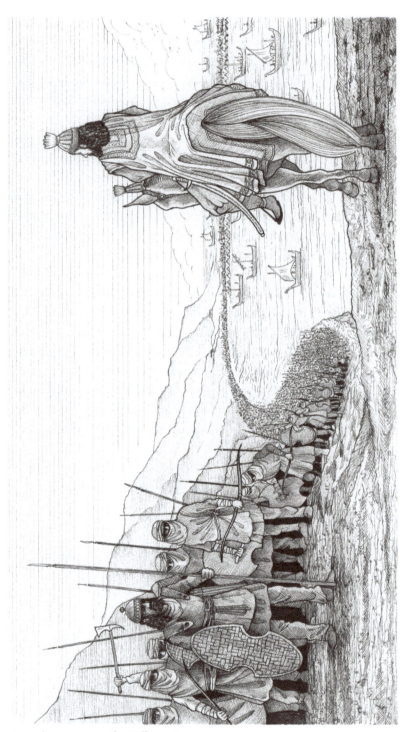

1. *Xerxes' army crosses the Hellespont*

Introduction: Encountering Xerxes

When in 480 BC Xerxes crossed the Hellespont from Asia into Greece, he stepped simultaneously into the imagination of the Greeks whose homeland he endeavoured to conquer. The bridge of boats across which his vast army marched (Plate 1) would become an enduring symbol of the transgression of a boundary – both physical and moral – by an arrogant king who dared to defy the will of the gods in his attempt to join two continents. The course of events which followed – first documented at length by Herodotus and retold in abbreviated form by successive generations of Greek writers – is familiar to those with even a passing acquaintance of Greek history of the period, although the precise details are often the source of scholarly conjecture. Although many Greeks surrendered to the invaders, the advance of the Persian hordes through Greece was blocked at the pass of Thermopylae by a small band of troops led by the Spartans under their king, Leonidas, and vastly outnumbered by Xerxes' army; the Spartans who fought there were assured of immortality in commemorative traditions which would portray their defeat at the hands of the Persians as a heroic stand for Greek freedom. A simultaneous naval engagement at Artemisium proved indecisive when storms beset the fleet, but the ensuing clash at Salamis was to be the battle in which the Greeks – under the leadership of the Athenian general Themistocles – achieved their most celebrated naval victory against Xerxes' fleet. That was not before the king's army had ransacked an abandoned Athens and torched the Acropolis, however; this particular act of irreverence – repeated in 479 by the remnants of the king's army – would live long in the collective memory. After his failure at Salamis the king himself withdrew to Persia, leaving behind his general Mardonius in charge of an army which would suffer its final defeat at the hands of a Greek force at Plataea in 479 BC. Plataea marked the end of Xerxes' attempts to gain military domination over

Greece; for the victorious Greeks, however, their defeat of Xerxes would become a defining moment in their history, and the memory of this glorious triumph would endure for centuries.[1]

Their struggle against Xerxes was not the mainland Greeks' first encounter with a mighty Asiatic foe; ten years previously, the Athenians and their Plataean allies had secured at Marathon a decisive victory over the Persian force sent to Greece by Xerxes' father Darius. Yet, where Xerxes set foot on the Hellenic soil which he intended to claim as his own – and in the course of his expedition committed the ultimate act of desecration in burning the sacred buildings of Athens – Darius had remained in Persia and instead sent his generals to carry out his campaign. As a result it was Xerxes, not his father, who subsequently entered into the Greek cultural encyclopaedia both as the archetypal destructive and enslaving eastern king and as a symbol of the exotic decadence, wealth and power of the Persian court. The narratives of his exploits are rich in motifs and episodes with which he came to be associated: the whipping and branding of the sacred Hellespont which mirrored both his mission as would-be enslaver and his brutal treatment of subordinates; his awe-inspiring army which was said to have drunk dry the rivers on its journey to Greece; the elaborate throne from which he observed his troops in battle; and the sexual politics of his palace, to name a few. The king himself, whose defeat at Salamis would be for the Greeks a lasting cause for celebration, was a figure who could inspire both fear and hatred, and whose image would at the same time become a source of enduring fascination in a literary tradition whose echoes would continue to resonate for centuries. The central concern of this volume is to explore the richness and variety of Xerxes' afterlives within the ancient literary tradition.

The historical encounter between Xerxes and the Greeks has been the focus for several recent scholarly endeavours, with attention being paid to particular texts[2] or episodes[3] in which Xerxes features; meanwhile other works have unpicked the sources to evaluate the historical accuracy of the accounts of

---

[1]   On the broader traditions relating to the commemoration of the Persian Wars as a whole see Clough (2003), pp. 25–32. Bridges, Hall and Rhodes (2007) provide a series of case studies which demonstrate the richness and diversity of responses to the Persian invasions since antiquity.

[2]   For example, recent editions of Aeschylus' *Persians* (Garvie, 2009) and Ctesias' *Persica* (Stronk, 2010; Llewellyn-Jones and Robson, 2010) and recent commentaries upon books of Herodotus dealing with Xerxes' expedition (Flower and Marincola, 2002, on Book 9; A. M. Bowie, 2007, on Book 8) as well as a new English translation of his work (Holland and Cartledge, 2013).

[3]   On Salamis, see Strauss (2004); on Thermopylae, Cartledge (2006).

his invasion,[4] collated and analysed the sources for Achaemenid Persia,[5] or provided an insight into scholarly analysis of Persian history.[6] While the process of disentangling the ancient testimonies in order to establish a narrative of Xerxes' reign and his invasion of his Greece is a rich field for study, however, my concern here is not to produce a biographical account or a cohesive picture of the 'real' historical king who spearheaded the second Persian invasion of Greece. Instead it is to draw together for comparative analysis the range of literary approaches to the figure of this king with a view to considering the ways in which these adaptations and deformations of the Xerxes-traditions – from the earliest appearance of Xerxes on the tragic stage in 472 BC and the portrayal of his character in Herodotus' fifth-century historiographical narrative to the biographical works of the Roman tradition and the moralizing texts of the Second Sophistic – were shaped by the diverse contexts within which they were produced. These successive re-imaginings from a variety of cultural and historical perspectives demonstrate that the figure of the king who played such a key role in events of the fifth century BC inspired an astonishing array of responses; in this sense the 'real' historical Xerxes has become inseparable from the literary character(s) who developed in his wake.

The earliest surviving cultural response to the figure of Xerxes is that seen in Aeschylus' *Persians*, his tragic drama of 472 BC which envisaged the reaction at the Persian court to the news of the defeat at Salamis and culminated with the return of the king himself, in rags and with a mere fraction of his vast army, to Susa. The reversal of fortune of this theatrical Xerxes and his transformation from intimidating aggressor to wretched failure acted as a reminder to the Athenians of their celebrated achievement in driving back the Persian foe. My first chapter investigates the ways in which Aeschylus' text assimilated the Persian king into this extraordinary piece of tragic theatre – the only extant Athenian tragedy based on a historical, rather than a mythical, theme – within which an actor was called upon to assume the guise of Athens' great barbarian adversary. While Aeschylus' text begins with the Chorus' remembered image of Xerxes as terrifying invader in the parodos, this picture is gradually eroded throughout the course of the play as the scale of the disaster at Salamis is revealed. Aeschylus uses the perspectives of the other characters in his

---

[4] Wallinga (2005).

[5] Briant's monumental 2002 work on Achaemenid Persia remains the most comprehensive study of the sources for Xerxes' reign. Kuhrt (2007) provides an exhaustive collection of the ancient sources in English translation.

[6] Harrison (2011). On the evolution of Achaemenid scholarship since the advent of the Achaemenid History Workshops in the late 1970s see further p. 75 below.

drama – the Queen, the messenger and the ghost of Darius – to build up the spectators' anticipation of the eventual appearance of the king himself. In doing so he draws on a series of striking images: the Queen's dream, which allegorizes Xerxes' failed mission and foreshadows his desolation upon his return to Susa; the messenger's report of the scene at Salamis, in which he describes the watching king's reaction to the defeat; and the rich and exotic appearance of the ghost of Darius, who represents here a contrasting model of successful Persian kingship against which Xerxes' failure is measured. The arrival of Xerxes himself, distraught and in rags, is the play's climactic moment, in which the king performs a sung lament; the full spectacle of his humiliation is thus played out on stage before the audience. A sung lament by the king would also feature in a later poetic and performative response to Xerxes; Timotheus of Miletus' late fifth-/early fourth-century BC citharodic nome was also entitled *Persians*, but represented an art form very different from the tragic drama of Aeschylus. This interpretation of the aftermath of the Persian defeat at Salamis – by a poet who in his time was thought of as a musical revolutionary – demanded a performer's sung impersonation of the imagined words of Xerxes in his melodramatic response to the destruction of his fleet. Chapter 1 also looks at the relationship between Timotheus' composition and Aeschylus' play, as well as considering the possible influence of the Xerxes-image upon the comic barbarians of Aristophanes' plays.

While the negative image of Xerxes as marauding invader would come to dominate many later interpretations of the king's persona, it is also possible to find strands of the Xerxes-tradition which look beyond this image of an irascible and impious despot in order to reflect upon other elements of his imagined character. As early as the *Histories* of Herodotus we encounter him as a more human figure, one susceptible to the vacillations of fortune and at the mercy of the course of history as well as deeply conscious of his position within the Persian royal dynasty. This Xerxes is epitomized in the scene early in Herodotus' seventh book which takes place at Abydus before the invasion of Greece: having surveyed the scale of the huge military force under his command, the king at first congratulates himself on this affirmation of his power but then, in a flash of insight which encapsulates a key theme of Herodotus' text and transcends any notion of a polarity between Greeks and barbarians, weeps as he acknowledges the transient nature of human existence. Chapter 2 considers the ways in which Herodotus' narrative weaves a complex picture of Xerxes and utilizes this king in order to exemplify one of the underlying ethical premises of his work – that human fortune does not reside for long in one place – as well as considering how the *Histories* might use the story of Xerxes as a way of reflecting upon the political realities of Herodotus' own day. It is also in Herodotus' text that we find the beginnings of a strand of the Xerxes-tradition which looks beyond his invasion of Greece and ventures behind the closed doors of the Persian court to explore the personal rivalries, sexual scandal and political intrigue within the king's harem. This interest in Persian 'harem politics' was to inspire a whole swathe of later texts and demonstrates that the boundary between historiography and what we might now describe as 'romantic fiction' was far from clear-cut in the ancient literary tradition.

Although these earliest Greek traditions and many of their literary descendants were inspired by Xerxes' invasion of Greece, it is striking that no surviving source from Persia itself makes any reference to this military campaign which took place on what was the western fringe of the Persian empire. This omission acts as a reminder that the dominant verdict upon the king, as pronounced by western society, is largely coloured by the response of that society to his military campaign. An analysis of the contemporary Persian sources for Xerxes thus allows us to unearth an entirely different perspective upon his reign; it is this perspective which is the subject of Chapter 3. The Achaemenid Persian sources differ from the Greek texts in both their emphasis and their form; here we find not literary narratives but instead material evidence in the shape of boastful official inscriptions and the sculptural decoration which adorned the royal palaces of Persepolis and Susa. An analysis of this source material provides a picture of the way in which the projected ideology of the Achaemenid kings – developed during Darius' reign and appropriated by his son and later successors – shaped the image of Xerxes which was communicated to his subjects and to posterity. Here the emphasis is overwhelmingly upon continuity with the past and the eternal tenets of Persian kingship rather than upon the specific character traits of the individual monarchs. This imagining of the king's character emerges as having been as much a construct, and a product of its cultural and political backdrop, as the western retellings of his story.

My fourth chapter returns to the Greek tradition, moving forward in time to the fourth century BC and a Greece which was increasingly fragmented in political terms. Within the body of extant Athenian literature from this period the Persian Wars are still a pervasive presence – forming in particular a significant part of the catalogue of Athenian exploits in the *epitaphioi* (funeral orations) – as a result, at least in part, of the presence of Persia as a player on the Greek political stage from the late fifth century onwards. We also detect here an interest in developing ideas about kingship; references to the government of

Persia feature in fourth-century texts as part of broader discussions of the nature of power and political theory. While several writers display an awareness that the theme of Athenian resistance to Persia was by now something of a cliché, in this new political context the most prominent vision of Xerxes which we see here is that of the great panhellenic foe. For some, like Lysias, the memory of resistance to this archetypal foreign enemy was a reminder of Athens' glorious past; others – most prominent among them the orator Isocrates – used the spectre of Xerxes in their own anti-Persian rhetoric, conflating him with the Persian rulers of their own day as a means of advocating a new expedition against the Persians which would serve to unite the disparate and warring Greek states. Here we find a much-reduced literary portrait of Xerxes which relies on a repertoire of key elements of the tradition to serve writers' rhetorical purposes: the king is identified by his extreme anger and impiety, and motifs symbolizing his attempted enslavement of Greece (for example, the Hellespont bridge) loom large in accounts of his invasion. This was a brand of rhetoric which would also later be taken up by the Macedonian kings; for Alexander in particular Xerxes seems to have become the focal point of a propaganda campaign in which, in order to garner political support in Greece, he presented himself as leading a moral crusade to seek vengeance from Persia for past wrongs done to the Greeks. Chapter 4 demonstrates too, however, that the negative image of Persian kingship as personified by Xerxes was not the sole possible response to the Persian monarchy in this period; in particular Xenophon's *Cyropaedia*, a fictionalized biography of Xerxes' maternal grandfather Cyrus the Great, provides a eulogistic portrait of a ruler whose reign is seen there as the high point of imperial Persian history.

While for the orators of fourth-century Athens it was the image of Xerxes as the formidable panhellenic enemy which proved most useful, alternative strands of the tradition were being developed simultaneously by other writers. These versions of Xerxes, whose origins might be traced back to Herodotus' closing chapters, have as their common setting the king's court; they take their readers behind the closed doors of the Persian palace into an exotic and decadent world populated by influential women, eunuchs and powerful courtiers whose conflicting interests could lead to corruption and intrigue. Chapter 5 examines the array of prose narratives inspired by the theme of the Persian court; these texts, despite the disparate cultural milieux from which they originate, are united by a shared fascination with this indoor realm and by the position which they occupy at the interface between historiography and romantic fiction. This chapter begins with the fourth-century BC *Persica* of Ctesias of Cnidus whose role as doctor at the court of Artaxerxes II allowed him access to the Persian royal traditions which formed the basis of his narrative. It then considers the ways in which vase paintings of this period share an interest in conjuring up images of the Persian court before looking at the way in which a particular story – that of the adventures in Persia of the Athenian commander Themistocles after his ostracism by his countrymen – allows the reader of Diodorus' much later (first-century BC) historiographical account access to Xerxes' palace. It is not only in the Greek-derived traditions, however, that the Persian court occupies a prominent role. An examination of the Old Testament book of Esther demonstrates here that the palace of Xerxes (named Ahasuerus in the biblical version), with all its richness and decadence, could become the location for a story which originated in the Jewish tradition. This chapter ends by looking at other later imagined narratives – the Greek novel, and the ekphrasis-writing of Philostratus during the Second Sophistic – which, in their use of the Persian court setting, illustrate a far-reaching fascination with the motifs long since associated with the most notorious of the Achaemenid kings.

Even several centuries after the Persian invasions of Greece, at a time when the political world-map had been redrawn by the advance of Roman domination in the Mediterranean, the theme of Xerxes' aggression retained its appeal. Chapter 6 investigates the ways in which the image of Xerxes was revisited in a world ruled by Rome. It looks at the contexts within which the Romans, as the new world-conquerors, engaged with the broader Persian Wars traditions before examining the ways in which elements of the Xerxes-narrative feature in Latin literature (particularly in the rhetorical schools, as seen in the *suasoriae* of Seneca the Elder and compilations of rhetorical examples such as those produced by Valerius Maximus) as a moral paradigm, whether as providing negative *exempla* of the types of behaviour to be avoided by contemporary leaders or as illustrating a wider theme of the mutability of fortune. Within the context of the Roman tendency to look to the past for such *exempla* the recollection of Xerxes' arrogance and immorality also provided a point of comparison for the conduct of particular individuals; this is particularly apparent in the work of authors hostile to the emperor Caligula, who would himself become a stereotypical symbol of debased tyranny in the Roman historiographical tradition. Yet during the Roman period we also find a thought-provoking alternative to this casting of Xerxes as the definitive villain; in the works of the Jewish historian Josephus, Xerxes appears as a pious ruler who is fêted for his tolerance and support of the Jews in his empire. Josephus' Jewish perspective reminds us (like the Persian sources discussed in Chapter 3) of the extent to which the mainstream tradition was shaped by the responses of Greeks who bore the scars of Xerxes' invasion. This chapter looks also at the continuing presence of Xerxes in the collective consciousness of Greeks who lived under Roman rule, considering the ways in which references to Xerxes at a time when Greece was subject to a powerful foreign empire – that of Rome – might carry subversive undertones (as seen in, for example, the geographical writing of Pausanias) before examining Plutarch's more cautious use of the Xerxes-themes. Here we find a writer whose work demonstrates his awareness of the potential for negative comparisons between the Persian king and the Roman emperor in a period when the notion of the 'freedom of the Greeks' was a delicate one given the Greeks' subjection to the government at Rome. The chapter concludes by considering the way in which a Latin satirical take on Xerxes by Juvenal subverts the image of the king as an artificial literary construct.

The Xerxes-tradition did not evaporate with the decline of classical literature; far from it. In the post-classical period, the lasting appeal of the Persian Wars narratives has given rise to their treatment in diverse forms of literary and artistic media; representations of Xerxes have thus found their way into a staggering range of literary genres, artistic media and cultural settings up to the present day, from the earliest portrayals in fifth-century BC drama and historiography through to the most up-to-date elements of twenty-first-century mainstream culture including graphic novels, movies and video games. While exhaustive treatment of the multifarious post-classical responses to Xerxes falls outside the immediate scope of this volume, my epilogue looks at one specific example of the way in which Xerxes has been re-imagined in the modern world. By considering the presentation of the king in the 2007 film *300* and its 2014 follow-up *300: Rise of an Empire* it highlights both the continuing audience-appeal of Xerxes as a figure with the ability to fascinate and entertain and the ongoing capacity, almost 2,500 years after the historical Xerxes' invasion of Greece, of portrayals of his character to incite controversy.

The strands of the Xerxes-traditions explored in the chapters of this book reveal a Persian king who assumes multiple guises, each of them shaped in varying degrees by developing traditions and by the authorial choices of those who engaged in the act of imagining him for fresh audiences and in new historical and artistic contexts. For some he is the brutal despot at the head of a massive army, whose enslaving mission is reflected in his whipping of subordinates or his cruel mutilation of those who arouse his displeasure. Elsewhere he becomes the converse of this fearsome dictator, either as the wretched and lamenting king stripped of both his royal garb and his dignity, or as a casualty of the vacillations of fortune, driven back to his homeland humiliated and with only a single ship to carry him there. He can also be pensive, exchanging arrogant self-congratulation for a moment of contemplation which highlights a broader truth about human existence. In other contexts too he becomes part of a bigger picture – that of the dynasty into which he was born. Here he is his father's son and his grandfather's grandson, a representative of the unchanging values of the Achaemenid royal line and the upholder of stability and continuity for his subjects. On rare occasions Xerxes can be generous, pious and tolerant, dispensing largesse to those who seek his assistance. Meanwhile he is envisaged by others as enthroned in the inner chambers of his palace, a decadent playboy at the centre of a vision of lascivious sensuality, court intrigue and harem politics. This astounding array of images, with their potential for inspiring drama and romance, their ability to provoke reflection or criticism, and their capacity to educate and entertain, bears witness to the far-reaching literary impact of the Greeks' historical encounter with Xerxes.

2. *Atossa's dream*. Based on a 1778 sketch by George Romney

1

Staging Xerxes: Aeschylus and Beyond

The viewer of an artistic depiction of the dream-vision seen by Aeschylus' Persian queen (Plate 2, based on George Romney's 1778 sketch, 'Atossa's Dream')[1] could be forgiven for failing at first to identify the figure who lies prostrate in the foreground. Raising his hand to his head in a gesture of despair, and stripped bare of the rich royal garments which might provide clues about his status or identity, he lies humiliated and pathetic, cast out from his chariot and watched over by an anxious bearded spectator – the ghost of his father – who is powerless to intervene. The women who stand over him, personifications of Asia and Greece, are no longer restrained beneath the harness attached to his chariot; his attempt to join them together in subjection to his command has been catastrophically thwarted. The wretched character seen here – unrecognizable as the fearsome warring king who marched on Greece with a military force of millions at his disposal – is the imagined Xerxes whom Aeschylus chose to present to the audience of his *Persians*. He is a Xerxes created within the theatrical context of a tragic drama; pictured by the Chorus at the start of the play as the formidable invader who struck terror into the hearts of the Greeks, the king is transformed in the course of the tragedy into a grief-stricken spectacle who eventually appears before us in rags and bereft of his vast army.

By envisaging the reaction at the Persian court to news of the Athenian victory at Salamis the *Persians* – the only surviving text of an Aeschylean trilogy produced in 472 BC, with Pericles as *choregus*[2] – presents to us a Xerxes who at

---

[1] For an alternative artistic rendering of the queen's dream see also John Flaxman's 1795 illustration from his *Compositions from the Tragedies of Aeschylus* (reproduced by Hall 1996, p. 32).

[2] The hypothesis to the *Persians* tells us that the other plays in the trilogy, and the accompanying satyr play, were on mythical themes; see Hall (1996) pp. 10–11 for a discussion. On the question of whether, as *choregus*, Pericles could have exercised any control over the play's subject matter or content see Garvie (2009), pp. xviii–xix.

first displays many of the characteristics which would come to be adopted in later literary depictions of the barbarian invader.[3] Here was an enemy capable of inspiring terror and awe, who had threatened the homeland and the lives of the Greeks; in articulating the absolute fear felt at his advance, the ultimate victors were also able to express their pride in their own success at overcoming the Persians against all odds. At the same time, however, Xerxes' defeat – precisely because it had seemed at first that all was weighted in his favour – reduced the king, in the eyes of the triumphant Greeks at least, to a pathetic figure, one who might be viewed with derision or perhaps even pity.[4] For the Athenian spectators in the Theatre of Dionysus in 472 BC, many of whom would actually have fought at Salamis, Aeschylus' tragedy – the first Greek cultural response to the figure of Xerxes which survives in its entirety and the only extant example of a tragic play based on a historical theme[5] – evoked memories of events which had taken place less than eight years previously. As a piece of tragic theatre, this first configuration of Xerxes is shaped by the requirements of the drama; this has an impact upon the presentation of his character in terms both of the play's moral dimension and the visual and aural elements of the way in which he is envisaged. An analysis of the play's presentation of the Persian king will demonstrate the ways in which Aeschylus' audience encountered his version of Xerxes – a theatrical impersonation of the then still-living barbarian ruler[6] – and the dramatic process by which the play uses the tools at the tragedian's disposal to

[3]　The role of Xerxes here cannot be divorced from the play's ideological construction of Persia. Said (1978, p. 21) saw *Persians* as an early example of the phenomenon of 'Orientalism', describing it as a 'highly artificial enactment of what a non-Oriental has made into a symbol for the whole Orient'. The construction of the opposition between Greeks and barbarians in the play was first explored in detail by Hall (1989), pp. 56–100; this is updated in Hall (2006), pp. 184–224. See also Hall (1993) and Harrison (2000). On the suggestion that the play presents an ideological opposition between democracy and tyranny as political systems, see below, p. 20 n. 28. Note, however, that the presentation of Darius in the play as representing a more benevolent and sagacious style of kingship than that of his son complicates the picture of a straightforward Greek/barbarian dichotomy or a clear-cut opposition between democracy and tyranny; the differentiation of the kings in this way reflects negatively on Xerxes as an individual. See pp. 26–30 below.

[4]　On the possibility of a variety of audience responses to Aeschylus' Xerxes see p. 35.

[5]　Tragedies on historical themes are attested prior to this date, but none has survived. Earlier examples include Phrynichus' *Sack of Miletus*, thought by most scholars to have been produced in the late 490s BC, which dramatized the capture and destruction of Miletus by the Persians in 494, during the Ionian revolt. Later Phrynichus produced another historical tragedy, the *Phoenician Women*; the ancient Alexandrian hypothesis to Aeschylus' *Persians* suggests that Aeschylus' play was modelled upon Phrynichus' tragedy and quotes the opening line as well as asserting that in the play the defeat of Xerxes was reported by a eunuch who was setting out thrones for officials. See Rosenbloom (1993) and Roisman (1988). Hall (1996), pp. 7–9 provides an overview of the ancient testimonies regarding later Greek tragedies on historical themes. See Garvie (2009), pp. ix–xv for a detailed discussion of *Persians* as 'historical tragedy'.

[6]　Xerxes was assassinated seven years later, in 465 BC. See pp. 131–2 below.

erode gradually the magnificent image of a fearsome enemy which is envisaged in the parodos.

Despite the focus on the defeat of Xerxes' force at Salamis the king himself actually appears only after over 900 lines of the text.[7] Although he is literally absent from the stage for much of the play, however, his presence is felt throughout in the words spoken by the Chorus and by other characters: the Queen, the messenger and Darius. This chapter will explore the ways in which their perspectives on Xerxes both anticipate his eventual arrival at the Persian court and create a series of images highlighting significant elements of his personality and behaviour as conceived in the early stages of the evolution of the Xerxes-traditions. By using striking visual imagery in the words of the Chorus, the Queen's report of her dream foreshadowing Xerxes' failure, and the messenger's description of the actual defeat at Salamis, when the prophecy seen in the dream becomes a reality, Aeschylus stages the decline of his offstage protagonist. Before Xerxes himself appears we are also offered an image of what might have been, in the form of the ghost of his father Darius, whose dramatically contrived presence in the play as a representative of past royal splendour and success serves to highlight the inadequacy of his son; Xerxes' predecessor also pronounces an ethical judgement on his actions. Xerxes' eventual appearance on stage is the final spectacular chapter in the tragic drama, which culminates with an outpouring of emotional anguish from the Greeks' vanquished foe; he embodies the Persians' humiliation and, by association, the triumph of the Greeks. This tragic Xerxes would inspire a range of literary responses throughout antiquity and beyond; the present chapter will also examine closely one performative re-interpretation of his character, a dithyramb composed by Timotheus of Miletus sixty or more years after Aeschylus' *Persians*, which illustrates the way in which Aeschylus' theatrical character could be adapted in a new artistic and historical context.

---

[7] For this reason some commentators have seen the *Persians* as a *nostos* play, that is, one whose focus is on the return of a central character from a mission or expedition (as with Odysseus' homecoming in the *Odyssey*): Taplin (1977), p. 124. The *nostos*-theme is alluded to early on in the play, when the Chorus divulge that they are worried about the king's homecoming (νόστῳ τῷ βασιλείῳ, 7). Xerxes is already conspicuous by his absence in the play's opening lines: he is among those Persians who have 'gone to Greece' (1–2), and attention is drawn to the fact that the Chorus of elders have been appointed to oversee matters in his absence (3–7).

First impressions: The formidable foe

It is within the parodos of the *Persians* – sung by a Chorus of elderly Persian advisors who express their anxiety about the condition of the Persian army and its commander[8] – that we find the play's first image of the as yet absent Xerxes, set in the context of his leadership of the expedition to Greece. It is an image of royal splendour and one which conveys a sense of the fearsome appearance of the mighty king and his vast army; the Chorus' description also reflects the haughty self-assurance of the king as he set out on his mission to Greece. This is a king imagined at the height of his power and confidence, shaped by Aeschylus' need at the start of his play to set up his Xerxes for the crushing fall which will be enacted in the course of the tragedy. Having set the scene by listing the contingents of the Persian force and its commanders in an epic-style catalogue[9] which serves to emphasize the size of the military force under Xerxes' command, the Chorus conjure a mental picture of the king as he undertakes his expedition:[10]

> The King's army, which annihilates cities,
> has already passed over to our neighbours' land opposite,
> crossing the strait named after Helle,
> Athamas' daughter, on a floating bridge bound with flaxen ropes,
> yoking the neck of the sea with a roadway bolted together.
>
> The raging leader of populous Asia
> drives his godlike flock against every land
> in two movements: an equal of the gods, born of the golden race,
> he trusts in his stalwart
> and stubborn commanders both on land and on the sea.
>
> He casts from his eyes the dark
> glance of a lethal snake;
> with numerous soldiers and numerous sailors
> he speeds on in his Syrian chariot,
> leading an Ares armed with the bow against famous spearsmen.

---

[8] Here, as throughout the play, the Chorus voice the perspective of Xerxes' Persian subjects on the actions of their king, as contrasted with the obviously royal viewpoints from within his immediate family which are later provided by the characters of the Queen and the ghost of Darius. Schenker (1994) suggests that the Chorus provide a 'national' perspective on the situation, as contrasted with what he describes as the 'personal' view of the Queen.

[9] On epic language and imagery in the play see further Saïd (2007), pp. 76–9.

[10] Translations of *Persians* used in this chapter are those of Hall (1996).

No one is so renowned for valour
that they can withstand such a huge flood of men,
and ward them off with sturdy defences.

(Persians 65–89)

The Chorus' recollection of the sight of Xerxes, sacker of cities, at the head of his immense army, offers a visual snapshot of the king in his role as powerful invader and incorporates several of the key *topoi* relating to Xerxes – recurring literary motifs which would come to characterize him in discourse surrounding the Persian Wars. The impression created here is one which draws primarily on Xerxes' capacity to induce terror; the image also highlights themes which were to become embedded in the Greek imagination as symbolizing his invasion of Greece. Of crucial significance is the reference to Xerxes' bridging of the Hellespont, an episode which in later texts would come to function as shorthand for the arrogance and transgressive behaviour of the king. References to the crossing from Asia into Greece in the literary tradition, beginning with Aeschylus' play, also turned the actual event into something with a deeper symbolic meaning; it would come to represent Xerxes' exercise of his despotic power and imperial ambition as well as his mission to enslave the Greeks in order to incorporate them into his already vast empire. The image here of the sea as having a yoke (ζυγόν, 71)[11] placed about its neck metaphorically implies that it is a living being, to be tamed, just as Xerxes attempted to subdue Greece and its inhabitants with the 'yoke' of slavery (at line 130, too, the sea is also described as ἀμφίζευκτον, 'yoked from both sides'). The noun τὸ ζεῦγος had been used since Homeric times to refer to a pair of beasts joined together (e.g. *Iliad* 18.543), and the verb ζεύγνυμι also applied to the action of yoking, harnessing or fastening together; with this suggestion of binding action it could also, like the English term 'wedlock', be used to refer to marriage. Aeschylus' play is, however, the earliest evidence of the application of vocabulary relating to yoking to the joining of opposite banks with bridges. While the metaphor is a logical one in the context, the fact that frequently in Greek literature from this point on the term is applied to Xerxes' bridge might indicate that the Persian invasion itself suggested this particular usage of the terminology. Elsewhere in

---

[11] In relation to the crossing itself the most striking image of yoking is in the Queen's account of her dream; see pp. 19–21 for an analysis. Darius also describes Xerxes as having treated the sea like a slave by using 'fetters' (δεσμώμασιν, 745) and 'hammered shackles' (πέδαις σφυρηλάτοις, 747) to constrain it. On the significance of the image of the yoke throughout the play see further Michelini (1982), pp. 81–6 and M. Anderson (1972), pp. 167–8. Hall (1996), *ad* 50 analyses the link between 'yoking' and political subjugation in early Greek thought. See further Brock (2013), pp. 108–9 on the use of imagery relating to the control of animals in relation to Persian conquest.

the play the Chorus assert that the inhabitants of Tmolus are 'set on casting the yoke of slavery (ζυγὸν ἀμφιβαλεῖν δούλιον) onto Greece', and later the Persians themselves are described as being 'yoked' under Xerxes' regime (591–4, where they imagine themselves as being able to speak freely once this yoke has been removed).

While the Hellespont crossing acts here as shorthand for the invasion as a whole, aggression and hostility are Xerxes' defining personal characteristics in the image conjured up by the Chorus. Their description of him as θούριος ('raging', 74) relates to the Iliadic epithet for Ares,[12] the god who personified the brutality and bloodshed of war, and whose name is also used in this description as a metaphor for the army led by Xerxes; the king himself is imagined as a deadly snake, or dragon (the Greek here is δράκων, 82), whose very gaze is sinister.[13] Meanwhile his army is one which fights not with the spear, like the hoplite soldiers of Athens, but with the bow (85), which came to symbolize Persian warfare in Greek discourse;[14] here and throughout the play – notably at the end of the *parodos*, where the Chorus wonder 'Has the drawn bow won, or has the mighty pointed spear been victorious?' (147–9) – the two sides are distinguished from one another by the different weaponry which they use.[15] The thematic significance of the chariot from which Xerxes commands his troops, although not emphasized here, will also later become clear with the Queen's recollection of the dream which symbolizes his defeat.

The deadly combination of Xerxes' overwhelming power and his potential for causing destruction is accompanied too by a sense that here is a leader deemed to be no ordinary mortal. The Greek translated here as 'an equal of the gods' (ἰσόθεος φώς, 80), emphasizes Xerxes' status as φώς, a mortal, yet suggests a comparison with the divine either in his actions or his attitude, although the suggestion that the Chorus think of him as actually being a god does not come until later in the play (157, where they refer to him as θεός); later Darius too is described as both δαίμων (620) and θεός (643). While there is no evidence

---

[12] Hall (1996), *ad* 73, referring to *Iliad* 15.127. The Queen also refers to Xerxes as θούριος when describing to Darius his expedition (718, 754). Garvie (2009), *ad* 73–80 notes that the Chorus intend their use of the epithet as a compliment, but that the Queen's use of the same adjective carries a negative connotation.

[13] Garvie (2009), *ad* 81–6 offers a detailed summary of the literary precedents for this description.

[14] Hall (1989), pp. 85–6; see also Sancisi-Weerdenburg (1993b), p. 130. Root (1979), pp. 164–9 examines the association of the bow with Persian kings in Achaemenid art, suggesting that Aeschylus' play may reflect this tradition.

[15] Cf. 26, 31, 55, 239–40, 278, 555, 926, 1020–3. On Xerxes' reference to the empty quiver which he carries at the end of the play see below, pp. 33–4. Note too that at line 817 Darius refers to the spears which will destroy the Persians at Plataea as 'Dorian', in an acknowledgement of the role played by Sparta in that battle.

to suggest that the Persians actually believed their kings to be divine (see also below, p. 25 with n. 42, on the representation of the practice of *proskynēsis*), Aeschylus' misrepresentation of the Chorus' perception of their royal masters as gods serves a dramatic purpose here; for an Athenian audience to whom the notion of worshipping a mortal would be abhorrent it emphasized the Persians' difference from themselves as well as highlighting further the Chorus' status as slave subjects.[16]

At the same time the description emphasizes the Persians' imagined confidence in the mission which, they suggest here, cannot possibly fail (it will become apparent, however, that this confidence is at odds with the concerns voiced elsewhere by the Chorus for the safety of the king and his army). The notion that it would be impossible for anyone to withstand such an onslaught is reiterated throughout the parodos as the Chorus repeatedly stress the immense size of the force which Xerxes has at his command. They frequently highlight the fact that the *whole* of Asia has gone to Greece (11, 56–7, 61), and the use of words beginning with πολυ- (πολύανδρος, 'populous' at 74; πολύχειρ κὰι πολυναύτας, 'with numerous soldiers and numerous sailors' at 83) stresses the sheer size of the military force under the authority of the king. A Homeric-style simile later reinforces this impression of immeasurable numbers: 'all the cavalry and all the infantry, like a swarm of bees, have left with the leader of the army' (128–9, cf. *Iliad* 2.87–90).[17] This in turn allows Aeschylus to remind his audience of the awe and terror which Xerxes and his advancing army inspired in the Greeks whose homeland they invaded, as well as setting up the king for the overwhelming calamity whose aftermath will later be played out on stage for the gratification of the spectators in the theatre.

This vision of a formidable enemy thus acts as our introduction to Xerxes at the start of the *Persians*; yet despite his terror-inducing appearance he had ultimately been no match for the Athenians who routed his fleet at Salamis. From this point in the play there begins a process by which the picture of the fearsome aggressor is gradually eroded; the culmination of this is the eventual melodramatic appearance of Xerxes on the stage upon his return to Susa.

---

[16] Harrison (2000), pp. 87–91. While Hall (1996), *ad* 76–80 suggests that the reference to Xerxes as ἰσόθεος φώς carries 'overtones of excessive aggrandisement' in the context of a tragedy, note *contra* Garvie (2009), *ad* 73–80, asserting that the epithet, which frequently describes a hero in Homer, 'need not indicate Xerxes' *hybris* or presumption'.

[17] M. Anderson (1972), p. 169 considers the significance of this simile. Harrison (2000), pp. 66–75 explores the emphasis on Persian numbers, discussing the link between this and the theme of the 'emptiness' of Asia which is highlighted in the play. On the use of the term πλῆθος, which is associated in the play both with abundance and with multitudes of people, see also Michelini (1982), pp. 86–96.

Already by the end of the parodos the Chorus' tone has reverted from the awestruck reverence for their leader seen in the description of Xerxes and his army to something which resembles the foreboding which they expressed at the very start of their song (8–11). Despite their apparent confidence in the invincibility of the Persian army the elders remain uneasy about the invasion (92–100), musing on the fact that mortal men may find it hard to avoid both the cunning deception of a god and the lure of *Atē*.[18] They go on to suggest that although fate, ordained by the gods, dictated that the Persians should engage in wars of conquest (102–5),[19] it was the act of setting their sights on the sea which meant that they overstretched themselves.[20] This train of thought again reminds the Chorus of the crossing of the Hellespont (113–14). It is specifically this element of the expedition, rather than the mere fact of the attempted subjugation of Greece, which is the source of their fear (116), and their reflections lead to a prediction of the scenes of mourning in Susa which will result from the Persians' defeat (121–5); the vision here of the women of Susa tearing their clothes in the act of lamentation foreshadows the play's final scene where it is in fact Xerxes and the Chorus who rend their garments (1030, 1060). At this point it is noteworthy that Xerxes himself is not yet singled out for explicit censure; his subjects, despite their concerns, express no disapproval for his personal conduct, instead referring to the Persians as being collectively responsible for this course of action. This is perhaps unsurprising given the Chorus' subordinate status and the emphasis which they have placed on the supreme power of the king. It is only later in the play, once the extent of the disaster has become clear, that they become more explicit in apportioning blame to Xerxes (see below, pp. 24–5 and p. 33).

---

[18] *Atē* is here the personification of the delusion sent by the gods to lead mortals to reckless action and thus disaster. The notion that the gods conspired against Xerxes is also reiterated by the messenger (361–2, 373; see below, p. 22) and by the Queen (472–3; see p. 24). Winnington-Ingram (1973) considers the level of blame which is apportioned to divine agents by the play's different characters. On the question of the degree of personal responsibility which is carried by Xerxes, see Podlecki (1993), pp. 58–64.

[19] On the suggestion in the *Persians* that Xerxes was under pressure to measure up to the standards set by his ancestors, see below, p. 28. We might also compare here the Herodotean picture of Xerxes as following in the footsteps of his forebears in embarking on a war designed to foster imperial expansion (discussed at pp. 61–2).

[20] The suggestion that the Athenians are naturally accustomed to seafaring as contrasted with the Persians, who are very much presented as a land-based power, recurs throughout the play: Pelling (1997, ed.), pp. 6–9.

Defeated in a dream

It is the Queen who next gives voice to the sense of foreboding which is apparent by the end of the parodos.[21] Introduced by the Chorus as 'the mother of the King' (151) and then addressed by them as 'aged mother of Xerxes and Darius' wife' (156) she is defined here in terms of her relationship to Xerxes and his father[22] and creates a strong visual impression as she enters the stage on a chariot and in her finery.[23] Her primary role here is to articulate a dramatic vision which foreshadows the news of Xerxes' defeat and his later arrival on the stage. The Queen's anxiety relating to the expedition focuses primarily on Xerxes' personal safety (168–9) and has been brought about by the image she has seen in a dream. The vision she describes (181–99) expands upon the Chorus' allusion to Xerxes' bridging of the Hellespont and the 'yoking' of two continents;[24] here, however, her son is powerless and demeaned, no longer the imposing commander seen in the Chorus' opening song.

The Queen describes having seen two women whose clothes (one wears 'Persian' robes, the other 'Doric' garments, 182–3) signify that they are personifications of Persia and Greece; when the two quarrelled Xerxes 'tried to restrain and mollify them; he harnessed them both beneath his chariot and put a yoke-strap beneath their necks (ἅρμασιν δ' ὑπο / ζεύγνυσιν αὐτὼ καὶ λέπαδν' ὑπ' αὐχένων / τίθησι)' (190–2). This reference to Xerxes' attempt to subjugate Hellas and join it to Asia mirrors the imagery used by the Chorus earlier; significantly, too, the reference to Xerxes' chariot – used here as a tool in the exercise of his rule – calls to mind the Chorus' earlier description of him (84) as riding in a chariot when commanding his troops.[25] By contrast with the Chorus' presentation of his unassailable power, however, on this occasion Xerxes' exercise of

---

[21] Critical responses to the Queen – who is not named in the text but has been identified with Atossa, the daughter of Cyrus, who is found in Herodotus' account (Broadhead 1960, p. xxvi) – vary in their assessment of how far the audience is expected to sympathize with her: Sancisi-Weerdenburg (1983), p. 24, for example, sees her as a 'model of motherly care', while Harrison (1996), p. 82–3 suggests that her very appearance in a political context implies a negative judgement and plays on Greek perceptions of the influence of royal women at the Persian court (cf. Brosius 1996, p. 105). McClure (2006) considers the Queen's primary role in the play as one in which she is used as a means of framing Xerxes' return and intensifying his public humiliation at the end of the play. For an overview of the scholarly debate on her character see Dominick (2007), pp. 436–41.

[22] On the notion that she is the wife and mother of Persian gods (expressed at 157) and the implied suggestion that the Chorus therefore believe both Darius and Xerxes to be divine see Garvie (2009), *ad loc.*

[23] See 607–8, with Hall (1996) and Garvie (2009), *ad loc.*

[24] See above, p. 15. Saïd (2007), pp. 88–9 discusses some of the ways in which the images presented in the Queen's dream relate to the rest of the play.

[25] On the depiction of the royal chariot in Persian art, and its significance in Persian ideology as part of the royal insignia, see Briant (2002), pp. 223–5.

imperial command is challenged by what follows. Although one of the women submits to the yoke, the other resists aggressively, tears the harness from the chariot and smashes the yoke in two; Xerxes falls from the vehicle (196). By being violently hurled from the chariot which was a distinctive feature of his appearance in the Chorus' earlier description, Xerxes is symbolically stripped of one of the material assets used to define him in the play.[26] In the dream as well as in the reality recently experienced by the Greeks Xerxes' attempt at control has been thwarted; in the Queen's vision he is reduced to a state of passivity and helplessness. While Darius can only look on in pity Xerxes tears his robes in grief (198–200): these elements of the dream-scene prefigure both Darius' later appearance in the play and Xerxes' own onstage response to the disaster (to be discussed below, pp. 26–30 and 30–5).

The Queen's premonition of the outcome of Xerxes' expedition is accompanied too by a bird-omen, the defeat of an eagle by a hawk (207–10), which mirrors the theme of the defeat of an apparently stronger power by a weaker one. Yet despite her terror as witness to these portents (210–11) the Queen remains confident in her son's supreme authority over his own people (212–14). While a successful outcome would win him admiration, her words make it clear that so long as he is still alive, his position as king is secure, for, as sole ruler, he is unaccountable to the community (οὐχ ὑπεύθυνος πόλει, 213).[27] The implied contrast between the rule exercised by Xerxes and the political system at Athens is later highlighted in the Queen's questioning of the Chorus as to the identity of the Athenians who, she learns 'are neither the slaves nor subjects of any single man' (242).[28] As conceived of by the Queen, then, any disaster is one whose consequences for Xerxes himself relate more to the king's personal humiliation

---

[26] On the question of whether Xerxes is in a chariot when he eventually appears on the stage, see below, n. 56.

[27] For Herodotus, the accountability of individuals in positions of power is specifically associated with a *democratic* constitution (see Hdt. 3.80).

[28] Here the Queen uses the Greek term ποιμάνωρ, 'shepherd' (241) in formulating her assumption that the Athenians must be subject to a sole ruler; this echoes the Chorus' earlier description of Xerxes' army as his 'flock' (ποιμανόριον, 75). On the significance of the Queen's questioning of the Chorus in relation to the construction of an ideological opposition between Athens (as a democracy) and Persia (as a tyranny), see Goldhill (1988) and Harrison (2000), pp. 76–91. This contrast between Greek and Persian political models in the play is also discussed by Kantzios (2004) in the context of a study of the use of fear as an instrument of rule. On the broader issue of the relationship between the performance of tragedy and civic ideology see Goldhill (1987 and 2000). Rhodes (2003) argues that some features of tragedy which have been ascribed to its performance in the context of a democracy relate more broadly to *polis* ideology rather than specifically to *democratic* ideology; see also Griffin (1998), suggesting that, while some individual plays deal with political themes, the phenomenon of tragic performance cannot be seen as primarily political in its motivation. Griffith (1998) discusses some of the ways in which tragedy explores socio-political relations and suggests (pp. 43–8) that elements of the Athenian audience may still relate to the notion of elite political rule, and perhaps even feel nostalgia for this during the evolution of democracy.

than to any notion that his position as ruler might be called into question.[29] It is this humiliation which is later played out on the stage as the ragged Xerxes laments the loss of his forces; with the arrival of the messenger the audience is taken one step closer to this final vision of the disgraced king.

The dream becomes reality

The messenger's narrative of events at Salamis is the means by which the Queen and the Chorus first learn what the theatre audience already knows – that Xerxes' navy has been defeated and that he is on his way back to Persia with what remains of his fighting force. To begin with the onstage characters are left in suspense as to the condition of the king himself; the messenger's initial emphasis is on the great losses sustained by the forces, as he announces melodramatically that 'the whole barbarian force has perished' (255). His first exchange with the Chorus makes no mention of Xerxes, providing instead a summary of events which links with the Chorus' earlier description of the size of Xerxes' force by focusing on the numbers of Persian dead (260, 272–3, 278). The emphasis on numbers, both of the size of the fleet, and of the Persian dead, is a striking feature of the messenger's speech and mirrors the way in which Aeschylus builds up a picture of the scale of the disaster throughout the play.[30] It is the Queen's interruption which brings the focus back to her son, as she asks which leaders have survived and which perished (296–8); the messenger correctly interprets her question as a demand for news of Xerxes and reports that 'Xerxes himself lives and looks upon the light' (299).

The Queen's expression of her relief at the news of her son's survival (301–2) is followed by the messenger's catalogue of the Persian commanders who lost their lives in the battle. By contrast with the catalogue of the parodos which advertised the extent of Xerxes' power, this list of the fallen serves to create the impression of total disaster and begins the dramatic process by which Aeschylus reveals the full extent of the humiliation of Xerxes' defeat. The scale of the reversal is given further emphasis as the messenger reminds his audience

[29] This of course accords with the historical reality that Xerxes' power apparently remained undiminished by his failure in Greece. No territory was lost, and the campaign related only to a proportionally small frontier of the vast Persian empire; in fact many Greeks had fought alongside Xerxes rather than against him, and many remained Persian subjects in the years after the invasion of mainland Greece. By contrast it suited the rhetoric glorifying the Athenians' achievements to present the defeat as a total disaster for Xerxes.
[30] Saïd (2007), pp. 71–3.

that the king's fleet vastly outnumbered that of the Greeks: a thousand or more Persian ships as opposed to the Greeks' 300.[31] Once again we are reminded of the parodos, and the Chorus' expression there of their belief that numerical superiority will guarantee a Persian victory; the Queen suggests here too that Xerxes' own confidence in the size of his navy may have spurred him on to engage in the sea battle (352).

While the messenger's account of the actual battle (384–432) is focused primarily upon evoking a sense of the sights and sounds of the action at sea, his analysis of the prelude to this examines Xerxes' role, raising the issue of causation and the moral question – crucially important in the context of a tragic drama – of where the blame for the disaster should fall. In keeping with the Chorus' earlier assertion that mortals might be deceived by an ill-willed deity (92–100; see above, p. 18) he too suggests that divine interference is at least partly responsible for what has occurred (354).[32] Significantly he also alludes to the ruse by which Themistocles tricked the Persians into fighting in the narrow strait,[33] highlighting Xerxes' error of judgement in falling for the trick. On two occasions here the messenger explicitly refers to a failure of understanding on Xerxes' part (361–2, 373);[34] the king's tactical ineptitude is thus implicitly contrasted with the brilliant strategic abilities of the Athenians' naval commander. It is at this point in the narrative that we can detect the early beginnings of a strand of the Xerxes-tradition in which the king, on the basis of his failings, might (at least from the perspective of the Athenian audience) be perceived as an object of derision. Although, like the Chorus earlier in the play, the messenger makes no overt criticism of his master, there is nonetheless a suggestion here that – despite having apparently had the odds stacked in

---

[31] The Greek text here is ambiguous and could be taken to mean that the Persians had either a thousand or 1207 ships; the number of Greek ships could be either 300 or 310.

[32] Winnington-Ingram (1973) examines the way in which religious ideas are presented in the *Persians*, pointing out that, while the Chorus and the messenger refer to the gods' jealousy and deceit as a cause of the disaster, Darius attributes it to the Persians' own acts of *hybris*, punishable by Zeus. He suggests that this apparent contradiction is crucial to the structure of the play and that it draws attention to the notion of human responsibility as well as acting as a warning against acts of *hybris*.

[33] The story, in which Themistocles was said to have been responsible for devising the plan to lure the Persian fleet into battle, is related by Herodotus (8.75). Aeschylus' version does not name Themistocles (no individual Athenian is named in the play); the messenger gives only a brief outline of the story in which 'a Greek man' (355) is said to have come from the Athenian force with the message that the Greeks were planning to flee. Podlecki (1999), pp. 15–26 argues for a pro-Themistoclean reading of the play as a whole. Although the date of Themistocles' actual ostracism (whether before or after the performance of *Persians*) is disputed, he was certainly under attack at Athens by 472. On the chronology of his career see Lenardon (1959).

[34] See also 391–2 where he alludes to the terror of the barbarians in general once they realized that they were 'mistaken in their expectation'.

his favour owing to the vastly superior size of his force – Xerxes' military failure could be ascribed to a lack of foresight. This error of judgement would also form a key element of Herodotus' assessment of Xerxes' expedition (see pp. 66–7).

Acting on the false information, and without pausing to consider the possibility of a trick, Xerxes is said to have called his fleet to action immediately (361). The king's pre-battle address, related by the messenger using indirect speech,[35] briefly outlines the plan to position his fleet in order to engage the Greek navy (364–71) and culminates in a threat to have his men universally beheaded if all does not go according to plan (369–71). The meting out of violent and arbitrary punishment in the form of bodily mutilation came to be associated with the idea of barbarian tyranny in Greek thought in the fifth century BC;[36] Aeschylus' play is our earliest evidence for the association of Xerxes with this practice. The portrait of the king presented by the messenger here thus combines a sense of his potential for inducing fear (this time among his own subjects rather than among those against whom he was fighting) with the suggestion of tactical ineptitude as well as a deluded confidence in the inevitability of a Persian victory.

The ensuing description of the naval catastrophe and loss of Persian life (presented in the messenger's account as unprecedented in its scale, 431–2) is bracketed by references to Xerxes' commanding role; this allows the audience an insight into his character as seen in the context of his military leadership.[37] The total disaster at sea is further compounded by the hoplite engagement on Psyttaleia (447–64), in which the troops sent there by the king are trapped and slaughtered by Greek soldiers. Once again the messenger places emphasis on Xerxes' failure to anticipate this outcome (454).[38] It is in the description of Xerxes' reaction to the disaster, however, that we find the most striking visual image of the king in the messenger scene (465–70):

---

[35] The use of reported speech here, and the way in which it distances the listener from the words of the king, contrasts strongly with the immediacy of the messenger's report of the stirring patriotic battle cry of the Greeks at 402–5, which is rendered in direct speech and which calls for the liberation of Greece.

[36] Hall (1989), pp. 158–9. On bodily mutilation as practised by Xerxes as a form of punishment in Herodotus' account see below, p. 48. Persian sources suggest that this was not merely an imaginative construct on the part of Greek writers, but that it had some basis in Persian practice.

[37] Schenker (1994), p. 287 n. 13 points out that, by contrast with the Queen's focus on Xerxes himself, the messenger's report 'emphasizes the national rather than the personal'. Despite this the episode is structured in such a way – with reference to Xerxes' role at the beginning and end of the account of Salamis – as to focus attention on the question of the extent to which the king is to blame for the disaster.

[38] Darius too comments on Xerxes as having been deluded in his actions: see pp. 27–30 below.

Xerxes wailed aloud as he saw the depth of the disaster. For he had a seat with
a clear view of the whole militia, a high bank close to the sea. He tore his robes
and shrilly screamed, and straightaway gave an order to the infantry, rushing
away in disorderly flight.

The messenger's recollection of Xerxes sitting on his throne, observing the course
of the battle, evokes an image which was to become firmly established in literary
treatments of the Persian invasion, appearing in narratives of Thermopylae as
well as of Salamis.[39] At this point he is distanced from the action, an observer of
the battle rather than a participant in it, whose own life is not in peril yet whose
misguided decisions have brought about the deaths of hordes of Persians. His
reaction to the disaster, described here by the messenger, provides – like the
image of Xerxes seen in the Queen's dream – another example of the way in
which reported action in the text prefigures the action which will take place on
the stage at the end of the play; the rending of his garments and wailing aloud
anticipates Xerxes' performance of these same actions in the play's final scene.
Despite his distress at Salamis, however, he still continues to act as tyrannical
ruler over his subjects, giving orders to his infantry; this too can be seen to
anticipate the play's final scene in which he reverts to his role as master over the
Chorus, directing their actions as they mourn the Persians' losses (see p. 34).

The reaction of the onstage listeners to the messenger's report of events at
Salamis returns the theatre audience's attention to the question of responsibility
for the disaster. While the Queen's immediate response is to blame a deity for
deceiving the Persians (472–3), she also frames the expedition as a whole as
a quest for vengeance against Athens on Xerxes' part, and suggests too that it
is his actions in this regard which have brought suffering upon the Persians
(473–7):

> The vengeance my son planned to exact from famous Athens turned bitter on
> him, and the barbarians whom Marathon destroyed were not enough for him.
> My son, expecting to exact requital for them, has brought on a multitude of
> afflictions.[40]

Her analysis here mirrors the messenger's suggestion that a combination of
divine malevolence and Xerxes' own lack of foresight has brought about the
calamitous outcome. Soon afterwards, the Chorus too go further than before in

---

[39] See below, pp. 54–5, on the image of the throne in Herodotus' narrative.

[40] The mention of Marathon here reminds the audience of Darius' previous campaign against Greece;
   this is perhaps designed to prepare us for the raising of his ghost in the next scene.

assigning a degree of blame to the king himself; in their ode sung shortly after receiving the news of the catastrophe they lament (547–54):

> For now the land of Asia mourns
> emptied out of its men
> Xerxes led them away *popoi*,
> Xerxes destroyed them *totoi*,
> Xerxes wrong-headedly drove everything on in seafaring ships.

The naming of Xerxes as a cause of the disaster, with the repetition of his name at the beginning of three lines,[41] is striking, and the notion of total destruction articulated by the Chorus here ties in with the pervasive emphasis placed on the annihilation of the entire Persian force throughout the play. Here the Chorus also make their first implied comparison between Xerxes and his father – a contrast which will later be developed further – by recalling that Darius brought no harm to his citizens (555–7). Later in this same ode (584–94) the Chorus go so far as to suggest that the king's power has itself been destroyed, that Xerxes' subjects will no longer submit to his rule, and that now the 'yoke' of his power has gone his people will speak freely against him; nor will they prostrate themselves before him any longer (οὐδ' εἰς γᾶν προπίτνοντες / ἄρξονται, 589–90). The allusion here to the practice of *proskynēsis*, which for the Greeks should be performed only before gods,[42] is another reminder of the difference between Xerxes' rule over his barbarian subjects and the freedom enjoyed by the citizens of Athens. The Chorus' assessment of the consequences of Xerxes' defeat here also goes further than the Queen's suggestion at 212–14 that though Xerxes, if defeated, would fail to win admiration, he would not be subjected to public scrutiny; their picture of a Xerxes who is weakened politically as well as having had his military force destroyed taps into the triumphalist rhetoric of the Athenian victors. This Xerxes is a far cry from the all-powerful leader envisaged in the parodos; in this way we are brought closer to the anticipated revelation of his wretched physical condition.

---

[41] The translation given here mirrors the structure of the Greek text in this sense.

[42] Hall (1996), *ad* 152 emphasizes the Greeks' view of this as a degrading practice (see also Couch 1931), although Garvie (2009), *ad* 152 suggests that here it is merely an example of Aeschylus' 'presenting the Persians as behaving in the way that his audience would expect'. Briant (2002), p. 222 notes that, as performed by the Persians, 'contrary to what the Greeks deduced from it, the rite did not imply that the king was considered a god'.

In the father's shadow: Darius and Xerxes

Where often in tragedy a messenger scene immediately precedes the arrival of the central character,[43] in the case of the *Persians* the arrival of Xerxes onstage is deferred by the episode in which Darius' ghost is raised. The spectacle of necromancy, while providing the theatre audience with an exotic and visually striking display for their entertainment and therefore shaped to a large degree by the dramatic requirements of a stage performance,[44] also allows Aeschylus to explore in detail the ethical comparison between Xerxes and his father. The scene performs a further thematic and structural role in preparing us for the entrance of the recently defeated king; Darius' pronouncements concerning his son's actions inform the audience's perception of Xerxes, and the evocation of a contrast between father and son is a crucial element of Aeschylus' presentation of Xerxes' character. The presence of the deceased king on stage also calls to mind his role in the Queen's dream, where he was described as standing by and pitying the defeated Xerxes (καὶ πατὴρ παρίσταται/Δαρεῖος οἰκτίρων σφε, 197–8), although father and son are never actually brought face to face in the course of the play. Darius' assessment of Xerxes' conduct is, however, far more explicitly judgemental in the ghost-raising scene than in the Queen's description of her dream; it is the spectre of Xerxes' predecessor who draws the audience's attention most clearly to the moral dimension of the invasion.

It is the Chorus who first draw attention to the comparison between father and son; their hymn summoning Darius' ghost (634–80) stresses their love and respect for the deceased king (652–5; cf. 555–7, 671):

> For he never killed our men
> through the ruinous waste of war.
> He was called godlike in counsel for the Persians, and godlike in counsel
> He was, since he steered the army well.

By implication Xerxes, insofar as he failed to avert the Persians' military catastrophe, is to be judged by the standards set by his father. The contrast between the two kings is stressed still further by Darius himself; on learning of recent events he comments that never since kings have ruled Asia has such a disaster befallen the city of Susa (759–61), later boasting, 'I went on military campaigns with a large army, but I never brought such a great catastrophe on the city'

---

[43] Taplin (1977), pp. 82–5.

[44] Griffith (1998), p. 59 summarizes the visual and aural impression created by the figure of Darius' ghost. On the staging of the scene see also Taplin (1977), pp. 114–19.

(780–1). The Chorus' lavish eulogy of Darius' rule after the departure of his ghost (852–907) reinforces this impression; it begins with an exaggerated nostalgic reflection on the excellence of Darius' rule, obsequiously describing him as 'the old all-sufficing undamaging invincible godlike king Darius' (855–6), then going on to praise the dead king's military exploits and to list the lands over which he ruled.[45] For the contrast with Darius to work here some subtle manipulation of history is required, with the omission of any suggestion that Darius' own policies created a precedent for Xerxes' actions. In fact his campaign against Greece, which was thwarted at Marathon, was the forerunner of the more recent invasion, and elsewhere he had suffered a great military humiliation when, having invaded the Scythians' territory (having accessed it by bridging the Bosporus, which for Herodotus could serve as a parallel for Xerxes' crossing of the Hellespont), he was outwitted by them and forced to retreat. Where Herodotus' account would implicitly bring out the similarities between the campaigns of Darius and Xerxes,[46] the opposite is true of Aeschylus, who uses the contrast of father and son as a means of drawing out a moralizing strand in his assessment of Xerxes.

It is the joining of Europe and Asia by means of the Hellespont bridge which becomes the focus for Darius' criticism of Xerxes' actions. His incredulity that his son has implemented such a plan (723) overlooks the fact that the building of a bridge between continents is something which he too accomplished as king of Persia; his subsequent analysis of the question of responsibility combines a reflection upon the role of the gods with a denunciation of Xerxes for his youthful folly and – mirroring the messenger's assessment – his error of judgement. Darius' initial acceptance of the Queen's suggestion that a δαίμων is responsible for affecting Xerxes' mind (724–5) later gives way to a more detailed analysis of the situation in which he suggests that it is Zeus who has carried out the destruction of the Persian force in fulfilment of prophecies; Xerxes' rashness, however, hastened this pre-ordained disaster (739–42). It is not the expedition itself but the crossing of the Hellespont which becomes for Darius the manifestation of Xerxes' folly (744–51):

> And this was achieved by my son, uncomprehending (οὐ κατειδώς) in his youthful audacity (νέῳ θράσει), the man who thought he could constrain with fetters, like a slave, the sacred flowing Hellespont, the divine stream of

---

[45] Hall (1996), *ad* 852–907 notes that many of the states in this list were Greek communities which were once under Persian control, but which had been liberated by 472 BC: 'The play's ostensible lament for the Persians' lost domains functions for the audience as a celebration of the autonomy of numerous Greek city-states.'

[46] On Darius' bridging of the Bosporus see Herodotus 4.87–8, cf. 3.134–4. For a discussion of further parallels between Xerxes and Darius in Herodotus' account, see below, pp. 59–60.

the Bosporus. He altered the very nature of the strait, and by casting around
it hammered shackles furnished a great road for his great army; although only
a mortal, he foolishly thought that he could overcome all the gods, including
Poseidon. Surely this must have been some disease affecting my son's mind?

The description of the 'enslavement' of the sea here mirrors imagery used earlier
in the play while at the same time introducing the idea that Xerxes – emphatically presented here as a mere mortal, yet acting in a manner more appropriate
for a god – interfered with divinely ordained boundaries by attempting to
enslave what the gods intended to be free;[47] once again his action serves as a
metaphor for the attempted subjugation of the Greeks.[48] Darius' emphasis on
Xerxes' incomprehension of the situation stresses his youth, a characteristic
which had been mentioned by the Chorus in the parodos (13), and which is
highlighted again by Darius at 782 (overlooking the fact that Xerxes was around
forty years old at the time of Salamis); this also seems designed to draw attention
to the artificially constructed contrast between 'aged' (γεραιός, 854) father and
childlike son. The decision to launch the expedition is cast here, in the realm
of Aeschylus' tragic vision of the Persian dynasty, as the result of an error
of judgement, perhaps attributable to some kind of mental affliction (νόσος
φρενῶν, 750). It is the Queen who then suggests that Xerxes was urged on in
his folly by 'wicked' men who influenced him with taunts that staying at home
would not help to augment his father's legacy; there is perhaps a suggestion here
of the pressures brought about by dynastic succession which are explored at
greater length in Herodotus' account of Xerxes' arrival at the decision to invade
Greece (see pp. 61–3).[49] Darius' summary of the reigns of the previous kings
of Persia (765–81) reinforces this impression, culminating in his boast that his
own military campaigns did not bring such a disaster on Susa, and concluding
with a repetition of the assertion that no other king has been responsible for so
much suffering (785–6).

Darius' assessment of the disaster and the culpability of Xerxes goes beyond
the events at Salamis and looks ahead to the final Persian defeat at Plataea,
which falls outside the play's chronological scope. In prophesying this new

---

[47] Winnington-Ingram (1973), pp. 215–17.
[48] M. Anderson (1972), p. 168 notes that 'Xerxes' transgression of the inviolable boundaries set
    between Greek and Persian is clearly one of the fundamental conceptions of the tragedy; yet it is
    hardly mentioned in explicit terms by the dramatist'.
[49] On the problem of dynastic rule in Aeschylus' play, and the link with Xerxes' supposed youthful
    rashness, see Griffith (1998), pp. 53ff. Griffith's discussion of the father/son relationship in *Persians*
    offers a reading which demonstrates that the play highlights the problems faced by elite males – in
    particular sons of successful dynasts – who are measured against the achievements of their fathers
    and ancestors.

failure he once again returns to the notion of his son's lack of foresight: in leaving troops behind in Greece Xerxes is 'deluded by false hopes' (κεναῖσιν ἐλπίσιν πεπεισμένος, 804). It is also in Darius' speech predicting events at Plataea that we find the play's only references to *hybris* (808, 821). Initially the accusation of *hybris* is not attached explicitly to Xerxes himself; it is the troops left in Greece who will suffer as punishment for their *hybris*, defined here by Darius as the act of violating and vandalizing shrines and sanctuaries (809–12).[50] The speech on Plataea then reflects more broadly on the implications of the invasion as Darius asserts that the slaughter of the Persians will act as a warning to future genera-tions against thinking excessive thoughts: 'for *hybris* flowers and produces a crop of calamity (*atē*, cf. 99, with p. 18 n. 18, above), and from it reaps a harvest of lamentation'. Ultimately it is Zeus who assesses and punishes mortal arrogance (827–8); with this pronouncement Darius exhorts the Chorus to 'use sensible words of warning to admonish Xerxes to behave temperately and stop offending the gods with his boasts and excessive confidence' (829–31). Thus the father concludes his condemnation of his son's actions; in his absence Xerxes is characterized as arrogant, impetuous and ultimately misguided in his attempt to conquer Greece.

In the analysis offered by Darius, then, the failure of the Persian expedition, while pre-ordained by the gods, was accelerated by Xerxes' personal weaknesses. This condemnation of his son's character flaws also has implications for our understanding of the play in relation to Aeschylus' presentation of the Persian monarchy. It is not possible to read the *Persians* as merely presenting us with a straightforward criticism of Persian kingship in opposition to Greek freedom or Athenian democracy;[51] rather, the contrast which is drawn between Darius and Xerxes serves to focus our attention on Xerxes himself as an example of a flawed human being whose failings have set in motion a disaster on an unprecedented scale. The image of Xerxes with which we are provided in the ghost-raising

---

[50] Fisher's extensive 1992 study of the concept of *hybris* demonstrates that it is not merely a form of excessive pride but that it involves the deliberate infliction of shame or dishonour on other mortals or gods by treating them in a degrading manner. His analysis of the *Persians* (pp. 256–63) sees the play as being structured around Xerxes' punishment for *hybris*.

[51] Easterling (1984), p. 38: 'Xerxes becomes an example of humanity over-reaching itself, not just of an essentially Persian mode of behaviour.' See also Kantzios (2004), pp. 13–14. The character of Xerxes might also be compared with Aeschylus' Agamemnon in this regard: both kings pay a heavy price for behaving in a way which is contrary to accepted norms, and both the *Persians* and *Agamemnon* explore the interplay of divine causation and personal responsibility for the disaster which befalls each king. The comparison is explored by di Benedetto (1978), pp. 156–65. See also Gantz (1982), pp. 11–13 and M. Anderson (1972), p. 174 n. 1. Rosenbloom (1993), pp. 191–2 suggests that the dramatization of the characters and fates of both Xerxes and Agamemnon (both of whom set out as naval leaders) may be partly intended to stimulate the audience's reflections upon Athens' own naval hegemony.

scene differs considerably from the strikingly visual descriptions offered by the Chorus, the Queen and the messenger; although here we are not provided with a mental picture of Xerxes instead the ghost of Darius acts as a photographic negative of his son and an image of the kind of king Xerxes could have been. Aeschylus constructs an image of the father as old, wise, and perceptive, as contrasted with a son who is young, impetuous and witless – characteristics borne out by his actions and the devastating consequences to which they have led.[52] The appearance of Xerxes, now a broken man, on the stage in the final episode reinforces visually the contrast with his father, who is seen appearing in all his kingly glory even from beyond the grave.[53]

From riches to rags

Darius' parting instructions (832–8) are directed at the Queen as he advises her to bring suitable clothing for Xerxes, who has torn his robes in his distress at the disaster; only she, he suggests, will be able to calm her son. The reference to Xerxes' tattered garments mirrors the emphasis placed on his clothing earlier in the play both in the Queen's dream (198–200) and in the messenger's account of the king's reaction after the defeat at Salamis (468).[54] The Queen declares that the thing which grieves her the most is the fact that Xerxes 'is disgraced by the clothes about his body' (846–8) and leaves the stage in order to carry out Darius' instructions. Her attempt to conceal the outward signs of his disgrace by bringing fresh clothing[55] does not materialize within what remains of play, however, and it is the appearance of Xerxes on stage in rags which reveals him as the physical embodiment of the disaster suffered by the entire Persian force. The construction of this theatrical Xerxes, impersonated on stage by an Athenian actor, is shaped entirely by the context of Aeschylus' play as a piece of performed tragic drama. This impacts upon every element of the presentation

---

[52] Garvie (2009), p. xxi: 'Aeschylus is not writing history; the contrast between the two kings is dramatically required, and it must be stark.'

[53] See, for example, 656–62 where the Chorus describe Darius' appearance with 'yellow-dyed slippers' and 'kingly tiara', and 694–6 where they express their awe at his presence before them. Taplin (1977), pp. 126–7 considers the visual impact of the contrast between Darius and Xerxes; on this contrast see also Saïd (1981), pp. 31–36 and Saïd (2007), pp. 88–9.

[54] The image of tearing clothes was first introduced in the play by the Chorus, who used it in their visualization of the reaction by the *women* of Persia to a possible disaster (125; cf. 116 where they employ similar imagery in relation to their own fear: 'the black robes of my heart are rent with terror').

[55] McClure (2006), p. 74, pp. 91–6.

of his character here, from his dress and his body language to the tragic lament which he sings.

Xerxes' eventual entrance, so long delayed, is a spectacle quite different from that envisaged by the Chorus in their imagining of the king at the start of the play. Dressed in rags (1030) and unaccompanied (1000–1, 1036), this is a king whose appearance has been altered dramatically from that described in the parodos;[56] the fearsome invader at the head of a vast army has been replaced by a wretched figure who from his very first words is able only to lament the misfortune which has befallen him. The Chorus' response to the entrance of their master contrasts markedly with their reactions to the arrival of the Queen and Darius earlier in the play; there is no prostration,[57] nor any of the honorific greetings lavished upon the Queen (152–8), and an absence of the ceremony which attended the appearance of Darius' ghost (623–80). Xerxes receives no formal greeting whatsoever from the Chorus, whose first words to him (917ff.) are in response to his opening lament.[58] This adds to the impression gradually created in the course of the play that this king, in contrast with his father, has been stripped of the trappings of royalty.

The arrival of the king in tatters is the moment which has been anticipated throughout the play;[59] every character has, prior to this point, presented us with their own imagined version of the king, yet none drew for the audience a picture which quite compares with the vivid image before them now. The all-powerful warrior king envisaged by the Chorus in the parodos – despite the hints of foreboding there – was far-removed from the shabby Xerxes of the final scene; both the Queen and the messenger told of a defeated king who tore his robes, yet the dream-vision and the report of the aftermath of Salamis could not match the impact of his physical presence; meanwhile Darius, scolding father of an impetuous youth, was presented to the viewer as the antithesis of the figure who

---

[56] The departure of the Queen into the palace at line 851 also means that when Xerxes enters at line 908 he is the only character on stage with the Chorus. Taplin (1977), pp. 121–3 also argues that Xerxes entered on foot, suggesting that this would offer a striking contrast with the spectacle of the Queen's first entry on a chariot (607) and with other royal entrances in tragedy. See also Garvie (2009), p. 339. The reference to Xerxes' 'curtained car' or 'wheeled tent' (σκηναῖς / τροχηλάτοισιν) at line 1000–1 may suggest, however, that he arrived on this vehicle (so Hall, 1996, *ad* 999–1001), which could perhaps be rendered as an appropriately shabby alternative to the war chariot mentioned earlier at line 84.

[57] On *proskynēsis* in the play, see above, n. 42. The apparent absence of this gesture here might remind the audience of the Chorus' prediction at 589–90 that Xerxes' subjects will no longer do obeisance to him.

[58] Kantzios (2004), p. 8: 'the news of the disaster at Salamis transforms the encounter of the king with the elders into an occasion of profound mourning and empathy, temporarily suspending the rituals and rhetoric of subordination'.

[59] Thalmann (1980); Saïd (2007), pp. 87ff.

appears before us at the end of the play. The impact of Xerxes' appearance lies in the fact that it both draws upon and takes to the furthest extreme this gradual revelation of the effect of the disaster in Greece upon the person of the king and, by extension, upon Persia itself.

As well as acting as a visual spectacle, the final scene of the play, which takes the form of an extended lament in which both Xerxes and the Chorus participate, is also aurally arresting. That Xerxes does not actually speak but only sings this *thrēnos* is the defining feature of his performance here and would require considerable skill and exertion on the part of the actor playing him; in this respect he is unique among the leading characters of extant tragedy.[60] Just as the tearing of his robes described in this scene (1030) mirrors the descriptions of Xerxes earlier in the play, so too his singing of a lament echoes the messenger's earlier description of the king's emotional outburst after Salamis, in which we were told that he 'tore his robes and shrilly screamed' (ῥήξας δὲ πέπλους κἀνακωκύσας λιγύ, 468). It is this scene which was the precursor to Timotheus' *Persians*, in which a virtuoso performer re-enacted in song Xerxes' response to the naval defeat at Salamis (see below, pp. 37–43). The influence of the image of a singing Xerxes also seems to have extended far beyond the classical Greek period; as late as the second century AD Aelius Aristides' rhetorical panegyric in honour of Athens would feature a Xerxes who 'sang a palinode' (παλινῳδίαν ᾖδεν, *Panathenaicus* 166) before his retreat from Salamis. Taken together in Aeschylus' play, the rending of Xerxes' clothing and his high-pitched lamentation may be seen to suggest the feminization of the king, a feature of his characterization which recurs in later versions of the tradition, and which is connected more broadly with barbarians in Greek discourse.[61] The association of funerary lamentation with women in Greek thought[62] and the language used to describe the actions of both Xerxes and the Chorus indicate that their behaviour is of a kind more usually associated with women than men. Just as Xerxes is referred to in the messenger's speech as tearing his *peplos* (a garment usually worn by Greek women), so too the king instructs the Chorus in this scene to tear their *peploi* (1060).[63]

---

[60] Hall (1999), p. 96. For broader surveys of singing in tragedy see also Hall (1999 and 2002).

[61] Hall (1996), p. 169 and Hall (1999), p. 100 and pp. 116–17; on the presentation of barbarians as effeminate see also Hall (1993). Georges (1994), pp. 102–9 also considers the inversion of gender roles in the *Persians*.

[62] Alexiou (1974), pp. 5ff. summarizes the evidence. See also McClure (1999), pp. 40–7. On the association of female characters with lamentation in tragedy see Foley (1993). Note, however, Garvie (2009), p. 340, suggesting that this kind of ritualized mourning, while a sign of the Persians' humiliation, need not necessarily be indicative of the feminization of Xerxes and the Chorus.

[63] Hall (1996), *ad* 468 also notes that the shrill screaming of Xerxes after Salamis is more usually associated with women in both epic and tragedy.

The antiphonal lament of Xerxes and the Chorus also takes up the play's moral theme of the extent to which the king himself is to blame for the disaster. While Xerxes begins by asserting that a god (δαίμων, 911; cf. 942) is to blame for the Persians' misfortune,[64] his ensuing lamentation that, 'I have become a miserable blight upon my family and my fatherland' (933–4) may suggest a move towards acceptance of his own responsibility for the disaster. The Chorus too now assign a degree of responsibility to Xerxes; while they acknowledge the role of the gods (921, 1005), it is Xerxes whom they blame for having killed the horde of young men and for having 'crammed Hades with Persians' (923–4).[65] Meanwhile the Chorus' lists naming Xerxes' now-lost comrades (956–61, 967–72, 981–5, 993–9) echo their catalogue of Persian troops at the start of the play; these have become catalogues not of triumph or victory but of failure and loss.[66] This Xerxes is a king humiliated and humbled, whose elaborate lament for his fallen subjects expresses the depth of his despair and the scale of the disaster which his actions have brought about.[67] The play's exodos thus – in keeping with the dramatic context of the tragedy – acts as a communal expression of grief in which king and Chorus are seen in an outpouring of emotion as they mourn the fallen troops and give voice to their anguish at the Persians' military failure.

After Xerxes' self-pitying lamentation in which he wishes that he too had died along with his men (907–17) his expressions of anguish for his own situation (931–4, 941–3, 950–54) and the loss of his troops (962–66, 974–7, 987–91, 1014–15) are alternated with the Chorus' mourning for the Persians' losses. In what follows Xerxes draws the clearest connection yet between his shabby appearance and the destruction of his army (1017–23):[68]

> Chorus: Is anything left of the Persians, O man of great calamity?
> Xerxes: Do you see what remains of my outfit?
> Chorus: I see, I see.

---

[64] Later in the scene (942) he again suggests that a δαίμων has turned against him, suggesting at one point that it was Ares who favoured the other side (950ff.). Winnington-Ingram (1973), p. 218 suggests that Xerxes' call upon Zeus (915) reminds the audience of Darius' words and highlights his failure to understand Zeus' role in the disaster.

[65] By contrast with Darius' analysis of the situation, however, there is no suggestion here that Xerxes or the Persians are being punished for *hybris*: Garvie (2009), *ad* 922–4.

[66] Some of the names listed here also appeared in the Chorus' earlier catalogue, as well as in the messenger's account of Salamis. For a full discussion of the individual names see Garvie (2009), *ad* 955–61, 966–73, 981–5 and 992–1001.

[67] See, for example, Schenker (1994), p. 291–2 (although it is quite a leap to suggest, as he does, that 'Xerxes has paid for his errors, and in the process he has learned enough never to repeat them') and Favorini (2003), p. 106.

[68] The clothing metaphor is later alluded to again at line 1036 when Xerxes uses the word γυμνός ('bare' or 'naked') to refer to the fact that he has been 'denuded' of his escorts: γυμνός εἰμι προπομπῶν.

Xerxes: And this quiver …
Chorus: What is this that you say has survived?
Xerxes: … the storehouse of arrows?
Chorus: Little enough out of so much.

Thus the king's ragged robes become analogous with the sorry state of his army, and the empty quiver stands for Persia, emptied of its men (cf. 761, where Darius refers to the emptying of Susa). No mention is made here of the bow, as the symbol of Persian military power; its absence, along with that of the arrows from Xerxes' quiver (or, in the terms of the metaphor, the men of his army) is indicative of the Persians' military failure.[69]

Following his revelation that the Persian force is in as sorry a state as his tattered robes and his empty quiver the relationship between Chorus and king undergoes a change, as Xerxes, with a series of commands using the imperative, stage-manages the Chorus' actions until the close of the play. He directs both their vocal utterances (with instructions variously to weep and shout in response to his own cries: 1038, 1040, 1042, 1048, 1050, 1058, 1066, 1071) and their actions (these comprise: 'rowing' gestures, 1046; breast-beating, 1054; plucking their beards and hair, 1056 and 1062; robe-tearing, 1060; and weeping, 1064). While in one sense the king has reverted to a position of command over his subordinates, it is a far cry from the status which he held in the minds of the Chorus at the start of the play. Although there is nothing here which conveys a sense that the king has been toppled from his position of power, we are left in no doubt that he has been utterly stripped of his dignity. The humiliation which he has suffered is, by implication, the humiliation of Persia itself.[70] This identification of the king with the state as a whole had been implied from the very beginning of the episode, where the language used by Xerxes to describe his condition was echoed in the Chorus' description of their country. Where Xerxes, in his opening lines, cried that 'The vigour has gone from my limbs' (λέλυται γὰρ ἐμῶν γυίων ῥώμη, 913), the Chorus used the metaphor of bodily weakness shortly afterwards in exclaiming, 'The land of Asia, O King of the country, has terribly, terribly been brought to her knees' (Ἀσία δὲ χθών, βασιλεῦ γαίας, /αἰνῶς αἰνῶς ἐπὶ γόνυ κέκλιται, 929–30). By the time the play closes, with Xerxes escorted from the stage by the wailing elders (1077), Aeschylus' audience have witnessed the full spectacle of his degradation. His enemies, the

---

[69] See above, p. 16 and Thalmann (1980), p. 272.
[70] Taplin (1977), p. 123: 'Seen in its full dramatic context one man embodies the ruin of a nation, his few paces the disaster of retreat.' See also Harrison (2000), p. 91 and Saïd (2007), pp. 91–2.

Athenian spectators in the theatre, although denied from witnessing in real life the imagined disgrace which followed on from Xerxes' departure from Greece, were thus afforded the opportunity to see the extraordinary spectacle played out on the stage before them.

The question arises here as to the extent to which the audience might be expected to sympathize with the figure of Xerxes. Scholarly readings of the *Persians* have ranged from interpretations of it as a jingoistic celebration of the Athenians' victory to the suggestion that, despite the subject matter, it might be seen as a human tragedy with a universally applicable message about the fragility of the human condition.[71] In responding to the dramatic character of Xerxes as presented here either – or both – of these reactions to his reversal of fortune is possible.[72] The play thus offers us within a single staged text a series of artistic responses to Xerxes which encapsulate both the image of the terrifying invader, to be hated and feared, and that of the failed conqueror, shabby and disgraced; this latter Xerxes, his reaction enacted on stage by an Athenian performer, is one to whom an audience might respond either with the triumph of victors deriding a defeated foe or with, if not pity, the horror of witnesses to the devastation of a fellow human being whose demise had been played out before them. It was this combination of the terrifying and the pathetic which, in varying degrees, would come to inform many of the subsequent portrayals of the Persian king discussed within this volume.

Dramatic variations on the Persian theme: Staging Xerxes after Aeschylus

Despite the absence of any further surviving fifth-century theatrical representation of Xerxes after that produced by Aeschylus it is nonetheless possible to detect traces of the continuing resonance of the image of the Persian king on the stage. While no other extant tragedy deals with the Persian Wars[73] it is on the comic stage where we find the clearest clues relating to the theme's ongoing

---

[71] Harrison (2000), p. 51ff. with p. 135 n. 1 offers a summary of the scholarly argument with comprehensive bibliographical references for each side of the debate.

[72] So Pelling (1997, ed.), p. 17, suggesting that 'we should not think of the audience responding monolithically'. Similarly Griffith (1998), p. 51 proposes a mix of responses. Hall (2006), pp. 208–11 discusses the way in which an audience of the *Persians* might experience both jubilation and pain as they remembered their own experiences of the war with Persia.

[73] A papyrus fragment from the fourth century (*tr. fr. adesp.* 685) seems to be part of a lament for Persian royalty, and may have been the inspiration for the Apulian 'Darius vase' discussed below (p. 134–5, with n. 33).

dramatic influence later in the fifth century.[74] Aristophanes' *Acharnians* (10) suggests that in around 425 BC some of Aeschylus' plays were enjoying a revival, and in the *Frogs* of 405 BC explicit reference is made to Aeschylus' *Persians*, which would appear to indicate a degree of audience familiarity with the tragedy.[75] Such a familiarity perhaps underlies allusions in Aristophanes' comedies which exploit stereotyped barbarian characters or create a humorous picture of Persian kingship; although Xerxes is not named in any of the extant comedies[76] elements of some of the plays appear to draw on a generic image of Persian kings which was, at least in part, generated by the presentation of Xerxes earlier in the fifth century.[77] *Acharnians*, for example, features an Athenian ambassador to Persia who reports upon the life of luxury which he has enjoyed while he has been away (68–78).[78] On the arrival of the ambassador at the Persian court the king – in an image which combines comic crudeness with a hint at both the military might of Persia and the presumed extravagance of the king's lifestyle – is said to have been away with his army 'shitting for eight months on the golden hills' (80–82); upon his return he served the ambassadors whole baked oxen (85–6). The suggestions of luxury and idle leisure seen here perhaps owe something to images of Persian royalty generated by mainland Greek memories of Xerxes' invasion.[79] The

---

[74] Even the earliest Athenian comedy appears to have shown an interest in eastern themes; the Suda records a *Persians* or *Assyrians* by Chionides, and we know of Magnes' *Lydians* from a brief fragment. Both poets seem to have been active in the 480s and 470s BC. Later, the title of Pherecrates' *Persians*, of which only scant fragments remain (*PCG* 132–41), reflects an ongoing interest in the theme (Edmonds 1957 suggests a date of 425 BC for this comedy). Long (1986), p. 4 lists titles of comic plays which appear to suggest a particular interest in non-Greeks, although these are not restricted to Persian subjects. Schmitt (1984) discusses 'Persian colouring' in old comedy, and Daumas (1985) provides a survey of references to Persians in the Aristophanic corpus. See also Tuplin (1996), pp. 141–52.

[75] *Frogs* 1026–9: here Aristophanes has his Aeschylus say that his *Persians* taught the Athenians always to be eager to defeat their opponents; Dionysus then comments on his enjoyment of the ghost-raising scene and the Chorus' wailing.

[76] Sommerstein (1980) identifies a possible exception at *Acharnians* 100 where he suggests that in the gibberish spoken by Pseudartabas we can 'detect traces of the names Artaxerxes and Xerxes'.

[77] Some scholars have attempted to draw connections between Aristophanic scenes and specific episodes in the course of Xerxes' invasion of Greece. Ketter (1991), for example, argues that the entrance of Lamachus at the end of *Acharnians* parodies the exodos of Aeschylus' *Persians*, where the defeated Xerxes appears. Byl (2001), pp. 35–6 suggests a link between the burning of the *phrontistērion* in *Clouds* and the burning of the sanctuary (*telestērion*) of Eleusis by Xerxes' forces (Herodotus 9.65). Such connections are rather tenuous and difficult to prove with any certainty.

[78] During the Peloponnesian War the forging of an alliance with Persia was a real possibility for both Athens and Sparta: see Rhodes (2007), pp. 36–8 for a summary of the historical context here. M. C. Miller (1997), pp. 109–33 looks at the evidence for embassies to Persia throughout the fifth century and considers the significance of these as a means of cultural exchange.

[79] A generic image of Persian kings – this time one which plays on the idea of their outlandish appearance – also lies behind the description in Aristophanes' *Birds* of the cockerel, the 'Persian bird' who 'first ruled the Persians before all those Dariuses and Megabazuses' (484–5); he 'struts around like the Great King with his headwear (crest) upright' (486–7). It is possible that this may relate to the appearance of Darius' ghost in Aeschylus' *Persians*, where the Chorus draw attention to the king's tiara (661).

ambassador has brought with him Pseudartabas, the 'King's Eye',[80] a caricature of a Persian official whose bizarre appearance is ridiculed by Dikaiopolis (94–7) and who speaks nonsensical Greek (100, 104).[81] Elsewhere the Chorus of old men in *Wasps* reminisce about their role in the wars against Persia (1070–90), using these memories to justify their own ongoing bellicosity; they appear to conflate the invasions of Darius and Xerxes, referring to a land battle which is presumably that at Marathon,[82] yet describing the barbarian as having set fire to Athens (1078–9), an event which occurred during Xerxes' invasion of 480 BC, and then later at the hands of the troops left behind with Mardonius in 479 BC.[83]

Re-enacting Salamis: Timotheus of Miletus

The most detailed performative response to the figure of Xerxes which survives from the period after Aeschylus' play was composed not by an Athenian but by a Milesian, Timotheus (c. 460–c. 350 BC).[84] His *Persians*, the date and location of whose first performance are unknown (although the final decade of the fifth century seems likely),[85] is a citharodic nome – that is, a poetic composition designed for solo performance to the accompaniment of the lyre.[86] Until the early

---

[80] Balcer (1977), pp. 256–61 assembles the rather sparse evidence for the role of the 'King's Eye' in Achaemenid Persia. See also Hirsch (1985), pp. 101–34, suggesting that evidence from Xenophon's *Cyropaedia* indicates that Greek assumptions about the existence of such an office in the Persian administrative system were erroneous.

[81] Pseudartabas is one of several non-Greek Aristophanic characters who are mocked for their incomprehensible speech; other examples are the Triballian god of the *Birds* who speaks gibberish (1615, 1628–9) and the Scythian archer of *Thesmophoriazusae* who speaks oddly distorted Greek (1001–7, 1082–97).

[82] The presentation of old men as 'Marathon-fighters' (Μαραθωνομάχαι) is a recurring element of Aristophanes' comic presentation of the older generation (and disregards the fact that it is unlikely that by the late fifth century any veterans of the Persian Wars still survived): see, for example, *Acharnians* 181, *Knights* 781–85.

[83] On a similar conflation of the actions of Persian kings in fourth-century Athenian oratory, see below, pp. 105–6 and 110–11.

[84] Much of what is known about Timotheus' life is anecdotal. Hordern (2002), pp. 3–8 collates the evidence.

[85] Hansen (1984) provides a useful summary of scholarly opinions on the date and location of the first performance; for a more detailed discussion see Janssen (1984), pp. 13–22, favouring a date of around 407 BC and a first performance in Athens. Rosenbloom, however (2006), pp. 149–50 argues for a distinctly non-Athenian perspective, with a first performance in 394 BC, on the grounds that this was when the Spartan king Agesilaus led an invasion of the Persian Empire; he suggests that the performance took place in Ephesus, the only Greek city except Timotheus' homeland of Miletus which is mentioned in the extant section on the sea battle. Without the complete text, however, this latter point is difficult to prove.

[86] See West (1992), pp. 215–17 on the meaning of the term 'nome'. Hordern (2002), pp. 25–33 looks at the history of the genre and the context of citharodic performances. Van Minnen (1997), pp. 254–5 also outlines the musical and mimetic characteristics of Timotheus' *Persians*. For discussions of so-called 'New Music' and the context – musical, social and political – within which Timotheus was working, see Csapo (2004) and D'Angour (2011).

twentieth century, all that remained of this poetic text consisted of fragmentary quotations in the works of Plutarch, who records that it was re-performed as late as 205 BC, at the Nemean games, in a patriotic tribute to the Greek commander Philopoemen who had led the Achaean confederacy to victory against the Spartans at Mantinea and subsequently held out against Roman domination of Greece.[87] The discovery in 1902 of a papyrus roll in a necropolis at Abusir, Egypt, brought to light around 250 more lines of the Greek text, some of which are badly mutilated, but which are nonetheless complete enough to give a clear sense of the subject matter.[88] The papyrus, thought to date to the fourth century BC, is thus one of the earliest surviving examples of a Greek 'book'. To judge from what remains of the second half of the nome, the surviving text is a vivid imagining of a series of episodes during a sea battle, which bears several resemblances to Salamis as described in Aeschylus' *Persians*.[89] The picture which is created here is one of utter chaos in the aftermath of defeat, with the sights and sounds of the battle evoked in extravagantly descriptive passages which conjure up images of devastation;[90] these narrative pieces are interspersed with the speeches of individuals who articulate their own experiences of drowning or being slain by the Greek victors, and the account of the battle culminates in the appearance of the king himself.

Although neither the subject matter nor the concept of dealing with the Persian defeat from the perspective of the enemy was original, Timotheus' handling of the battle of Salamis represented an innovative approach. Seen as a musical revolutionary in his own time and by the critics of later antiquity, Timotheus seems not always to have been appreciated for the innovations which he brought to his poetry – even the epilogue of his *Persians*, where he comments on Spartan censure of his work (206–12), suggests that his novel methods may have met with disapproval. He was said to have experimented with metre, rhythm and language, as well as by blending various other genres

---

[87] Plutarch, *Philopoemen* 11.2. On the use of this song in celebration of Greek collective identity see also Hall (1994), pp. 48–60, revised in Hall (2006), pp. 273–5. Plutarch also refers to Timotheus' poetry at *On Listening to Poetry* 11.1 and *Agesilaus* 14.2 (see *PMG* 788–790).

[88] Wilamowitz edited the first published version of Timotheus' *Persians* in 1903. Line references in the discussion which follows are those used in the 2002 edition of Hordern. The line numbering in Janssen's 1984 edition is slightly different.

[89] Rosenbloom (2006), pp. 151–3.

[90] The destruction of the ships is described in vivid detail at 5–28. Elsewhere we are given other visually striking images: the sea reddened with blood (31–3); a Phrygian frantically trying to save himself from drowning (40–71); and the vast quantities of corpses in the sea and along the shore (94–7). The aural impact of the performance is indicated by references to the lamentations of distraught survivors (100–104, 139, 169–70), along with the rendering of the words of individual sailors in their death throes (72–81, 150–62) or in response to the horror of the situation (105–38).

into his compositions, thereby pushing the flexibility of the nome to the limit;[91] meanwhile the mimetic aspect of performances of his poetry is well attested, with other titles attributed to him including the *Birth Pangs of Semele, Scylla, Cyclops,* and *The Madness of Ajax.*[92] Such sensational roles appear to have been conceived as special challenges to the vocal skills of a citharode. The portrayal on stage of a barbarian dying or in distress might therefore also be seen as a similarly extraordinary feat; the poem affords ample opportunity for dramatic licence, most notably with its use of 'barbarian' dialect and the lamentation of the dying enemies.[93]

It is within this context of musical and dramatic innovation that the character of Xerxes is rendered as one of several barbarian figures who are individualized in Timotheus' piece.[94] This image of the Persian king, as impersonated by a Greek performer, bears a close theatrical relationship to the Xerxes of Aeschylus' *Persians* – not least in that he sings in lamentation of the Persians' losses at Salamis – yet at the same time we might also detect a shift in the way in which he is represented. Left unnamed in Timotheus' version (as he would be too in many subsequent literary treatments of his invasion of Greece), the king, simply identified here as βασιλεύς (171, 174), is nonetheless instantly recognizable, both from the setting of the poem and his actions and words. Our first reminder of Xerxes comes before his actual appearance, however, as the first drowning barbarian addresses the sea itself and recalls his master's bridging of the Hellespont (72–81):

> Once before in your audacity you were yoked (καταζευχθεῖσα) and had your turbulent neck in a flaxen bond; now my lord, mine (ἐμὸς ἄναξ ἐμὸς), will stir you up with pines born of the mountains, and enclose your navigable plains with his roaming sailors, you who are maddened by the gadfly, ancient object of hate, faithless and embraced by the winds rushing to dash you.

---

[91] Hordern (2002), pp. 36–62 analyses the style, language and metre of Timotheus' *Persians*.

[92] Herington (1985), pp. 153–4, with notes 14–20 (pp. 274–5) collates the ancient testimonia relating both to the perception of Timotheus as a musical revolutionary and to the 'dramatic realism' of his performances. See also Hall (1994), p. 66: 'histrionic representations of persons undergoing physical and psychological disturbance seem to have been one of Timotheus' fortes'.

[93] See, for example, the reference to the dying Phrygian's words as 'interweaving Greek speech with Asian' (146–7) and the mock-Greek which follows (150–61); Hall (1994), p. 63 notes that this kind of linguistic caricature is rare in extant Greek literature, but that it is in a similar vein to the Greek spoken by the Scythian archer in Aristophanes' *Thesmophoriazusae* (411 BC) and by the Phrygian in Euripides' *Orestes* (408 BC). See also Wright (2008), pp. 45–7. The distinctive sound of the Persians' lamentation is also evoked by Timotheus at lines 169–70; the 'Asian lament' is described as σύντονος, 'intense' or 'high-pitched'.

[94] The text's presentation of barbarian stereotypes and its relationship to Greek cultural identity has been analysed in detail by Hall (1994, revised as Hall 2006, Ch. 9, both with particular reference to the significance of the drowning barbarians' inability to swim as a mark of 'otherness').

The familiar image of the yoking of the sea evokes both Aeschylus' description of Xerxes' bridge and the Herodotean treatment of the Hellespont crossing.[95] Meanwhile the reference to Xerxes' sailors and 'mountain-born pines' (the wooden oars of his ships) as enclosing the sea also hints at the motif of the vast number of Persian forces. Shortly afterwards, the second Persian in distress also appears to refer to the Hellespont crossing; while the text is badly mutilated here references can be detected to 'navigable Helle' (113) and perhaps to 'the cover providing a passage, (which) my master (ἐμὸς δεσπότης) built far from home' (114–16). The speaker goes on to say that had it not been for this he would never have left Tmolus or Sardis to make war in Greece; the focus on Xerxes' crossing as the starting-point for the Persians' ills might be seen to echo the Aeschylean emphasis on the symbolic significance of the bridge as well as the stress placed (at least by the character of Darius) in Aeschylus' play on the responsibility which Xerxes carried for the disaster (see above, pp. 26–30).

When Xerxes actually makes an appearance in Timotheus' poem, it is amid a scene of Persian chaos; as his troops flee in the aftermath of the battle they perform characteristic gestures of mourning rather like those of Aeschylus' Chorus, rending their garments and clawing at their faces with their fingernails (162–66). Seen at the site of the battle, Timotheus' Xerxes fuses elements of the description given by Aeschylus' messenger with the Xerxes seen on stage at the end of the tragic drama (173–95):

> The king, when he had looked upon his army rushing in confusion in backward-travelling flight, and had fallen to his knees and mutilated his body, said, as he surged in his misfortunes: 'Oh, the destruction of my house, and the destructive Greek ships, which killed the young men of my ships, a great throng of my contemporaries; the ships will not take them away backward-travelling, but the smoky strength of fire will burn them with its fierce body, and there will be lamentable sufferings for the Persian land. Alas, wretched misfortune that brought me to Greece! But go, delay no longer, yoke my four-horse chariot, and you, take my countless riches onto the wagons, and set fire to the tents, so that they may have no benefit from our wealth!'

Like Aeschylus' Xerxes, this version of the king observes and reacts to the unfolding disaster, performing the actions associated with mourning as he falls to his knees and injures his own body. The naval metaphor κυμαίνων τύχαισ{ιν}

---

[95] On Herodotus' treatment of the theme see below, pp. 56–8. The barbarian's personification of the sea here perhaps also recalls the Herodotean description of Xerxes' 'punishment' of the Hellespont – as if it were a slave – with whips and chains for destroying his bridge in a storm (Hdt. 7.35).

(177, translated here as 'as he surged in his misfortunes') associates him with the ordeal undergone by his sailors yet at the same time reminds us of his own physical detachment from the action; there is no risk to his own life, by contrast with the men whose death throes the audience has already observed being enacted by the singer. The king's speech here highlights too his distance from the voices which we have already heard; where the drowning figures spoke (or sang) distorted 'barbarian' Greek, Xerxes' words are couched in perfect Greek,[96] and the tone becomes distinctly tragic.[97] The emphasis here on the number and youth of the Persians who have been lost carries Aeschylean resonances (cf. Aeschylus' *Persians* 922–7); Xerxes' lament at the 'wretched misfortune' which brought him to Greece (ἰὼ βαρεῖα συμφορά, 187) also echoes the Aeschylean Xerxes' anguish (cf. Aeschylus' *Persians* 1044: βαρεῖα γ' ἅδε συμφορά·). Unlike Aeschylus' Xerxes, however, Timotheus' Persian king offers no suggestion that he accepts any personal responsibility for the disaster; nor do the gods feature in this version as having played any part in bringing about the defeat.

It is in the final lines of Xerxes' lament, however, that Timotheus' version differs most strikingly from that of Aeschylus. His orders to his subordinates place a clear emphasis on the preservation of Persian wealth, and a wish to ensure that the victorious Greeks will not be allowed to benefit from this wealth. The wealth of Persia is not in itself a new theme,[98] yet the king's command to retrieve his riches and burn the Persians' tents is one not seen elsewhere in the extant sources; by contrast, Aeschylus' *Persians* suggests that the Persians' ὄλβος had been destroyed by the defeat at Salamis (251–2, 826; cf. 163–4).[99] A fragment of the text preserved by Plutarch (*Agesilaus* 14.2 = *PMG* 790) appears to suggest that Persian wealth may have been a theme elsewhere in the poem: it reads 'Ares is lord; Greece has no fear of gold'. It is tempting to see in Xerxes'

---

[96] Hall (1994), p. 64.

[97] Van Minnen (1997), p. 251, noting that Xerxes' words have a tragic rhythm and incorporate a phrase from Aeschylus' *Choephoroe*, as well as echoing Aeschylus' *Persians*. Hordern (2002), pp. 218–24 detects echoes of Aeschylus' *Persians* throughout the Xerxes-scene in Timotheus' text.

[98] See, for example, Aeschylus' *Persians* 3, 45, 53, 80, 159. The image of the extravagance of the Persian camp and Xerxes' tent, however, is more familiar to us from Herodotus' account (7.118–20; see below, pp. 55–6). Herodotus' version (9.82), by contrast with that of Timotheus, suggests that Xerxes left his tent behind with Mardonius; it is this which occasions Pausanias' comparison of Spartan poverty with Persian luxury after Plataea. M. C. Miller (1997), pp. 49–55 examines the evidence for the luxurious tents of Persian military campaigns.

[99] Timotheus' text uses both ὄλβος (191–2) and πλοῦτος (195) to refer to the Persians' material possessions. On the use of these two terms and the apparent distinction which is drawn between them in Aeschylus' *Persians* see Gagarin (1976), pp. 44–5 with n. 35 (pp. 180–1), suggesting that πλοῦτος refers to 'wealth' or 'riches' and that ὄλβος is used to suggest a more general idea of 'prosperity' or 'well-being'. Rosenbloom (2006), pp. 153–4 contends that Timotheus' allusion to the preservation of Persian wealth should be seen in the context of Persian financing of Sparta's navy towards the end of the Peloponnesian War.

intention to deny the Greeks access to his material resources an allusion to the historical context of the composition of Timotheus' poem; after 479 BC Persia repeatedly tried to exert influence by subsidizing some Greek states against others,[100] and the presence of Persia as a key player on the Greek political stage in the late fifth century made for a very different set of circumstances from those surrounding the performance of Aeschylus' *Persians* in 472 BC. In 412/11 BC, in the latter years of the Peloponnesian War, Thucydides (8.18, 8.37, 8.58) reports a series of treaties between Sparta and Persia (with the king represented by the Persian satrap Tissaphernes) which secured Persia's financial and military support for the war against Athens;[101] the first of these treaties immediately followed the revolt from Athenian control of Miletus, Timotheus' homeland.[102] Both this and the second treaty between Sparta and Persia agreed to hand to the Persian king, Darius II, control of all territory which had previously been held by him or his predecessors. A third agreement apparently revised this clause, limiting Persia's claim to the Asiatic mainland, which included Miletus.

Although the precise date of Timotheus' composition remains open to conjecture his re-imagining of Xerxes at a time when the king's descendant had been involved in financing a war being waged between Greek states thus had as its historical backdrop an international political situation which was very different from the Persian Wars aftermath during which Aeschylus staged his version of Xerxes. Produced by a Greek who hailed originally from a politically strategic city outside Athens, this new poetic *Persians*, the production of which entailed the overt impersonation of an infamous Persian king from the past, might be seen to offer an ironic comment on contemporary political affairs. In light of Persian support for Sparta towards the end of the fifth century, Xerxes' insistence in the poem on denying the Greeks access to Persian wealth could be used to highlight the contrast between the past – when Hellenic states united against an external foe – and the contemporary political landscape, in which Greece was divided to the point where rival states now sought alliance with their erstwhile arch-enemy. At the conclusion of Xerxes' lament Timotheus provides his audience with a picture of the victorious Greeks (identified here only by the use of the definite article οἱ, 196) setting up trophies to Zeus and performing an honorary paean (196–201); no particular state is singled out for mention here, which might support a panhellenic reading of the text. This

---

[100] See Lewis (1989).

[101] Lewis (1977), pp. 83–135 examines Persia's role in the later stages of the Peloponnesian War. On the context of the political manoeuvrings see also Andrewes (1992).

[102] See Gorman (2001), pp. 215–42 on the history of Miletus in the fifth century.

was certainly the spirit in which, according to Plutarch, this poem was appropriated in honour of Philopoemen, defender of Greek freedom, around two centuries after its composition.[103] In the decades which followed the image of Xerxes as the archetype of the hostile Persian ruler was to become a focus for panhellenic sentiment in Athenian rhetoric, most notably in the works of Isocrates (see below, pp. 107–12); Timotheus' Xerxes might therefore be viewed as a forerunner to these appropriations of the king in the service of a call for Hellenic unity. The requirements of the orators differed, however, from those of the poets; the emphasis in their speeches would lie less upon the dramatic spectacle of the humiliated Xerxes than upon on the image of a mighty invader whose onslaught had been resisted by the Greeks against all the odds. For Aeschylus and Timotheus, inventing a melodramatic Xerxes and imagining his distraught reaction to events at Salamis allowed them to create arresting theatrical performances for their audiences' entertainment; it was this vision of the Persian king as a shadow of his former self, with his extravagant lamentation, his torn clothing and his broken pride, which was the tragic theatre's bequest to posterity.

[103] Hordern (2002), p. 129.

3. *Xerxes contemplates the brevity of human existence*

2

Historiographical Enquiry: The Herodotean Xerxes-Narrative

Before embarking upon the crossing of the Hellespont from Asia to Europe, the Herodotean Xerxes pauses at Abydus to take in the view of his military force. Perched upon a throne of white stone he congratulates himself upon the sight of his vast army and navy, which fills the land and sea as far as the eye can see. It is what happens next, however, that is astonishing: the king's happiness is short-lived, and he begins to weep. On being questioned by Artabanus as to the reason for his change of mood Xerxes gives a response which encapsulates a key ethical premise of the *Histories* in a single sentence of the Greek text (7.46.2):[1] he remarks that he was reflecting upon the brevity of human life, and upon the fact that not one of the men he sees before him will still be alive in a hundred years' time (Plate 3). This extraordinary moment in Herodotus' narrative embodies the multi-faceted vision of Xerxes explored by the historian: here the Persian king is at once both the fearsome invader with all of Persia's might at his command and a far more recognizably human figure whose invasion of Greece is used by Herodotus to explore the fleeting nature of power and the changing fortunes of mankind.

This chapter will examine the ways in which Herodotus' narrative constructs our most detailed insight into the character and actions of Xerxes, who is given a more thorough treatment than any other Persian in the *Histories*. One aspect of this representation inevitably concerns those episodes which relate to his role as a brutal barbarian despot, the enslaving and cruel tyrant who transgressed both physical and moral boundaries and behaved with disregard for the gods of the Greeks. These features of Xerxes' characterization relate closely to the Athenian

---

[1] On the issue of how best to render the episode at the Hellespont into an English translation, see Willett (2000). For a more detailed discussion of the scene and its relationship to the *Histories* as a whole see also below, pp. 64–6.

traditions – voiced most strikingly in Herodotus' account by Themistocles – in which Xerxes was the epitome of the hated invader. Herodotus' work is also the most extensive exploration which we possess of some of the key literary motifs, or *topoi*, relating to the figure of Xerxes; here we find detailed descriptions of the striking images – Xerxes' vast army, his Hellespont bridge and Athos canal – which, in abridged and much-simplified form, would later come to be reused time and again by the Athenian orators and the later inheritors of the traditions they transmitted. Yet a close reading of the text will also reveal that the negative elements of his character do not constitute for Herodotus the whole picture. Instead these are accompanied in the historian's retelling by aspects which highlight Xerxes' essential humanity; this is a far more nuanced presentation than those of later accounts, and one which allows Herodotus to examine Xerxes' role within the Persian dynasty. Here is a king who, as the last of the four successive kings – after Cyrus, Cambyses and Darius – who feature in Herodotus' exploration of the history of his world, is compelled by his position in Persian history and the burden of the kingship which he has inherited from his father to undertake the expedition to Greece. Ultimately there lies beneath the tyrannical façade a flawed human being whose inability to learn from his mistakes and to understand the nature of the Greeks whose territory he endeavoured to conquer leads to the failure of his mission. Herodotus' account also looks beyond the failed invasion of Greece and into the world of Xerxes' harem; the tale of court intrigue which he recounts at the end of his *Histories* is the earliest instance of the 'romantic' element which would later become a key feature of several prose narratives based on the Xerxes-traditions.

The brutal barbarian?

> For we did not achieve these things, but it was the gods and heroes, who were jealous that one man – unholy and reckless (ἀνόσιόν τε καὶ ἀτάσθαλον) – should be king of both Asia and Europe: a man who made no distinction between what is sacred and what is secular, one who burned and tore down statues of the gods, and who whipped and fettered the sea. (Hdt. 8.109.3)

Themistocles' words to the Athenians after their victory in the naval battle at Salamis, imagined here in Herodotus' account, provide a summary of the key elements of Xerxes' character as received in the dominant Athenian tradition and its literary descendants. The speech presents an image of a cruel and impious despot, bent on imperial supremacy, whose disregard for all that is sacred led to acts of outrageous transgression. Xerxes' destruction of sanctuaries is seen here as the ultimate manifestation of his irreverence, and his mission to enslave Greece is encapsulated within the image of the Hellespont itself as being flogged and bound like a slave. Meanwhile the defeat of Persian imperial ambition is presented as the work of divine forces jealous of this one man's arrogant attempts at territorial expansion. This Xerxes comprises features already familiar from Aeschylus' dramatic presentation of his character;[2] the voice of the commander of the Greek fleet, presented in direct speech in Herodotus' account, offers a version of the Athenians' response to the Persian king who had invaded their territory and burned their city.[3]

The reader of Herodotus who seeks examples of the behaviour of a brutal and sacrilegious despot is, on first glance, well served where Xerxes is concerned.[4] Actions of the kind which are alluded to in Themistocles' speech appear regularly throughout the historian's account of the invasion of Greece; these are the deeds which lend credence to the image of Xerxes as a formidable figure who brought terror to the Greeks whom he intended to enslave. The very first mention of the king in the *Histories* is one which foreshadows much of the later discourse about his role as destroyer of all things sacred; at 1.183.3 Xerxes is said to have stolen a sacred golden statue from a temple in Babylon, and to have killed the priest who tried to stop him from doing so.[5] This is one of several such instances of theft and sacrilege: in the course of the invasion of Greece

---

[2] See Saïd (2002), pp. 137–45 for a detailed comparison of Herodotus' and Aeschylus' interpretations of Xerxes' invasion.

[3] Fisher (2002), p. 224 notes the irony 'that this neat summing up of Xerxes' moral punishment is delivered by the cleverest and most morally ambiguous of [Herodotus'] Greek characters, who according to Herodotus was already planning a possible escape route to the court of this same impious and outrageous Xerxes, who constantly displayed his greed, and who was soon to play a leading role in the earliest stages of Athenian imperialism'. On Herodotus' treatment of Themistocles, see Fornara (1971), pp. 66–74 and Blösel (2001). Podlecki (1975) and Lenardon (1978) both offer surveys of the literary and archaeological evidence relating to Themistocles' life. For discussions of Themistocles' relationship with Xerxes in the works of later Greek writers see below on Diodorus (pp. 137–9), Philostratus (pp. 152–4), Cornelius Nepos (pp. 163–4) and Plutarch (pp. 183–5).

[4] The verdict of Georges on Herodotus' Xerxes (1994), p. 201 is typical of assessments which focus primarily on the negative elements of his characterisation in the *Histories*: 'In sum, Xerxes is purblind and sacrilegious in the environment of Greece to that extreme epitomized by the immense hubris of his armada itself.' Similarly Immerwahr (1966), pp. 176–83 emphasizes the negative aspects of Herodotus' Xerxes: 'Xerxes is the typical Persian in extreme form, both in magnificence and in cruelty' (p. 177). Hartog (1988), pp. 330–4 stresses the transgressive and despotic aspects of the behaviour of Xerxes and other Persian kings. Evans (1991), pp. 60–7 offers a more balanced view; cf. Romm (1998), pp. 166–70.

[5] The image of Xerxes as remover (and destroyer) of sacred objects is one which is noteworthy in the later works of Strabo (see below, pp. 177–9) and Pausanias (pp. 180–2) in particular. The 'guidebook' style in which Herodotus is writing on Babylon here foreshadows these geographical works in which Xerxes' impact on the material environment is of particular significance.

he sends his army to sack the sanctuary at Delphi and to bring the treasures to him (8.35ff.), and his impiety reaches its height with the sack of Athens, which culminates in the slaughter of those who had sought refuge in the temple on the Acropolis and the burning of the sacred site (8.53.2).

Throughout the invasion, the wrath of Xerxes also manifests itself against particular individuals who become the personal victims of the campaign. The first casualties are the men responsible for the construction of the original bridges across the Hellespont, which are destroyed by a storm; they are beheaded on the orders of Xerxes (7.35.3). It is in the story of Pythius the Lydian, however, that Herodotus' account offers an extended narrative which is illustrative of Xerxes' characteristic cruelty. At 7.27–9 Xerxes had seen fit to reward Pythius generously for his hospitality in entertaining the Persian army en route to Greece and for his offer of financial support for the campaign. Shortly afterwards, however, we see Pythius requesting that Xerxes should spare his eldest son from taking part in the expedition (7.38). Xerxes' reaction may be seen to demonstrate a terrifying potential for inconsistency; he becomes furiously angry (κάρτα τε ἐθυμώθη, 7.39.1) and has the son in question cut in half so that the army can march between the two halves of the corpse. This kind of apparently callous and exhibitionist cruelty reaches its peak in Xerxes' display of anger against Leonidas after Thermopylae (7.238); then, we are told, the Persian king ordered the Spartan leader's head to be cut off and fixed on a stake.[6] This, Herodotus says, goes against any usual practice of Persians since they, more than any others, honour men who have died in war; the historian reasons, therefore, that Xerxes must have felt greater anger against Leonidas than against any other man alive (ὅτι βασιλεὺς Ξέρξης πάντων δὴ μάλιστα ἀνδρῶν ἐθυμώθη ζῶντι Λεωνίδῃ, 7.238.2).[7] By contrast, Pausanias' reaction to the suggestion after Plataea that he should behead and impale Mardonius as revenge for Xerxes' treatment of Leonidas is one of outrage, in which he declares that to insult a dead body in this way would be to do something more fitting for barbarians than for Greeks (τὰ πρέπει μᾶλλον βαρβάροισι ποιέειν ἢ περ Ἕλλησι, 9.79.1); yet Greeks in Herodotus' narrative are by no means above acts of cruelty such as those perpetrated by the Persians under the direction of Xerxes (see below, pp. 68–9).

---

[6] Lateiner (1987), pp. 92–3 considers the various occasions on which we see 'barbaric' mutilation of the human body in Herodotus' narrative. Steiner (1994), p. 155 interprets the beheading of Leonidas as one of a series of triumphalist actions on the part of Persian kings.

[7] The anger of Xerxes has already been seen at Thermopylae when, as the Persians are still anticipating the retreat of the Greek force without an engagement, Xerxes loses patience and becomes enraged (θυμωθείς, 7.210.1) before sending the Medes and Cissians to attack.

Further manifestations of Xerxes' anger appear later in the text. At Salamis, the Phoenician sailors who lose their ships try to claim that this was a result of the Ionians' treachery (8.90); on seeing an Ionian ship fighting particularly well, Xerxes, οἷα ὑπερλυπεόμενός τε καὶ πάντας αἰτιώμενος ('exceedingly displeased and critical of everyone'), vents his wrath on the Phoenicians by having them beheaded. Elsewhere there is evidence of the fear inspired by Xerxes among his own troops: at 8.65, before Salamis, Demaratus warns Dicaeus not to reveal the portent which he has witnessed apparently heralding the destruction of Xerxes' force, for fear that Xerxes will have his head. Later (8.69) the Persian commanders are convinced that Artemisia's attempt to dissuade the king from engaging in battle at Salamis will result in her punishment; on the contrary, however, Xerxes is pleased with her advice (although choosing nonetheless to ignore it). On the journey home from Greece too we hear of a further tale relating to the king's potential for committing acts of brutality. In an alternative version of Xerxes' retreat related at 8.118, Herodotus tells the story of Xerxes' crossing of the Hellespont in a ship. When a storm arises, Xerxes asks the captain how they can survive it; the response given is that the only way is to get rid of some of the men on board and so Xerxes persuades the Persian nobles accompanying him to jump overboard to their deaths. On arriving safely ashore, Xerxes is said to have rewarded the captain with a gold crown for saving his life, and then to have cut off his head for causing the deaths of the other Persians. This story of the 'captain's reward' gives us pause, however, to consider Herodotus' particular perspective on Xerxes and his actions. On this occasion the historian expresses his own doubt at the veracity of this version of events, not because the notion of the punishment exacted is necessarily implausible but because surely, he says, if it were necessary to dispense with some of the men on board, Xerxes would have flung overboard not the nobles but the lowly Phoenician rowers (8.119). On the contrary, he goes on to say, the true version of the story of Xerxes' return home is that which relates his journey by road with the army. While there is no question in what Herodotus says here that the king is presented as deeming his slave subjects to be disposable chattels, this particular story is of significance for the way in which it demonstrates already in the fifth century the potential for elaborate anecdotes highlighting irrationality and brutality to be attracted to the imagined figure of Xerxes.

While, then, it is tempting to see the outbursts of anger and cruelty outlined above as facets of the barbarian character of Xerxes, presented as part of a negative image of the king with which we are familiar from Aeschylus' *Persians*, it is also possible to suggest that Herodotus' presentation is far less critical than a mere catalogue of Xerxes' misdemeanours such as that given here may suggest. It is certainly true to say that from an Athenian perspective – such as that expressed by the Herodotean Themistocles – these episodes are rich fodder for the creation of an image of a cruel and impious invader, yet closer examination suggests that the account of Herodotus is more subtle in its assessment of Xerxes' behaviour. Here we might compare the case of Cambyses, whom Herodotus emphatically describes as insane throughout the *Histories* (see, for example, 3.30.1, 3.33, 3.34.1, 3.37.1, 3.38.1, where Herodotus asserts that his acts of transgression and violence were a result of his madness).[8] By contrast, despite the violent and contemptible nature of some of Xerxes' actions, they are not attributable merely to irrationality or madness. Even the episode involving Pythius and his son could be seen as a response, in accordance with the principles of reciprocity, to Pythius' violation of the terms of *xenia*;[9] likewise, the punishment of the Phoenician sailors at Salamis, despite the cruelty of Xerxes' method here, is not merely an arbitrary act but a direct response to their mendacity and disloyalty. Within the wider context of Herodotus' narrative this type of behaviour is not peculiar to Xerxes alone but is part of a broader pattern which characterizes the actions of several Persian kings, including, as we shall see below, those of Xerxes' father Darius.

It is possible too to identify occasions in Herodotus' narrative where we see beyond the picture of tyrannical brutality. During the narrative of Xerxes' march to Greece (7.133) Herodotus tells us that Xerxes sent no demand for submission to Athens or Sparta because of what had previously happened to messengers sent by Darius; those at Athens were thrown into a pit for criminals, and those sent to Sparta were thrown into a well. The story told here continues with the Spartans' later sending to Persia of Bulis and Sperchias, volunteers who were to atone with their own lives for the deaths of the Persian heralds. The details of the episode provide an insight into familiar elements of the Greek/ Persian distinction: for example their conversation with the satrap Hydarnes en route offers the opportunity for the Spartans to espouse the joys of freedom as opposed to slavery (7.135.3), and the refusal of the two to perform *proskynēsis* before Xerxes underlines the difference between a nation of slave subjects who do obeisance to a mere mortal (7.136.1) and one where individual freedom is

---

[8] For detailed discussions of Cambyses' madness see Griffiths (1989) and Munson (1991). Lloyd (1988) examines the construction of Herodotus' narrative on Cambyses.

[9] On this interpretation of Xerxes' treatment of Pythius see Baragwanath (2008), pp. 269–80; cf. Ubsdell (1983), pp. 15–16. Note, however, Harrison (2011), pp. 60–3, advocating caution in dealing with revisionist views which may be too ready to explain away such episodes of violence.

a defining factor.[10] Xerxes' exchange with Bulis and Sperchias does, however, allow the king on this occasion to occupy the moral high ground (7.136.2): he magnanimously (ὑπὸ μεγαλοφροσύνης[11]) announces that he will not kill them and thus behave like the Spartans, who acted contrary to the customs of all men (τὰ πάντων ἀνθρώπων νόμιμα). Herodotus goes on to state that Xerxes would therefore not relieve the Spartans of the blame for their crime, relating that instead the real retribution later came when the sons of Bulis and Sperchias were sent on a mission to Asia but intercepted and taken as prisoners to Attica, where the Athenians put them to death (cf. Thucydides 2.67, recording this incident as having taken place in 430 BC).[12] Herodotus' narration of this story alerts the reader to the fact that the Greek/barbarian comparison in moral terms is not so easily defined as it might at first glance seem.[13] It is made clear here that Greeks too (Athenians and Spartans alike) are capable of morally dubious acts which violate established custom; Xerxes on this occasion demonstrates his moral superiority. The fact that the continuation of Herodotus' account looks beyond the chronological scope of his Persian Wars narrative to a moment in more recent history – the Athenians' killing of the sons of Bulis and Sperchias – also acts as a reminder that since then the Athenians have again perpetrated similar acts of violence;[14] this is a point which will be examined in more detail later in this chapter.

---

[10] See above, p. 25 n. 42, on Aeschylus' presentation of the Persians' practice of *proskynēsis*.

[11] On the interpretation of the Greek *megalophrosunē* as used by Herodotus see further below, pp. 56-7.

[12] Macan (1908), *ad* Herodotus 7.137 points out that the vengeance which eventually fell upon the Spartans carried no benefit for the Persians against whom the initial wrong was committed. On the themes of divine vengeance and ancestral guilt in relation to the story of Bulis and Sperchias see Gagné (2013), pp. 296-304.

[13] Hartog (1989) first posited the Greek/barbarian polarity in Herodotus' work in terms of 'self' and 'other' (see also, for example, Cartledge (2002), pp. 51-77). Note in particular, however, Dewald's review (1990), pointing out that this view 'requires a fairly fixed and uncomplicated Same and Other' (p. 220) and suggesting that Hartog oversimplifies the notion of polarity in Herodotus' narrative. Pelling (1997) provides an analysis which explores the blurring of the moral dichotomy between Greeks and Persians in Herodotus' account. See also Gruen (2011), p. 80, noting that Herodotus does not present a black-and-white cultural divide between Greeks and Persians but that, 'Heroes and villains appear on both sides.'

[14] Thucydides' version allows the Athenians to justify the killing of the Spartan ambassadors to Persia on the grounds that Spartans had killed at the start of the Peloponnesian War all Athenians whom they had captured at sea. By omitting any reference to such motivation Herodotus' account provides no precise justification for the Athenians' actions; his reader might therefore be more inclined to question the morality of the killings of Bulis' and Sperchias' sons.

In-depth narrative: Herodotus' exploration of the Xerxes-*topoi*

While our discussion of Aeschylus' *Persians* provided an insight into the earliest surviving references to key literary motifs relating to Xerxes, *topoi* which were to become inextricably bound up with the representation of this king in later literature, it is in Herodotus' detailed narrative account that we find the fullest literary exposition of the distinctive images which would come to symbolize Xerxes and his invasion of Greece. In accounts post-dating that of Herodotus – such as those of the Athenian orators, Roman exempla or later historical and biographical accounts of the Persian Wars – these are often reduced to somewhat formulaic, easily recognizable snapshots used as succinct ways of characterizing the king's behaviour. The king's vast army, the Athos canal and Hellespont bridge, and the throne and chariot from which he observed his troops would all serve in the later traditions as shorthand for a picture of an enslaving tyrant renowned for extremes of behaviour and surrounded by the wealth and luxury of a huge empire.

One of the most striking recurring themes of Herodotus' narrative of Xerxes' invasion is that of the size of the invading army. In references to Xerxes' army numbers feature as heavily here as in Aeschylus' portrayal;[15] this is undoubtedly a reflection of the very real fear which the inhabitants of Greece must have felt at the Persian onslaught. The epigram cited by Herodotus as having been composed for the Thermopylae dead cites three million as the total number of Xerxes' forces (7.228.1), and Herodotus himself describes the army as greater than any other which was known (7.20.2), and as dwarfing even that which Darius took on his Scythian campaign; he goes on to say that Xerxes took every Asian race with him to Greece and that, except for the great rivers, every stream was drunk dry by the army (7.21.1). This idea that the rivers were drained recurs later in Herodotus' account – at 7.108.2 we are told that the river Lisus was drunk dry by Xerxes' men, and at 7.109.2 the lake at Pistyrus is said to have been emptied by the pack animals alone. As well as damaging the physical landscape (a theme which recurs throughout the narrative of Xerxes' invasion, as we shall see below in relation to his crossing of the Hellespont and Athos canal) the army leaves an impact too on the peoples it encounters en route – at 7.118–20 Herodotus relates in depth the ruinous effects felt by those who were forced to host the king and his entourage at each stage of the journey, and with this in

---

[15] See above, p. 17, p. 21 and p. 33.

mind Megacreon, a citizen of Abdera, is cited as regarding it as a blessing that Xerxes is not in the habit of taking *two* dinners a day (7.120.1).

Elsewhere in the narrative more specific details about Xerxes' various contingents are given; Herodotus puts the number of Persian land forces at 1,700, 000 (7.60.1) and tells us that the king's navy consisted of 1,207 triremes, along with transport ships (7.89.1).[16] He devotes a total of 39 chapters (7.61–99) to listing the component sections of the army and fleet, thus – by the sheer scale of the detail which he provides – reinforcing the impression which his narrative creates of the vast number of men and resources at Xerxes' command. Xerxes himself, meanwhile, is seen to be acutely concerned with the scale of his military assets. He demonstrates a particular interest in reviewing and counting his troops; indeed, it is his desire to enumerate the force at Doriscus (7.59) which presents Herodotus with the occasion to provide a full catalogue of the contingents.[17] Here the historian relates the method by which the number of troops is calculated; ten thousand men are fenced into a small space, and then the rest of the army is measured in batches of ten thousand by herding them into this pen.[18] After the troops have been counted Xerxes holds a review in which he questions each contingent; the answers are recorded by his secretaries. He makes the survey of the army mounted in a chariot, then boards a ship and seats himself under a gold canopy in order to review the fleet (7.100).

It is apparent too from Herodotus' description that Xerxes trusts absolutely in the sheer force of numbers at his command;[19] at 7.32 he sends demands for submission from the Greeks in total confidence that those who previously refused to submit to Darius will now be frightened into doing so at his bidding. This is mirrored later in the narrative when the king, rather than executing Greek spies found in Sardis, has them shown the whole Persian force in the misguided belief that this show of Persian strength will encourage the Greeks to surrender without engaging in conflict; his underestimation of his enemy here, subsequently explored in more detail by Herodotus, will prove to be fatal. When Artabanus expresses his misgivings at Abydus, and his concern that Xerxes'

---

[16] On the question of Herodotus' accuracy concerning Persian numbers, see Briant (2002), p. 527.

[17] The ethnic detail which Herodotus includes in his catalogue is reminiscent of the way in which the contingent nations of the Persian empire are represented by their different costumes and appearance on the Persepolis reliefs. See below, pp. 80–1 and pp. 84–5.

[18] On Xerxes' preoccupation with observing the size of his force as a means of measuring his power see Konstan (1987). Christ (1994), pp. 172–5 explores the notion that Herodotean kings use counting as a means of testing their own greatness. Steiner (1994), p. 144 notes that the very act of enumeration and recording distances the king from his subjects; this is also seen in Xerxes' recording of the names of those who distinguished themselves at Salamis (8.90.4).

[19] So Dewald (2006), p. 157: '[Xerxes'] habitual assumptions about the vast extent of his own power effectively blind him to the possibility of failure.'

force may be brought down by the two most powerful things of all (7.47.2), Xerxes assumes that he refers to military powers and asserts that he can easily expand his own militia if necessary. As it turns out, Artabanus' prediction (7.49, immediately dismissed by Xerxes) that the land and the sea will conspire against Xerxes' troops is later borne out by Herodotus' narrative of the campaign.[20] The historian later ridicules Xerxes' 'laughable' (γελοῖον, 8.25.2) scheme – which, he says, fooled no one – to conceal all but a thousand of the twenty thousand Persian dead at Thermopylae, losses sustained when the need to fight in the narrow pass meant that the Persians were unable to take advantage of their superior numbers (7.211.2). The authorial interjection here draws attention to the fact that this is ludicrous behaviour on Xerxes' part, and it is possible to detect a triumphal note in the Greek version of events – despite the Spartans' defeat, the engagement at Thermopylae is portrayed here as a rather hollow victory for Xerxes in the light of the losses he sustained.[21]

Where naval tactics are concerned the size of the fleet works against it at Salamis; Themistocles outlines his tactical move to force the Persians to fight in the narrows at 8.60β, and the strategy results in the destruction of a large proportion of the Persian fleet (8.86). Here the contrast between Greek and Persian forces is not merely one of numbers but also relates to the Greeks' disciplined fighting as contrasted with the Persians' lack of order (8.86); we might compare here account of the messenger in Aeschylus' *Persians*, which emphasizes this same contrast of Athenian order and Persian disarray.[22] The losses sustained by army and navy while on operations are also compounded on Xerxes' march home with his army, many of whom are killed by plague or hunger (8.115.1–2), as Artabanus predicted. Ultimately we are left with the impression that the size of the force meant that the disaster which befell it was all the greater; in this respect Herodotus' account thus follows the lead taken by Aeschylus, who, as we saw earlier (p. 21 and p. 33) used this to create an impression of the scale of the Greek victory. The more spectacular the humiliation can be made to seem, the more glorious the victory for the Greeks.

The overwhelming size of the king's forces is just one of the attributes used to characterize Xerxes in Herodotus' account. Linked with the notion of the

---

[20] See Shapiro (2000), pp. 103–5 for a more detailed discussion of this exchange. On Artabanus as one of a series of 'warner' or 'wise adviser' figures in Herodotus' account see further Bischoff (1932), pp. 53–67, Lattimore (1939) and Pelling (1991), p. 130ff.

[21] Note too A. M. Bowie (2007), *ad* 24.1 (regarding the 20,000 said to have been lost by the Persians at Thermopylae): 'The rounded numbers here have all the exaggeration of traditions generated by the victors.'

[22] Disorder of Persian forces at Salamis: Aeschylus, *Persians* 422, 470, 481. Contrast this with the Greeks' order and discipline at 374, 399–401, 462.

ostentation of Xerxes' vast force is also the memorable image of the king's throne, from which he observes his troops. At Abydus Herodotus describes a throne of white stone (προεξέδρη λίθου λευκοῦ, 7.44.1) as having been specially prepared by the locals, on the king's orders; seated on a hill near the shore Xerxes is able to observe both the army and the navy.[23] At Thermopylae he is again seen observing the battle from his throne (this time the Greek gives ἐκ τοῦ θρόνου[24]), from which he leaps up three times in fear for his army (7.212.1). The throne not only sets him apart from the rest of the Persians – as such it is emblematic of his position of power – but also serves to emphasize his role not as an active participant but as a detached observer; by contrast with the Greek commanders who, like Leonidas at Thermopylae, risk their own lives, Xerxes himself is far from the danger of the battle. The chariot from which Aeschylus' Xerxes is seen commanding his troops also appears in Herodotus' account when he mounts it to make his survey of the army at Doriscus (7.100.1; cf. 7.40 where Xerxes is described as travelling to Greece in a chariot).[25] His later review of the fleet while on board a ship is conducted from beneath a golden canopy; the association of gold with Persian wealth hints too at the luxury enjoyed by the king elsewhere in Herodotus' text and the later traditions.[26] This theme is expanded still further with the description of Xerxes' camp and the extravagance of his dining arrangements at 7.118-20;[27] Herodotus claims that a single meal cost 400 silver talents and gives a lavish description of the preparations for the king's supper, listing the produce which was required and asserting that vessels of gold and silver were also manufactured for the purpose. While the rest of the army sleeps in the open air there

---

[23] For further discussion of the significance of this scene, see below, pp. 64–6.

[24] θρόνος is the noun most commonly used by Herodotus to describe the 'seat' of Xerxes; he refers to it in relation to the idea of dynastic succession at 7.8α.2 and it appears, for example, in the story of Artabanus and the dream (7.15.3, 7.16, 7.17.1); it is also used to refer to the seat of the sacred chariot at 7.40.4. The term προεξέδρη is used only once in Herodotus' work, at 7.44.1, although see below p. 59 on the use of the linguistically similar term προέδρα in relation to Darius.

[25] At 7.40 Xerxes' chariot, drawn by sacred Nisaean horses, follows behind the holy chariot of Zeus in which no mortal is allowed to sit. This juxtaposition could be interpreted as a recognition of Xerxes' acknowledgement of his status as human rather than divine. At 8.115.4 Herodotus tells us that Xerxes left the sacred chariot at Siris in Paeonia en route to Greece; he was unable to retrieve it on his return journey as the Paeonians had given it to the Thracians and pretended that the horses had been stolen. On Aeschylus' use of the chariot motif, see above, pp. 19–20.

[26] Aeschylus' *Persians* also frequently makes the association between the Persians and gold (3, 45, 53, 80, 159; cf. by contrast *Persians* 237–8 on the Athenian *silver* mined at Laurium, discussed by Kurke (1999), p. 306).

[27] We are also reminded of this extravagance at 9.82, after the defeat of Mardonius at Plataea, when Pausanias has a typically elaborate Persian royal meal prepared so as to draw the contrast between this and the Spartans' modest way of life.

is always a tent (σκήνη) ready for the king (7.119.3); again his detachment is emphasized.[28]

The nature of Xerxes' aspirations and his position are also reflected in particular actions en route to Greece which symbolize his imperial ambition as well as his role as tyrant king over a slave nation. The paired actions of the carving of the Athos canal and the crossing of the Hellespont serve to demonstrate both the king's transgression and alteration of natural boundaries[29] (thus implicitly relating to the act of attempting to subsume Greece into his Asiatic empire) and his role as would-be enslaver. Herodotus offers a detailed description of the construction of the Athos canal at 7.22.3, noting that the work was carried out 'under whips' (ὑπὸ μαστίγων, 7.22.1) by men from Xerxes' army. Such reminders that the king's subjects were slaves are never far away in Herodotus' story,[30] and later in the narrative this becomes a key point of contrast between the Persians and their Greek opponents, in particular during the exchange between Xerxes and Demaratus in which the Spartan royal exile asserts that the Greeks will do everything in their power to resist slavery (7.101ff.: see below, pp. 66–7). The historian concludes his account of the cutting of the canal by suggesting that this was an ostentatious gesture on Xerxes' part, commenting, 'Having considered it, I reckon that Xerxes ordered the digging only out of *megalophrosunē* (μεγαλοφροσύνης εἵνεκεν, 7.24.1), wishing to display his power and leave a monument to himself'. The translation of the Greek *megalophrosunē* here is open to conjecture. While some commentators and translators have favoured the English 'pride', with the word's concomitant negative connotations,[31] there is scope for interpreting the term, whose literal rendering is simply 'greatness of mind'[32] as less disapproving in its

---

[28] If, as Broneer (1944) argued, the tent of Xerxes was used as the *skēnē* for the Athenian theatre, it is possible that some of Herodotus' audience were particularly familiar with the image conjured up by this description.

[29] On the relationship in Herodotus' narrative between the crossing of physical boundaries and moral transgression, see Lateiner (1985), pp. 88–93 and Lateiner (1989), pp. 126–35. Immerwahr (1954), pp. 19–27 examines in detail the structural significance of the Hellespont in Herodotus' work as a whole. The notion that by these actions Xerxes turned land into sea and sea into land is not expressed by Herodotus, but would later become a literary commonplace.

[30] Also relevant here is the treatment of the Thebans who defect to the Persian side at Thermopylae (7.233.2). They are branded with Xerxes' royal *stigmata*, thus being marked out as the king's property and therefore as slaves.

[31] So, for example, How and Wells (1912) and Godley (1922); de Sélincourt (1954) offers the more moderate 'mere ostentation', while Waterfield (1998) has 'a sense of grandiosity and arrogance'. Holland's 2013 translation elaborates upon the Greek text here to give 'the sheer scale of Xerxes' relish for magnificence'.

[32] LSJ. s.v. See Fisher (1992), pp. 376–7 for a discussion of Herodotus' use of the term in relation to Xerxes. Note too Baragwanath (2008), p. 255 with n. 47, observing that the related quality of *megalopsychia* ('greatness of soul') can have positive connotations, as seen in Aristotle's *Nicomachean Ethics*.

meaning; it cannot necessarily be construed merely as an assertion that this is purely despotic megalomania on Xerxes' part.[33] The notion that the use of the word does not have to imply a wholly negative judgement becomes clearer too when we consider the other occasion where Xerxes is described as having acted because of *megalophrosunē*; as we saw earlier (pp. 50–1) the application of the term to his actions relating to Bulis and Sperchias suggests more readily the notion of 'magnanimity'. Allowing for the possibility that Herodotus' verdict on Xerxes is not necessarily wholly critical is a crucial element of any interpretation of the way in which his image of the Persian king is constructed.[34]

Like Aeschylus, Herodotus finds scope for exploring the parallel between Xerxes' enslavement of peoples, and the 'enslavement' of nature itself. In the Herodotean descriptions of the Hellespont bridge the yoking metaphor is again prominent; the verb ζεύγνυμι is first used in Herodotus' summary of Mardonius' selection of oracles relating to the proposed invasion of Greece (at 7.6.4 an oracle is cited which states that the Hellespont will be 'yoked' by a Persian). Shortly afterwards Xerxes announces, 'I intend to yoke the Hellespont and take an army through Europe into Greece' (μέλλω ζεύξας τὸν Ἑλλήσποντον ἐλᾶν στρατὸν διὰ τῆς Εὐρώπης ἐπὶ τὴν Ἑλλάδα, 7.8.β2). This image is carried over into the king's plans for the extension of the Persian empire; he intends that 'guilty and innocent alike shall wear the yoke of slavery' (δούλιον ζυγὸν, 7.8.γ3). In Herodotus' account of the building of the bridges too, these are repeatedly envisaged as 'yokes' across the water (7.33.1, 34.1, 46.1, 36.4).

The description of Xerxes' relationship with the Hellespont continues with the use of additional imagery relating to enslavement; when the first bridge is destroyed by a storm, the king, in his anger, orders the beheading of those who constructed it and demands that the sea should be given 300 lashes as well as having a yoke thrown into it (7.35).[35] At the same time, those ordered to carry out his commands are told to chastise the sea with the following words (7.35.2): 'Oh bitter water, your master (δεσπότης τοι) inflicts upon you this punishment because you did wrong to him, although he did not wrong you. But Xerxes the king will cross you, whether you wish it or not.' Later, however, we learn of Xerxes' actions immediately before the crossing began (7.54); here, after a

---

[33] Baragwanath (2008), pp. 254–9 considers the notion here that Xerxes has a practical purpose in mind for producing such a display, suggesting that this – as with his expectations regarding the size of his army – could be seen as both a strategic attempt to deter resistance and a way of demonstrating his place in Persian history (on which see further below, pp. 59–63).

[34] For other examples of Xerxes' generosity see for example 7.237.2, where he rebukes those who speak ill of Demaratus, and 9.107.3 where he rewards Xenagoras with the governorship of Cilicia for saving the life of his brother Masistes.

[35] Themistocles' summary at 8.109.3 (see above, pp. 46–7) clearly relates to this part of the story.

prayer for success, he is said to have thrown a golden cup and bowl and a sword into the Hellespont. Herodotus offers two possible explanations for his actions here: either these were offerings to the sun or they were a way of trying to make amends for his having lashed the Hellespont. The fact that Herodotus allows for the possibility that Xerxes is able to recognize and attempt to remedy his mistakes is crucial here;[36] the king's ability to make amends for his actions is also seen later in Herodotus' account, when, after the sack of Athens he has an Athenian-style sacrifice performed on the Acropolis by Athenian exiles serving with his forces (8.54). Herodotus suggests that he may have done so because a dream had suggested it to him, or because the burning of Athens was on his mind. This Xerxes – who considers the consequences of his actions carefully – is not simply the unalloyed villain found in many later retellings of the Persian Wars but rather a more multi-dimensional character whose behaviour on occasion reveals elements of a more restrained, human figure than that seen elsewhere.[37]

Like father, like son: Xerxes and the pressures of Persian kingship

Crucially Xerxes' crossing of the Hellespont – and indeed his apparent 'mistreatment' of the waters there – is not without precedent in the *Histories*. Other eastern kings before him had crossed rivers as part of their imperialist policies: Croesus, for example, crossed the Halys – the border between the Lydian and Median empires – so as to attack Cyrus (1.75),[38] and later, Cyrus himself undertook a river crossing, that of the Araxes, in order to attack the Massagetae (1.201–4). Herodotus' account of this event follows an earlier story in which Cyrus is described as having meted out a punishment to the

---

[36] Gruen (2011), p. 78: 'This is not the stereotypical tyrant.' This story also finds a potential parallel at 7.113.2, where the Magi are said to have sacrificed white horses to the River Strymon in an attempt to propitiate it. The treatment of an object in nature as being like a god is also apparent at 7.31, where Xerxes comes upon a plane tree so beautiful that he adorns it with gold ornaments and appoints a guardian to look after it. Aelian later related this story in his third-century AD *Varia Historia* (*Historical Miscellany*, 2.14), by which time it had become an example of what he called Xerxes' 'ridiculous' (γέλοιος) behaviour; the episode was one which was incorporated into the plot of Handel's 1738 opera *Serse* (see Kimbell 2007).

[37] On the more 'human' side of Xerxes' character as presented by Herodotus see further below, pp. 63–9.

[38] Here Herodotus asserts his own belief that there was already a bridge across the Halys, although he relates an alternative Greek version of the story which claims that Thales of Miletus' engineering skills made it possible to ford the river; this is more closely related to the meddling with nature seen in the traditions relating to Xerxes' crossing of the Hellespont. Xerxes' own crossing of the Halys is mentioned by Herodotus at 7.26.3.

river Gyndes on his march to Babylon (1.189); when one of his sacred white horses was swept away by the current, he decided to punish the river so that in future 'even women would be able to cross it easily without wetting their knees'. In order to achieve this he had his army dig in such a way that the river was split into 360 small channels. The pattern of this episode is closely linked with that of Xerxes' treatment of the Hellespont; in each case the channel in question behaves in such a way as to anger a king, and the king responds by treating the water in a manner apparently intended to inflict degradation upon it.

Where Xerxes' crossing is distinct from these earlier examples, however, is in the fact that the Hellespont was not a mere river; rather this sacred strait was part of the sea which divided two continents. Nonetheless, there is a closer precedent in Herodotus' account for this action. It is in relation to the Scythian campaign of Darius that the link between Xerxes' actions and those of a predecessor are seen most strongly. Darius too had bridged the distance between the continents, at the Bosporus (4.87). His scheme is first referred to in a conversation between Darius and his wife Atossa, in which the king uses language similar to the terms in which Xerxes' bridging of the Hellespont would come to be described; Xerxes' predecessor too announces (3.134.4), 'I have decided to yoke a bridge (ζεύξας γέφυραν) from this continent to the other, and to march against Scythia.' Later the designer of the bridge is said to have commissioned, with the money which he received as a reward from the king, a picture of the crossing. The image described by Herodotus has Darius seated on a throne (ἐν προεδρίῃ) while the army crosses the bridge; the term used here for 'throne' is similar to the προεξέδρη of Xerxes which is described when he reviews his troops at Abydus (7.44.1: see above, p. 55) and the overall picture is one which highlights the close resemblance of the actions of father and son. Whereas in the *Persians* of Aeschylus the contrast between Xerxes and his father was a feature of the way in which the playwright cast the character of Xerxes in a negative light (see above, pp. 26–30), we find here a very different pattern, one in which there is a clear parallel between the behaviour of the two kings. Furthermore, the emphasis on this connection is one way in which Herodotus presents us with an image of Xerxes as being acutely aware of his position in the Persian dynasty.

The notion of a parallel between the actions of father and son forms part of a broader schematic element of Herodotus' work in which Xerxes' invasion of Greece is placed firmly within the historical framework of Persian dynastic continuity. While in Aeschylus' dramatic picture Xerxes is presented as being inferior to his father, the actions of Herodotus' Xerxes can instead be seen to mirror those of Darius. The link between Xerxes' crossing of the Hellespont and Darius' bridging of the Bosporus is perhaps the most striking example of such parallels, yet there are further echoes of Darius' actions throughout the narrative of Xerxes' campaign. In particular it is important to note that, in comparison with the positive image of Darius which makes for such a dramatic contrast between father and son in Aeschylus' *Persians*, Herodotus' account shows Darius as being far from faultless. His ruthlessness in suppressing the Babylonian revolt, in which he had the city demolished and 3,000 prominent citizens impaled (3.159), surpasses any single act of brutality authorized by Xerxes; later his cruel treatment of Oeobazus and his sons – in which the sons have their throats cut when their father dares to ask that they be spared from military service (4.84) – prefigures the story of Xerxes and Pythius (see above, p. 40).[39] The presence of such negative stories relating to Darius in a fifth-century narrative raises the question as to why, in the ensuing reception of the Persian Wars tradition, it was instead Xerxes who became embedded in the collective Greek consciousness as the archetypal wicked barbarian king.[40] The answer may lie partly in the fact that, whereas Darius himself had not entered Greece, Xerxes' assault on Greek territory involved his own physical presence there; Greeks had actually seen him for themselves, and some were therefore first-hand witnesses to his appearance, his actions and the physical trappings of his kingship. This king was no distant orchestrator of a campaign waged from afar but one whose appearance in the flesh surely captured the imagination of those whose lives and homes were in peril. The king's supreme outrage in entering and burning Athens was no doubt instrumental too in creating the unforgettable image of the barbarian *par excellence*. Meanwhile the dominant cultural legacy of fifth-century Athens helps to explain why it should be the more negative version of Xerxes seen in Aeschylus' play which was perpetuated throughout antiquity and beyond.[41]

Our introduction to the character and deeds of Xerxes in Herodotus' work comes in the form of a description of events relating to his succession at the beginning of his seventh book (7.2–3). Herodotus relates a dispute between Xerxes and Artobarzanes, another of Darius' sons, as to who should succeed

---

[39] The connection between these two stories was later drawn by the younger Seneca for the purposes of his moral philosophy in the first century AD (*De ira* 3.16–18): see below, p. 170.

[40] For more detailed discussion of Herodotus' portrayal of Darius, and the negative elements of this, see Immerwahr (1966), pp. 169–76 and Waters (1971), pp. 57–65.

[41] On the ancient reception of the *Persians* see Hall (2007), pp. 170–3.

their father. Ultimately in this version Xerxes uses the argument put forward by Demaratus (the exiled Spartan king who had recently arrived at the Persian court) to convince Darius that he is the legitimate heir to the Persian throne. This argument draws not on Persian precedent, but derives from Spartan tradition, whereby the son born when his father was already on the throne would inherit the kingship.[42] Herodotus also alludes here to the influence of Xerxes' mother Atossa, daughter of Cyrus, suggesting here that even without Demaratus' intervention Xerxes would have become king, 'for Atossa held all of the power' (7.3.4).[43] Xerxes' legitimate inheritance of the kingship from his father – and his peaceful assumption of Persian rule upon Darius' death – contrasts strikingly with Herodotus' account of Darius' own accession to the throne by way of a palace coup.[44]

Immediately after his description of the succession issue, Herodotus goes on to demonstrate that Xerxes inherited not merely the throne, but also the Greek campaign, from his father.[45] Despite Xerxes' initial reluctance to invade Greece, the war hawk Mardonius is shown to have wielded his influence at the king's court to move the issue to the forefront, arguing that the Athenians should be punished for the harm which they have done to Persia,[46] that an invasion would enhance Xerxes' reputation and deter others from attacking Persia, and that the king of Persia ought to possess the beautiful land of Europe (7.5). Other parties are said to have used their influence on Xerxes (7.6), and it becomes apparent in Herodotus' detailed account of the decision-making process which follows that the pressure of his position as Persian king is credited here as a key factor in Xerxes' decision to invade Greece.

Xerxes' opening words to the leading Persians whom he has gathered in order to announce his plans emphasize his adherence to Persian *nomos* (law/custom); he stresses here that ever since his maternal grandfather Cyrus founded the empire the Persians have been continuously at war, and that therefore his

---

[42] On the succession question see Briant (2002), pp. 518–22.

[43] The notion of Atossa's influence here doubtless relates also to Herodotus' account (3.131–4) of the way in which, having been induced to do so by the Greek doctor Democedes, she first encouraged Darius' attack on the Greeks, by claiming that she desired to have some Greek slave girls. On the figure of Atossa in Herodotus' narrative see Sancisi-Weerdenburg (1983), pp. 23–6.

[44] 3.70–88. On the Persian accounts of Darius' succession, see also below, pp. 76–8.

[45] When announcing his plan to invade Greece, Xerxes himself alludes to the link with his father's campaign (7.8.β2).

[46] Mardonius does not make explicit here the wrongs which the Athenians have committed against Persians: Herodotus apparently expects his audience to recognize that his words refer back to the burning of Sardis during the Ionian revolt (5.101–2, where Herodotus states that this later became the Persians' pretext for burning Greek sanctuaries) as well as to the defeat of Darius at the battle of Marathon (6.113–17). Xerxes later alludes to both of these events in his speech declaring his intention to invade Greece (7.8β.3).

plan to launch an expedition to Greece is nothing new (7.8α.1). He goes on to assert that, having assumed the kingship, he must live up to the reputation of his predecessors by increasing the Persian empire and gaining glory. On announcing his intention to bridge the Hellespont and to march against Greece the king then introduces the notion of seeking revenge against the Athenians as a way of finishing what his father started before his plans were cut short by his death (7.8β.1–2). Taken together, these points can be seen as indicative of Xerxes' awareness of the weighty demands imposed upon him in his role as king; this is by no means presented by Herodotus as the rash action of an impetuous tyrant, but rather as a carefully thought-out decision which accords with past Persian policy.[47] Thus Xerxes, the final king in the line of Persian rulers used by Herodotus to explore the history of the world in the mid-fifth century BC, comes to represent the culmination of Persian power, with its problematic elements as well as its overwhelming might.

Despite Xerxes' explanation of the reasons for his decision, and Mardonius' ensuing endorsement (7.9), Artabanus feels compelled to express his own misgivings, reminding Xerxes too of the way in which he warned Darius against the Scythian expedition; then too his warnings fell on deaf ears (7.10α).[48] Initially angered by Artabanus' advice against the invasion (7.11.1), Xerxes later reaches the conclusion that he will abandon his plans (7.12.1) but is persuaded to change his mind when repeatedly visited by a vision in his dreams (7.12.2, 7.14). An elaborate ploy – in which Artabanus is persuaded to impersonate Xerxes – to 'test' the vision results in the appearance of the same dream-figure to Artabanus (7.17). The resulting conclusion of Artabanus is that the dream has been sent by a god and that the mission is therefore predestined: at 7.18.3 he describes Xerxes' desire to invade as δαιμονίη ('god-given'), Greece's impending ruin as θεήλατος ('driven by a god') and the vision as being ἐκ τοῦ θεοῦ ('from the god', with this notion of divine transmission of the message being repeated

---

[47] In the context of her wider study of the motivations at play in Herodotus' work Baragwanath (2008), pp. 243–53 offers a detailed analysis of Xerxes' decision to invade, considering both the Persian council and the dream, and presenting Xerxes 'not as a victim of personal lusts, but as a figure whose decisions are influenced above all by his understanding of the past' (p. 243). See also Pelling (2006), pp. 108–10. Solmsen (1974), pp. 7–24 also explores the reasons for Xerxes' decision to invade Greece, and de Jong (2001), pp. 104–12 offers an analysis in narratological terms of Xerxes' reasons for the expedition, as presented by Herodotus, summarizing these as 'revenge, inherited imperialism, and the attractions of Hellas' (p. 104). See also Immerwahr (1954), pp. 30–37.

[48] Grethlein (2009), pp. 197–205 looks at the 'Persian Council Scene' as what he calls 'an implicit commentary on the usefulness of the *Histories*' (p. 197) and Artabanus' contribution as a way of showing that 'the past as narrated by Herodotus can provide guidance in the present' (p. 202). See above, p. 54 n. 20 on the role of Artabanus as a 'warner' figure in Herodotus' narrative.

shortly afterwards in the phrase τοῦ θεοῦ παραδιδόντος). While Xerxes' own articulation of the reasons for the expedition offered a human explanation in terms of dynastic and imperial policy, the story of the dream adds a super-natural dimension and suggests that it is divinely validated.[49] Herodotus' Xerxes does not, therefore, act merely on his own reckless impulse, but is instead compelled to invade by three key factors: his status as Persian king; his nation's history of expansionist imperialism; and divine ordinance.

Beneath the façade: The humanity of a tyrant

As the preceding discussion has demonstrated, there is ample material in the Herodotean image of Xerxes which can be used to build up a negative picture of the barbarian king; yet already we have seen that this Xerxes is not merely a one-dimensional representation of the deplorable characteristics with which he came to be associated in the later western tradition. That Herodotus' judgement upon Xerxes is not so damning as that of alternative versions of the Persian Wars tradition can perhaps be detected in a comment which comes after Herodotus' summary of the Persian forces before Thermopylae (7.187.2). There Herodotus asserts that, despite the size of the Persian army, 'there was no one more worthy than Xerxes – on account of his beauty and size (κάλλεος τε εἵνεκα καὶ μεγάθεος) – to wield this power.' We find here too alternative insights into Xerxes which allow us to see evidence of piety in the king's behaviour; for example, on his journey to Greece he is said to have sacrificed a thousand oxen to the Trojan Athena,[50] and similarly at Halos in Achaea he shows respect for sacred ground (7.197). While gestures such as these may be interpreted simply as acts of Persian propaganda, they do allow us to see beyond the image of Xerxes as destroyer of all things sacred, showing him instead as a figure who is capable of respecting local religion.[51]

---

[49] Evans (1961) explores the link between the dream and the *nomos* of the Persians, arguing that the dream demonstrates that abandoning the Greek campaign would involve abandoning the *nomoi* of Persia.

[50] On the broader significance of this gesture as propaganda aimed at garnering support from the Asiatic Greeks for the campaign against Athens see Georges (1994), pp. 60–3, and Haubold (2007), pp. 54–8.

[51] This element of Achaemenid kingship is one which is played down in the majority of the Greek-derived sources; elements of the Jewish tradition, however, offer an insight into an alternative perspective which presents an image of greater religious tolerance. This positive response stems from the fact that it was the Persians (under Cyrus) who allowed the Jews to return to Judaea from their exile in Babylon. See further below, pp. 141–8 (on the biblical book of Esther) and pp. 173–6 (on Josephus).

This positive image is complemented by the fact that there is also much in Herodotus' account which allows us to see Xerxes as an essentially human character who not only is subject to the pressures of his position in history and his role as tyrant-king, but is also aware of the fragility of the fortunes of mankind.[52] This particular insight into Xerxes' character is especially apparent immediately before the crossing of the Hellespont in the exchange highlighted at the beginning of this chapter (7.44ff.). The episode is prompted by the king's desire to observe the scale of his military force and thus highlights once more the overwhelming power of the Persian empire, embodied in the person of the king. At the same time it is a scene which combines several of the symbols which characterize the image of Xerxes throughout Herodotus' text: the throne from which the king observes his troops, his desire to observe and enumerate his military resources (here he also has his navy engage in a rowing contest for his entertainment), and the notion of the vast size of this force (at 7.45 Herodotus writes that the whole of the Hellespont was covered with the king's ships, and the beaches and plains of Abydus filled with his men). Yet the abrupt change of Xerxes' mood from one of self-satisfaction to sorrow (Herodotus tells us, 'Xerxes then congratulated himself, but after this he wept': ἐνθαῦτα ὁ Χέρξης ἑωυτὸν ἐμακάρισε, μετὰ δὲ τοῦτο ἐδάκρυσε, 7.45; cf. 7.46.1) leads to a moment of insightful reflection which highlights the precarious nature of human life and fortune.[53] A literal translation of Xerxes' words (7.46.2) in reply to Artabanus' concerned enquiry as to the reason for his tears would read, 'A feeling of compassion came to me when I considered how brief human life is, [if] of all these, so numerous as they are, not one will survive to the hundredth year.'[54] Through this succinct statement, the brevity of which belies the magnitude of the far-reaching implications which it carries, Herodotus allows his Xerxes to articulate one of the key ethical premises which inform his narrative. Xerxes' reflection on the inevitability of death is a reminder that, no matter how great an individual's power, it cannot last forever. The sentiment he expresses here is one which is repeated later in Herodotus' narrative too, this time by one of the

[52] For a general survey of characterization in historiography (on which there has been little recent published scholarship) see Pitcher (2007); Pelling (1990), pp. 259–61 also raises some points which are relevant to the topic.

[53] Flory (1978) analyses the scene at Abydus as an example of what he refers to as the recurring 'laughter, tears and wisdom' motif in Herodotus' narrative. He sees Xerxes as 'childish' (p. 146) in his joy here and points out that the tears which Xerxes sheds are a result of the pain caused by reflection or understanding.

[54] So Willett (2000), p. 125. The Greek text here reads as follows: Ἐσῆλθε γάρ με λογισάμενον κατοικτῖραι ὡς βραχὺς εἴη ὁ πᾶς ἀνθρώπινος βίος, εἰ τούτων γε ἐόντων τοσούτων οὐδεὶς ἐς ἑκατοστὸν ἔτος περιέσται.

Persians who remains in Greece with Mardonius after Xerxes' return to Persia. There (9.16) the Persian officer, with a prescience which foretells the imminent defeat at Plataea, tells Thersander of Orchomenus that of all the Persian army, in a short time only a few will still be alive; the reflection causes him to weep, and he then reflects that no man has the power to prevent the occurrence of that which has been ordained by a god.[55] The echoes of Xerxes' own reflection at this point in the narrative, before the Greeks' final defeat of the Persian force, act as a reminder of the impermanence of the king's might.

Xerxes' contemplation of the brevity of human existence and the inevitability of death also chimes with a related theme – that of the mutability of fortune – which recurs throughout Herodotus' work. At the very start of his text the historian signposts the significance of the changing nature of human prosperity as he notes that cities which were once great have now become small and vice-versa (1.5.4); his acknowledgement here that good fortune does not endure for long in the same place acts as a programmatic statement which will inform the shape of his narrative. This motif is explored in more detail early in the first book of the *Histories* with the exchange between Croesus and Solon in which Solon reflects on the transience of happiness (1.29–32),[56] and indeed the story of Croesus taken as a whole can be viewed as a parable which invites reflection on the maxims 'look to the end' and 'call no man happy until he dies.'[57] Solon's words to Croesus concerning divine jealousy (1.32.1) are also echoed in Artabanus' response to Xerxes at Abydus, where he blames a 'jealous god' for the troubles of men (the Greek φθονερός at 7.46.4 is the same adjective used by Solon). While Solon's reflection on the unpredictability of shifting fortune highlights the fact that only at death can a judgement be made upon a person's life, Xerxes dwells not upon the capriciousness of fortune but rather on the utter inevitability of death; the dialogues are linked, however, by a recognition of the impermanence of an existence which is granted to us only by the favour of the gods. The parallel is emphasized still further in Artabanus' concluding remark, in which he advises Xerxes to 'bear in mind the well-put old saying that the

---

[55] 9.16.4: ὅ τι δεῖ γενέσθαι ἐκ τοῦ θεοῦ ἀμήχανον ἀποτρέψαι ἀνθρώπῳ.

[56] See Shapiro (1996) for a detailed discussion of the Solon/Croesus episode and its relationship with the theme of the mutability of fortune elsewhere in Herodotus' work. The story of Polycrates' ring (Hdt. 3.40–3) echoes the same sentiment.

[57] See, for example, Evans (1991), pp. 44–51; at p. 62 he also notes that the pattern of Xerxes' career 'invites comparison with the Croesus-*logos*'. Immerwahr (1966), pp. 154–61 acknowledges that elements of the story of Croesus can be related to the whole of humanity (these are what allow it to be seen in some sense as a parable), while also asserting that some features of the tale are particular to Croesus himself.

end is not apparent at the beginning' (7.51.3).[58] This 'reversal of fortune' motif, which had been played out dramatically by Aeschylus too, would also become a recurring theme in the later Latin and Greek moralizing traditions relating to Xerxes' story (see below, pp. 163–70). That Herodotus uses Xerxes as a means of exploring the twin themes of mortality and the transience of fortune – with the king's own reflections upon the inevitability of death occurring as he is about to embark upon the expedition whose outcome itself proved that might and wealth are no guarantee of future success – is key to our understanding of this historiographical version of the Persian king, the resonances of which would be felt throughout antiquity and beyond.

It is clear from the exchange at Abydus that Herodotus' Xerxes is far from being an unfeeling monster; the moment of insight displayed here demonstrates a more human side to his character than many later, more reductive, versions of the Xerxes-tradition allow. This understanding of Xerxes' mortality also throws into relief a peculiarly Herodotean explanation for his downfall – one which is distinct from the Athenian version which relies rather on a notion of divine punishment for reaching beyond the bounds of acceptable behaviour.[59] Like all mortals Xerxes is subject to the vacillations of fortune, and the magnitude of his power and wealth simply means that he has further to fall than most. This concept is expressed neatly by the message sent by the Greek allies before Thermopylae, in which they try to persuade other states to send troops (7.203.2). The message states that it is not a god but a mortal who is attacking Greece, and that all mortals must suffer an element of misfortune; this misfortune is greater for those who are themselves more mighty (τοῖσι δὲ μεγίστοισι αὐτῶν μέγιστα).[60]

Ultimately, of course, Xerxes' failed attempt to conquer Greece does demonstrate that he has human flaws. Despite flashes of insight such as that shown at Abydus, Xerxes' failure can be seen as the result of his misjudgement of the task in hand.[61] Nowhere is this more apparent than during the scene prior to

---

[58] On the nature of changing human fortunes see also Croesus' advice to Cyrus on his last campaign (1.207.2), where he talks about the cycle of human affairs in which the same individuals are not allowed to prosper forever.

[59] This is the explanation given by Herodotus' Themistocles for Xerxes' failure in Greece (see above, pp. 46–7); on the Aeschylean version of divine punishment see above, pp. 27–9.

[60] This emphatic assertion of Xerxes' mortality might be compared with the story of the Hellespontine man who, on seeing Xerxes making the crossing, mused, 'Oh Zeus, why do you make yourself look like a Persian man and assume the name of Xerxes instead of Zeus?' (7.56.2). The comparison of Xerxes with a god here serves to remind us of the fact that Xerxes is in fact merely a mortal, yet one with the grandest of designs and the utmost power and wealth.

[61] So Dewald (2003), p. 43: 'Xerxes is weakened by the traits of self-indulgence, irresolution, and bad judgement in the choice of advisor and advice, and he proves personally unequal to the demands of the gigantic despotic empire that he heads.'

Thermopylae where Xerxes interrogates Demaratus as to the character of the Greeks (7.101ff.). Demaratus' response – that the Greeks will resist an attempt to enslave Greece at all costs, even if they have only a thousand men in their army[62] – is met with scorn by the Persian king. His derisive laughter here (7.103.1) is symptomatic of his failure to understand the nature of the enemy he has taken on. There follows Demaratus' exposition of the Spartans' adherence to the rule of *nomos* at all costs: this too meets with laughter from Xerxes (7.105.1).[63] After Thermopylae, Demaratus' advice as to how best to defeat the Greeks is also rejected by Xerxes in favour of the advice of the king's brother Achaemenes (7.235–7).[64] As a result the Persian fleet heads for Salamis, where the Greeks are victorious thanks largely to Themistocles' tactical expertise (8.60, where he outlines his plan to engage the Persian fleet in the narrow strait) and cunning (8.75, where his pretence that the Greeks are about to flee draws Xerxes' fleet into battle). In underestimating the Greeks Xerxes has effectively doomed his expedition to failure; Mardonius remains in Greece with a portion of the army,[65] but the king himself flees (8.107; cf. 8.97, where Herodotus outlines Xerxes' fears for his own safety and his initial plan to escape).[66]

There is, then, a sense in which the image of Xerxes painted by Herodotus is one of a very human individual, not wholly unappealing but marred by character flaws and no less troubled by the vicissitudes of fortune than any other mortal. The flash of insight into this side of his character at Abydus reminds us that, despite the brutal and terrifying nature of his tyrannical behaviour seen elsewhere in Herodotus' account, an alternative view of Xerxes is indeed possible; his story provides us with a parable of 'how the mighty fall'. Herodotus' narrative leaves us with a complex picture not of an individual who is immoral to the core, but of one whose position at the head of the Persian empire – and

---

[62] Gruen (2011), p. 68 attempts to refute the suggestion held by many scholars that this dialogue is 'a linchpin for Hellenic identity as against eastern barbarism.' He points out that Demaratus speaks not for Greece as a whole but for Sparta alone and notes that it is a system of discipline (law as 'master') rather than a constitution of political liberty which he praises here.

[63] Lateiner (1977) looks at the phenomenon of laughter in Herodotus and shows that it functions as a warning from the author that disaster will follow for the character who laughs. On the link between humour and danger in Herodotus see also Dewald (2006). The other occasion on which Xerxes laughs in Herodotus' narrative is at 8.114.2, when the Spartans demand reparation for his treatment of Leonidas' corpse: his response, laden with irony, is that Mardonius will pay them what they deserve.

[64] For a detailed discussion of the role of Demaratus in the *Histories* see Boedeker (1987).

[65] Mardonius' later message to the Athenians (8.140α.3) reflects Xerxes' underestimation of the Greek resistance; he asserts that they will never be able to defeat the Persian on account of the extent of the power which he wields.

[66] Note here Artemisia's endorsement of the plan to leave Mardonius behind (8.102); she points out that if the plan works, Xerxes can take credit for the work of his slave, but if not and Mardonius is killed by the Greeks Xerxes need not worry about the death of one who is merely his slave.

the weight of the responsibility which this confers – places him in a situation where the invasion of Greece, and the shocking consequences of that action, become inevitable. In this respect his behaviour can be understood not as a consequence of his own individual personality but rather as part of a wider pattern of aggressive imperialistic overreach which replicates elements of the conduct of his predecessors – Cyrus and Cambyses, as well as Darius.[67]

The notion that tyrannical power carries with it this pressure to behave in ways which are often objectionable is an important one when we take into the account the historical context within which Herodotus' work was produced.[68] Several scholars have considered the way in which this history of the past can be used to shed light on contemporary political issues, with particular reference to potential parallels between Persian expansionist policy and Athenian imperialism in the second half of the fifth century BC.[69] In the context of a discussion of Xerxes' character it is therefore enlightening to consider the way in which his opponents are presented by Herodotus. Rather than inclining towards a straightforward moral opposition between Greeks and Persians, Herodotus' approach is far less clear-cut. While we might expect Xerxes to suffer by comparison with the virtuous Greeks (as seen in the terms framed by Themistocles' analysis of the situation cited at the opening of this chapter), on closer examination it becomes clear that here there is no such stark dichotomy between freedom-loving Greeks and enslaving tyrant; nor, it becomes apparent, can Xerxes' actions be seen as being distinctly Persian in the context of Herodotus' narrative.[70] Indeed at both the beginning and end of his account of Xerxes' invasion Herodotus alludes to an incident which casts doubt upon the ability of the Athenians (in particular, rather than the Greeks in general) to occupy the moral high ground. At 7.33, when describing the route taken by Xerxes to Greece, Herodotus alludes briefly to the story of the Persian Artaÿctes, the satrap of Sestos who was bound alive to a plank by the

---

[67] Dewald (2003) offers a study of the ways in which Herodotus' narrative problematizes the institution of tyranny, considering the negative influence of power on the individual who holds it. With particular reference to the factors which are said at 7.8 to influence Xerxes to invade Greece she writes (p. 48) that, 'As Herodotus presents it, what is dangerous about eastern imperial despotism is not the wickedness of the individual despot but the way he is, like everyone else, enmeshed in a structure that takes on a life of its own, that moves inexorably in the direction of its own further growth.'

[68] Evans (1979) offers a useful summary of the evidence for the publication date of the *Histories*, concluding that although exactitude is impossible this may have been as late as 424 BC.

[69] See, for example, Raaflaub (1987) and Moles (1996), both arguing that Herodotus' work can be interpreted as a warning to Athens against the dangers of excessive imperial ambition. The notion is one which was first explored in depth by Fornara (1971).

[70] See also above, pp. 50–1, on the story of Bulis and Sperchias as an insight into the blurring of the moral distinction between Greeks and Persians.

Greeks under the command of the Athenian commander Xanthippus. This Xanthippus was the father of Pericles. Herodotus returns to the story at the very end of his work, where he provides further detail. There (9.12) we learn that on entering Sestos after a siege the Athenian forces took Artaÿctes and his son prisoner; Xanthippus refused to accept Artaÿctes' offer of recompense for the treasure he had taken from the sanctuary of Protesilaus[71] and instead had him crucified – a punishment, like impalement, more usually meted out by Persians in Herodotus' narrative[72] – while his son was stoned to death before his eyes. This detail is one which carries echoes of the punishment of the offenders' innocent sons in the episodes involving Pythius and Oeobazus (see above, p. 40 and p. 60). That references to this act by an Athenian – and at that the father of the most influential Athenian statesman of Herodotus' own time – frame the Herodotean narrative of Xerxes' invasion of Greece is no mere coincidence.[73] The notion that Greeks too can carry out such acts of brutality is a reminder that neither side in the war is beyond reproach. Within this context Xerxes is not merely the hybristic and brutal barbarian seen in later versions of the tradition; nor does he simply represent a peculiarly Persian mode of behaviour.[74] Instead he is revealed as a figure who alerts Herodotus' audience to the fact that the potential to behave in morally unacceptable ways resides in us all.

---

[71] It is perhaps significant that on this occasion the removal of treasure from a sanctuary is not blamed on Xerxes himself; here the king is duped into allowing the theft by Artaÿctes, who falsely asserts that Protesilaus invaded Xerxes' land (9.116).

[72] Note that the Greek distinction between crucifixion and impalement is not always made clear by the vocabulary which is used: see Rollinger (2004) for a survey of these and other forms of physical violence in the *Histories*. See Flower and Marincola (2002), *ad* 9.120.4, and Desmond (2004), pp. 34–5, for a discussion of the precise meaning of the terminology used by Herodotus in relation to Artaÿctes' punishment. Other examples of impalement/crucifixion can be found at, for example, 3.125.3 (Polycrates' crucifixion at the hands of Oroetes), 3.159.1 (Darius' impalement of 3,000 leading Babylonians), 6.30.1 (the impalement of Histiaeus of Miletus by Artaphernes and Harpagus), 7.194.1 (Darius' crucifixion of Sandoces of Cyme, who was saved from death when the king had a change of heart). On the marking and mutilation of the body as a symbol of despotic power in Herodotus, see Steiner (1994), pp. 154–9.

[73] Boedeker (1988) analyses the use of the Artaÿctes story as a means of framing Herodotus' account of Xerxes' invasion, focusing on the punishment of Artaÿctes as a means of retribution for his violation of the sanctuary of Protesilaus, one of the great Achaean heroes at Troy; she also considers the significance of the location of Artaÿctes' execution (at the Hellespont) in relation to the Persians' transgression of this boundary.

[74] M. A. Flower (2006), p. 286: 'the distinction between Greek and barbarian has indeed become difficult to discern'. See also Pelling (1997).

Beyond the invasion of Greece: The Herodotean Xerxes at the Persian court

While for the most part Herodotus' portrayal of Xerxes is concerned with either the planning or execution of the expedition to Greece, the final detailed episode relating to the king in the *Histories* is one which looks beyond the military mission to turn our attention instead to the Persian court. This tale has thematic links with the beginning of the *Histories*, and the story of Candaules in which the Lydian king is destroyed by his wife (1.8–10);[75] in this sense it offers a conclusion to Xerxes' story which completes the cycle of Herodotus' discussion of the lives of the eastern kings. The Xerxes-narrative ends for Herodotus not with his departure from Greece nor with his assassination in 465 BC but with a tale of harem intrigue, scandal and violence at the Persian court (9.108–13). The king's lust for his sister-in-law (the wife of his brother Masistes: she remains unnamed in Herodotus' account) sets off a chain of domestic mishaps; having arranged for the daughter of Masistes' wife to be married to his son (Darius), in the hope that this would allow him easier access to the object of his affections, Xerxes then instead becomes infatuated with his new daughter-in-law, Artaÿnte. She in turn extracts a promise from the king that he will give her anything which she desires, upon which she demands an elaborately woven robe made for Xerxes by his wife Amestris. When Amestris finds that Artaÿnte has the robe and thus discovers the affair, she wreaks revenge by having Masistes' wife hideously mutilated (the motivation for Amestris' treatment of an apparently innocent party in this way is not made clear). As a result, Masistes plans to stir up revolt in Bactria in an attempt to gain retribution. The story ends with the assassination, on Xerxes' orders, of Masistes, his sons, and his troops. For the rest of Xerxes' story we must look beyond Herodotus' account; it was Ctesias who would later take up the narrative of Xerxes' assassination as a result of a palace coup.[76]

The desire to characterize Xerxes beyond his failed invasion of Greece which is apparent here offers an insight into a strand of the Xerxes-traditions which focused more upon the Persian court as a locus for domestic intrigue and sexual politics.[77] While Aeschylus' *Persians* took as its setting Xerxes' palace in Susa,

---

[75] See Flower and Marincola (2002), pp. 291–2.

[76] See below, pp. 131–2, on Ctesias' version of events. Diodorus also refers to Xerxes' death (see pp. 140–1).

[77] Note too here the significance of the domestic setting in relation to the invasion of Greece by Darius; the 'bedroom scene' in which Atossa persuades her husband to undertake his expedition (3.134) also reflects a Herodotean interest in the influence of family on Persian politics.

the drama nonetheless derived wholly from the Persians' imagined response to the defeat at Salamis;[78] Herodotus, in his closing chapters of Xerxes' story, looks beyond that scenario to consider the personal and political relationships behind the closed doors of the king's palace. This is thus our earliest surviving written text which attests to a developing fascination with the exotic world of the Persian royal household. As such it foreshadows in particular the work of the fourth-century writer Ctesias along with the works of a swathe of later authors whose interest lay less in the military ambitions of Xerxes than in the outlandish and decadent setting of the court, the royal harem, and the potential for corruption and scandal therein.[79] Herodotus' version of Xerxes thus opened up the possibilities for alternative re-interpretations of his character by later authors. While for some Greek authors – particularly the Athenian rhetoricians writing in the fourth century BC, whose works form the basis of my discussion in Chapter 4 – he would come to personify the panhellenic foe, terrifying and magnificent, for a whole range of other prose writers (discussed in Chapter 5) it was to be the vision of Xerxes as the epitome of the decadent palace playboy which would win out.

---

[78] The reaction at Susa to news of the defeat is dealt with briefly by Herodotus, at 8.99, where he asserts that the grief of the Persians stems not from the news of the loss of the fleet but from concern for Xerxes himself; there is perhaps a trace here of the anxieties of Aeschylus' Queen (see pp. 19–21, above).

[79] On the idea of decadence as a feature of Greek images of the Persian monarchy, see in particular Sancisi-Weerdenburg 1983 and 1987a. For a detailed discussion of literary and artistic treatments of the Persian court see Chapter 5 in this volume.

4. *Darius and his crown prince.* Detail of Persepolis treasury sculpture

3

Xerxes in his Own Write?
The Persian Perspective

Standing behind the enthroned king who features on the treasury reliefs of Darius at Persepolis is a second royal figure whose dress, distinctive square beard and posture mirror those of the seated ruler (Plate 4; see also Figures 1 and 2, pp. 84–5). It is this tableau of king and crown prince which perhaps best illustrates the image projected by the Achaemenid Persian dynasty to its subjects and to posterity. Here the sense of seamless continuity from the reign of one king to the next is rendered in a visual format in which the son is constructed as a carbon copy of his father; this is an idealized vision of dynastic stability which is also echoed in the Persian epigraphic sources. After Darius' assumption of the Persian throne in turbulent political circumstances an emphasis upon the peaceful transmission of hereditary power between generations would come to form a key element of the Achaemenid ideology crafted during his reign and later adopted by Xerxes.

This chapter will examine the ways in which the Persian sources offer a perspective on Xerxes which differs from that seen in the Greek texts, yet one which is itself as much a construct as the Greek versions of Xerxes.[1] It will use evidence from Darius' reign – in the form of inscriptions, architecture and sculpture – to provide an insight into this king's construction of a new Achaemenid ideology before going on to consider Xerxes' adoption of the image of Persian kingship promoted by his father. Examination of the epigraphic evidence from his reign reveals that Xerxes consciously fostered the construction of parallels between his kingship and that of Darius; the

---

[1] Root (1979), pp. 1–2 makes it clear that Achaemenid official art, as a reflection of the ideals and attitudes of the king, does not mirror 'objective historical reality' but can tell us about the 'subjective historical self-perception' of the Persian kings whose images it portrayed. Her study examines the process by which Achaemenid imperial iconography was created in order to project a vision of kingship and empire.

picture which emerges is one of a model monarch who is both righteous and all-powerful in the exercise of his rule. The so-called *daiva*-inscription, however, has been used in the past to suggest that Xerxes' rule marked a break from that of his father, and that he was less tolerant than his predecessor in the exercise of his power; here Xerxes alludes to his suppression of the worship of gods other than Ahuramazda, supreme god of the Persians. The final section of this chapter will demonstrate that to seek some concrete historical truth about Xerxes' personality from this, or indeed any other epigraphic source from his reign, is to overlook the fact that the inscriptions are themselves carefully constructed pieces of propaganda designed to create their own particular image of the king.

Perspectives on the Persian sources

The starting-point for the construction of the image of Xerxes which is projected by the earliest Greek sources is the series of events surrounding the Persian Wars; the resulting impression of the Persian king is to a large extent conditioned by the perspectives of those for whom he had represented a threat to their homeland, their freedom and their lives, and whose memory of their own extraordinary victory in war meant that the Xerxes-traditions which they created and transmitted were inevitably dominated by episodes in which he was cast in the role of the hated invader. Even if we allow for a reading of Herodotus which suggests a more nuanced approach to his character than that seen in Aeschylus' *Persians* it was nonetheless Xerxes' invasion of Greece which sparked the historian's inquiry. The sources originating from Persia which survive from Xerxes' reign differ, however, from the Greek sources in both their format and their emphasis. In contrast with the literary texts which transmitted the Greek traditions the Persian evidence relating to the figure of the king consists entirely of material remains, in the form of relief sculptures, buildings and inscriptions (these include some lengthier detailed statements of the king's policies which have been found on buildings as well as very short proprietorial statements carved on objects such as seals and precious items).[2] By contrast with the Greek texts, the surviving Persian sources make no mention of the invasion of Greece; the event which, for the Greeks, came to be seen as a defining moment in their

---

[2] Note too that 'treasury tablets' from Persepolis, some of which can be dated to Xerxes' reign, also survive. These are, however, administrative documents detailing payments for labourers at the site and, as such, provide no insight into the way in which the figure of the king was envisaged. For those dating from Xerxes' reign see Cameron (1948), pp. 98–191 (nos. 10–75).

own history and which captured the imagination of writers for centuries to come seems to have made little – if any – impact on the official Persian version of history and on the presentation within this of the figure of Xerxes himself.[3]

Since the work of the Achaemenid History Workshops, initiated by Heleen Sancisi-Weerdenburg in the late 1970s,[4] historians of Achaemenid Persia have sought to present a view of the Persian kings which looks beyond the Hellenocentric version as telescoped through the lens of the authors whose interest in Persia was sparked by the invasion of Greece; scholarly attention has focused on evaluating the Persian evidence on its own terms rather than seeking to use it as confirmation of what is thought to be 'known' from the Greek sources.[5] A clear example of the way in which the Persian evidence for Xerxes' reign might be misinterpreted by focusing first on the Greek sources and looking from the outside in is offered by Sancisi-Weerdenburg (1989, p. 551): 'If we know from a (clearly novelistic) tale in the *Histories* that Xerxes had a love-affair ... this 'fact' can be used to interpret Xerxes' building policy which leads furthermore to the 'conclusion' that is understandable that the 'Harem' was Xerxes' most impressive building.' No Persian testimony identifies the so-called 'harem' of Xerxes as such.[6] Similarly, Kuhrt and Sherwin-White (1987) have now shown that it was the Greek-determined view which coloured scholars' assessments of Xerxes' policy in Babylonia and which led to suggestions that Xerxes destroyed temples and pillaged the cult statue of Bel-Marduk there.[7]

To recognize that scholarly approaches might be conditioned by the perspective of the Greek sources is not to suggest, however, that by starting with the Persian evidence we are able to produce a flawless account of the 'real' historical Xerxes, and nor is that what the present study sets out to do. The Persian sources too – themselves a series of carefully crafted expressions of

---

[3] Briant (2002), p. 541 goes so far as to suggest, on the basis of the country-list in Xerxes' *daiva*-inscription (discussed below, pp. 89–96), that 'royal propaganda denied the defeats.' Note too, Kuhrt's assertion (2007, p. 239) that administrative documents show there to have been no disruption in, for example, building activities during Xerxes' reign: 'Such pieces of evidence help to balance our image of Xerxes' reign, reminding us of the dangers of letting a setback suffered in one campaign along the empire's north-western fringe define an entire reign of twenty-one years.'

[4] Kuhrt (2009) provides an overview of the origins and output of the Workshops.

[5] See Sancisi-Weerdenburg (1987c). Harrison (2012) examines in detail the scholarly reassessment of the history of Achaemenid Persia in recent decades, although he suggests that the 'imagined break with past scholarship and past understanding' (p. 15) has been exaggerated.

[6] Root (1979), p. 101 notes that the building in question was labelled as a 'harem' by archaeologists because of its relatively secluded position and the presence of a series of identical small compartments.

[7] For a discussion of the *daiva*-inscription – which, despite the fact that it names no specific country, was interpreted by some as confirmation of Xerxes' sacrilege in Babylonia (cf. Herodotus 1.183.3, discussed above at p. 147) – and the way in which scholars have used it as evidence for Xerxes' religious intolerance, see pp. 91–2.

imperial ideology presented to us entirely from a narrowly royal perspective – possess their own particular limitations and lacunae, and rather than offering us the opportunity to reconstruct a continuous historical narrative of Xerxes' reign or to unearth an objective view of his character they offer instead a window into the official Persian version of Xerxes' kingship. Artistic and epigraphic material from the reign of Darius on shows the development of a tradition – itself the product of a variety of Near Eastern cultural influences[8] – which would be perpetuated by his successors and which created a formalized public image of the Achaemenid kings. This royal Achaemenid vision served to emphasize the legitimacy and scope of the rulers' imperial power while at the same time advertising the dynastic stability which was brought about by hereditary transmission of that power from one king to the next.

Darius and the creation of Achaemenid ideology

Far more Persian evidence survives from the reign of Darius then from that of Xerxes, and it is during Darius' kingship that we see the establishment of imperial traditions which were to be perpetuated under his son's rule; an analysis of the ideological construction of Persian kingship which Xerxes inherited from his father thus forms a necessary prelude to our investigation of Xerxes' own use of those traditions. Darius was not a direct descendant of his predecessors Cyrus and Cambyses but had become king after his part in the overthrow of a usurper; having acceded to the throne during a period of political turmoil he then had to suppress a series of revolts throughout the empire in order to consolidate his position. These are the events which are recorded in extraordinary detail in the form of an extensive inscription (DB) found high on a rock face at Behistun (Bisitun).[9] This trilingual text, inscribed in Elamite and Babylonian languages as well as what is now called Old Persian,[10] is the longest extant document produced by a Persian king, consisting of five columns and a total of 414 lines

---

[8] Root (1979), pp. 28–42 outlines the influences upon the development of Achaemenid art.

[9] Inscriptions discussed in this chapter are referred to by standard abbreviations as found in Kent (1953). The single exception is XPl, which was discovered after Kent's volume was published: see Gharib (1968) and Kuhrt (2007), pp. 503–5. For the text of DB discussed here, see Kent (1953) pp. 116–34; see also Kuhrt (2007), pp. 141–57 for a translation and detailed notes. Translations of other inscriptions cited in the present chapter are those of Kuhrt (2007), with the exception that I have substituted the more commonly used 'Ahuramazda' where Kuhrt uses 'Auramazda'.

[10] Schmitt (1990), p. 302, outlines the chronology of the translations; it seems that Darius claims in the inscription to have instigated the creation of the 'Old Persian' script as a way of recording his own language.

of text; it is also the only surviving Persian inscription purporting to describe in detail specific political events. The inscription opens with details of Darius' genealogy as he asserts his connection with the Achaemenid dynasty, claiming that he could trace a familial link with the eponymous founder Achaemenes and thereby implicitly relating his family to that of Cyrus.[11] He then names the supreme god Ahuramazda as having bestowed upon him the kingship before going on to list the territories now subject to his rule. The majority of the inscription is, however, given over to Darius' account of the events which he claims took place in the first three years of his reign. It describes his seizure of the throne after a period of bloody political turmoil, incorporating a complex story of intrigue and violence in which, after Cambyses' secret murder of his own brother Bardiya an impostor, a magus named Gaumata, incited rebellion by pretending to be Bardiya and asserting his own claim to the throne.[12] Darius declares that, with the help of Ahuramazda and a small band of men, he killed the impostor and assumed the kingship himself. He then goes on to describe in great detail the subsequent resistance which he encountered and overcame, listing the provinces which revolted and over which he regained control as king, and including the names of individuals who supported him in these actions, as well as the locations of battles and the months in which these took place. Darius declares that his own actions demonstrate his opposition to those who follow 'the Lie' (DB col. I §10; cf. col. IV §54: the Old Persian term *drauga*, 'falsehood' implies political rebellion as well as carrying a religious meaning here)[13] and proclaims repeatedly throughout the text that this was all achieved by the favour of Ahuramazda, who is named a total of 63 times. The inscription was accompanied by a relief sculpture which acted as a visual echo of the message conveyed by the text.[14] Here Darius, life-sized and accompanied by weapon bearers, is shown before nine captured rebels, their hands bound, each one labelled with his name and nationality to represent the countries which Darius had subdued; the king's right foot rests on the prostrate body of a defeated foe,

---

[11] It is likely that Darius manipulated his genealogy in order to assert his claim to the throne: see Briant (2002), pp. 110–11.

[12] The story of Gaumata's imposture was retold in several variant versions in the ancient Greek and Roman texts, including that of Herodotus (3.61–79) who names the usurper as Smerdis. See Briant (2001).

[13] Briant (2002), p. 126; Kuhrt (2007), p. 152, n. 15. Cf. DB col. IV §55 and col. IV §64, in which Darius exhorts his successors to mete out similar punishments against those who rebel.

[14] Root (1979), pp. 182–226 analyses the Behistun monument in detail; for images see also Root (1979), plates VI–VIII and Boardman (2000), pp. 106–7; Kuhrt (2007), p. 150 provides an outline drawing of the figures on the relief.

labelled as the impostor Gaumata.[15] The scene is observed by the winged figure which symbolizes Ahuramazda hovering above.

The question of whether the Behistun inscription can be viewed as an accurate description of the process by which Darius came to be king and his role in the assassination of the alleged pretender Gaumata remains the subject of scholarly controversy,[16] yet despite the ongoing debate concerning the veracity of Darius' account of events there can be no question that the presence of such a conspicuous assertion of his authority acts as a powerful piece of imperial propaganda whose scale is unmatched by anything else in the corpus of surviving Persian sources. Both the narrative in the inscription and its accompanying pictorial rendering defined this new king as formidable in his authority and military might; they acted too as a visible declaration of the legitimacy of Darius' rule, under the divine authority of Ahuramazda. By asserting his claim to the throne in this way and proclaiming his triumph over rebellious subjects as well as appropriating for him the support of Ahuramazda the Behistun inscription loudly declared the scale of the new king's power; it can therefore provide us with an insight into the way in which this Achaemenid king created and promoted his own self-image.

This image is one which was perpetuated elsewhere in inscriptions produced under Darius, and although nothing survives which presents such a detailed Persian perspective on his rule, themes which are important in the Behistun inscription can be found elsewhere too. Declarations of the wide geographical extent of his empire in the Persepolis foundation tablets (DPh = DH) demonstrate the reach of his power and act as reminders that this was deemed to have been granted by the divine authority of Ahuramazda: 'King Darius proclaims: This (is) the kingdom which I hold, from the Saca who are beyond Sogdiana, from there as far as Kush, from the Indus as far as Sardis, which Ahuramazda, the greatest of gods, bestowed upon me.'[17] Ahuramazda reappears frequently

---

[15] On the identification of the figure in the relief as Gaumata see Sancisi-Weerdenburg (1999), p. 92 and Briant (2002) p. 125.

[16] Shahbazi (1993) provides a summary of the scholarly debate concerning the veracity of Darius' description of events in the Behistun inscription; key issues are also summarized by Kuhrt (1997), pp. 135–9. Wiesehöfer (1978) and Balcer (1987) provide detailed examinations of the evidence. For an analysis of the historical statements made in the Behistun inscription see also Tuplin (2005). Sancisi-Weerdenburg (1999) notes that the inscription is unique among surviving Persian documents in that it purports to record precise events, and considers more broadly the extent to which such texts can be used as historical sources.

[17] Cf. DPg §2 in which the king refers in broad terms to the geographical area from which those who built Persepolis came: 'With the protection of Ahuramazda, these (are) the lands, who did this, who gathered here: Persia, Media, the lands of other tongues, of mountains and plains, from this side of the sea to that side of the sea, from this side of the desert to that side of the desert, as I commanded them.' Similarly the Susa foundation charter, DSf (§7–13) lists the locations from which the building materials were brought, and the peoples who worked them; cf. DSz §7–12 and DSaa §4. Such statements act as expressions of the geographical reach of the king's influence and the extent of his power.

in the royal inscriptions, whether as bestower of the royal power (for example DPd; DSf §1–6) or protector of the king and his works (DSe §6; DSj). Elsewhere lists of tribute-bearing subjects advertise the king's position as ruler over a vast empire (DPe §2, and Darius' tomb inscription DNa §3). Such declarations of power over other nations could also find expression in visual form, such as on the colossal statue of Darius found at Susa which was made of Egyptian granite and possibly originally set up in Egypt after his reassertion of Persian control there in 519/518 BC.[18] The base of the statue depicts kneeling figures, hands raised as if supporting the figure of the king; the people are differentiated from one another by their dress and physical appearance and labelled in hieroglyphic text which identifies them as representing the lands over which Darius held sway.[19]

Perhaps the most visible signs of the king's authority were, however, the imperial palaces whose construction he inaugurated or developed; these bore witness both to his wealth and his power, and could serve as platforms upon which to display further idealized visions of his kingship in the form of inscriptions and sculptures. Nowhere is this more apparent than in the elaborate building programme begun under Darius at his new capital Persepolis[20] and the royal necropolis at Naqsh-i-Rustam a few kilometres away; at Susa too Darius undertook a major construction scheme.[21] The spectacular relief sculptures of the vast, columned Apadana, or royal audience hall, at Persepolis demonstrate the way in which such a building might be used as a way of promoting a vision of Achaemenid kingship.[22] The facades of its monumental stairways are adorned

---

[18] Root (1979), p. 71; see also Briant (2002), pp. 963–4.

[19] See Kuhrt (2007), p. 482 (fig. 11.4). The 'canal stelae' commemorating Darius' completion of the ancient Suez canal bear a similar image of kneeling figures, each of which is labelled with the name of one of the king's territories: Root (1979), pp. 61–8. The motif is one which also features on Darius' tomb. Briant (2002), pp. 172–83 analyses the representation of the king's subject peoples in inscriptions and sculpture.

[20] Kuhrt (2007), p. 470 points out that the site at Persepolis was not a new foundation by Darius, but that archaeological evidence suggests that Cyrus and/or Cambyses had built there previously. Nonetheless the vast terrace and palace complex begun during Darius' reign represented a significant development of the site; the fact that Darius established Persepolis as his capital marked a departure from Cyrus' use of Pasargadae and may suggest a conscious decision to represent himself as breaking with what had gone before. Darius did, however, also complete buildings at Pasargadae, and inscriptions there (CMa, CMb and CMc; see Kuhrt (2007), pp. 177–8) suggest that Darius claimed that Cyrus was an Achaemenid and therefore his ancestor. On the building programmes of Darius see also Briant (2002), pp. 165–71.

[21] See, for example, inscriptions DSe, which suggests that Darius remodelled the existing site at Susa, and DSf, relating to the building of a palace there and advertising the vast extent of Darius' empire by listing the regions from which the building materials and craftsmen came.

[22] A comprehensive series of photographs of the site at Persepolis is provided online by the Oriental Institute of the University of Chicago: http://oi.uchicago.edu/museum/collections/pa/persepolis/persepolis.html

with ostentatious carvings depicting parades of royal guards, Persian nobles
and tribute-bearers – distinguished by clothing and appearance to represent
the subject nations of the empire – carrying gifts for the king. These figures
converge on the enthroned king, his crown prince and attendants standing
behind him.[23] The foundation inscriptions (four copies of a trilingual text, DPh,
on gold and silver tablets found at each corner of the building) indicate that
Darius planned the construction of the Apadana; later inscriptions bearing
Xerxes' name (XPg) declare that his son completed the building work after
his father's death. It is likely too that the sculptural decoration was planned in
Darius' time but completed under Xerxes' rule (Root 1979, p. 91); the ongoing
construction at the site could thus serve as a conspicuous physical symbol of
Achaemenid dynastic and political continuity.

If the royal palaces at Persepolis and Susa, with their accompanying inscriptions and sculptural decoration, convey a sense of imperial majesty, it is in the
tomb of Darius at Naqsh-i-Rustam where we find a combination of this vision
of awe-inspiring power with a series of written statements which provide an
idealized view of the more personal qualities which an Achaemenid king might
be expected to possess.[24] The façade of the tomb displays a lengthy inscription
referring to Darius' achievements as well as a relief sculpture which mirrors the
idealized vision of the king's power beneath the watchful gaze of Ahuramazda
as seen elsewhere. Here the king, holding a bow which rests against his foot,
stands on a raised podium held aloft by two rows of figures representing the
different peoples of his empire and individually labelled as such. At either side
are Persian nobles and weapon bearers (two of whom are named as Gobryas
and Aspathines, which might be indicative of a more personal element to the
monument than is seen in the palace reliefs at Persepolis), and the winged
figure of Ahuramazda hovers above the scene. As the king's final resting-place,
the monument bears witness to the lasting image of his rule which Darius
wished to convey. The accompanying trilingual inscriptions (DNa and DNb,
each in Old Persian, Elamite and Babylonian) refer to Darius, his achievements as king and his admirable personal characteristics. DNa begins with
an invocation of Ahuramazda's role as creator and as Darius' benefactor (§1),

---

[23] Root (1979), pp. 86–95 details the sculptural decoration of the Persepolis Apadana. See also Brosius
    (2010) for a discussion of the audience scene in Achaemenid art and its role in representing the king
    as 'the absolute, but peaceful, monarch ruling over his subjects' (p. 141). The image of the enthroned
    king is one which the Achaemenids borrowed from Assyrian imperial iconography: M. C. Miller
    (1988), p. 82. On the representation of the crown prince see further below, pp. 83–7.

[24] See Kuhrt (2007), p. 500 (fig. 11.4) for a drawing of the tomb façade; Root (1979), pp. 72–6 gives a
    description of the sculptural decoration.

before giving Darius' titles and pedigree (§2: 'I am Darius the great king, king of kings, king of countries containing all kinds of man, king on this great earth far and wide, son of Hystaspes, an Achaemenid, a Persian, son of a Persian, an Aryan, having Aryan lineage') and then going on to list the twenty-nine countries which, by Ahuramazda's favour, the king declared he 'seized outside of Persia' (§3) and which brought him tribute. The inscription then goes on to refer to the accompanying sculpture as a visual representation of the countries over whom the king ruled (§4) before claiming Ahuramazda's support and protection (§5) and exhorting the viewer to follow the path commanded by Ahuramazda (§6).

While DNa offers a view of Darius as almighty ruler, and as Ahuramazda's representative on earth, DNb provides an insight into the way in which the king's persona was envisaged and projected within official Achaemenid royal ideology. This inscription too begins with a declaration of Ahuramazda's greatness but then differs from other royal inscriptions in that it acts as a eulogy of the personal attributes which gave Darius the ability to perform successfully his role as king. Crucially for the purposes of the present discussion, this text was also re-appropriated by Xerxes for his own use, with only the name of Xerxes being substituted for that of Darius (XPl) and little else altered;[25] the document therefore makes a highly significant contribution to our understanding of the way in which Xerxes' kingship was represented within the Persian empire. A complete translation reads as follows:[26]

> §1 A great god (is) Ahuramazda, who created this excellent (work) which one sees; who created happiness for man; who bestowed wisdom and energy upon Darius/Xerxes the king.

> §2a Darius/Xerxes the king proclaims: By the favour of Ahuramazda I am of such a kind that I am a friend to what is right, I am no friend to what is wrong. (It is) not my wish that to the weak is done wrong because of the mighty, it is not my wish that the mighty is hurt because of the weak.

> §2b What is right, that is my wish. I am no friend of the man who is a follower of the Lie. I am not hot-tempered. When I feel anger rising, I keep that under my control by my thinking power. I control firmly my impulses.

---

[25] Note that while DNb is trilingual, only an Old Persian version of the corresponding XPl has been found. Gharib (1968) presents a comparison of the language of XPl and DNb, pointing out that the differences are mainly grammatical and suggesting (p. 55) that both may have been copied from the same original draft.

[26] = Kuhrt (2007), Ch. 11, no. 17 (pp. 503–5).

§2c The man who co-operates, him do I reward according to his co-operation. He who does harm, him I punish according to the damage. It is not my wish that a man does harm, it is certainly not my wish that a man if he causes harm be not punished.

§2d What a man says against a man, that does not convince me, until I have heard testimony from both parties.

§2e What a man does or performs according to his powers, satisfies me, therewith I am satisfied; it gives me great pleasure and I give much to faithful men.

§2f Of such a kind (are) my intelligence and command; when you shall see or hear what has been done by me, both in the house and in battle – that (is) my ability in addition to thinking and intelligence.

§2g Moreover this (is) my ability, that my body is strong. As a fighter I am a good fighter. At once my intelligence stands in its place, whether I see a rebel or not. Both by intelligence and by command at that time I regard myself as superior to panic, when I see a rebel just as when I do not see (one).

§2h I am furious in the strength of my revenge with both hands and both feet. As a horseman I am a good horseman. As a bowman I am a good bowman, both on foot and on horseback. As a spearman I am a good spearman, both on foot and on horseback.

§2i These are the skills which Ahuramazda has bestowed upon me and I have had the strength to bear them. By the favour of Ahuramazda, what has been done by me, I have done with these skills which Ahuramazda has bestowed upon me.[27]

This inscription expands upon the portrait of an invincible and infallible king favoured by the supreme god Ahuramazda, acknowledging the god's role both in his own fortunes and in the creation of the building upon which the inscription was carved, then denouncing anyone who follows the 'Lie' and therefore rejects Ahuramazda (and, by implication, the divinely ordained rule of the king). As upholder of moral rectitude, the king is envisaged here as a just and upright ruler who seeks fairness for both weak and strong. The emphasis on doing what is right is accompanied by the characterization of the king as a man of self-control rather than rash impulse. Here is a ruler who rewards the generosity

---

[27] DNb has ten lines more than XPl, set apart from the main text by a space, and consisting of an exhortation to a subject, urging obedience.

and loyalty of others but who metes out due punishment to those who do him damage or betray him; a fair judge, however, he listens to both sides in a dispute before pronouncing a reasoned judgement. Meanwhile he is said to possess the mental and physical attributes which befit a fine military commander; his intellectual abilities confer tactical aptitude and calmness in the face of adversity while bodily strength and training in the arts of soldiery make him a competent fighter. The reference to skill with the bow as a positive attribute here contrasts with allusions to this particular weapon in Aeschylus' *Persians* where it acts as a symbol contrasting the Persians' (implicitly inferior) military tactics with those of the Athenian hoplite fighters (see p. 16 with n. 14). In the Persian context it becomes one of the ideal qualities of a model Achaemenid monarch which are immortalized on Darius' tomb. That Xerxes chose to replicate his father's conception of kingship almost word-for-word in an inscription found close to Persepolis demonstrates his desire, as successor to the throne, to stress continuity with the past and his place in the dynasty founded by his father. It also acts as a reminder to us that the text should be read not as an individualized characterization of a particular monarch but rather as outlining the ideal virtues of the perfect Achaemenid king; as such it is not merely a memorial to one king but also a manifesto to be adhered to by those to whom the throne will pass in the future. This emphasis upon continuity from one king to the next contrasts starkly too with Aeschylus' vision of Persian kingship in which the notion of clear distinction between father and son, with its emphasis on the youthful rashness of Xerxes in comparison to Xerxes' moderation, is of paramount dramatic importance (see pp. 26–30); it is closer, in fact, to the Herodotean vision of Xerxes as bearing the weight of dynastic responsibility in following on from his father (pp. 58–63).

Like father, like son

It was, then, the image of Achaemenid kingship created during Darius' rule, then inscribed and sculpted so prominently on the monuments to his power, which Xerxes would inherit from his father and upon which this king's own imperial propaganda would build. While the wholesale appropriation of Darius' tomb inscription by his son and successor is the most striking evidence of the emphasis which was placed upon dynastic continuity, the material remains pertaining to Xerxes' reign are rich in examples which demonstrate further the forging of an ideological link between father and son. It would seem that this link was already being cultivated during Darius' reign, before Xerxes' own accession to the throne; the need to carve out a secure future for the dynasty was crucial in the wake of the turbulent circumstances surrounding Darius' assumption of the kingship.

Figure 1: Council Hall: South jamb of east doorway of main hall depicting enthroned Darius with crown prince behind him. Image reproduced courtesy of the Oriental Institute of the University of Chicago.

Figure 2: Persepolis treasury: South portico of Courtyard 17 depicting audience scene with king and crown prince. Image reproduced courtesy of the Oriental Institute of the University of Chicago.

The mirroring of the kingly qualities of father and son seen in Xerxes' re-use of his father's tomb inscriptions finds its artistic parallel in several of the relief sculptures from Persepolis. Images from the treasury[28] and door jambs of the Apadana and Tripylon (council hall) depict the king seated on a throne and resting his feet on footstool; a royal figure, now usually identified as his crown prince, stands behind him (Figure 1).[29] The king and prince are on a raised platform and beneath a decorated canopy with a hovering figure of Ahuramazda overhead; the door-jamb reliefs show this podium being held aloft by figures representing the subject nations in a manner similar to that of Darius' tomb relief. Here the royal figures are beneath an elaborately decorated canopy, above which is the hovering figure of Ahuramazda. The treasury reliefs display the same tableau of king and crown prince as part of an audience scene in which the king receives a Persian dignitary (Figure 2).[30] Behind the royal figures stand

---

[28] The treasury reliefs are thought to have originally been installed on the Apadana and later moved: Cahill (1985), pp. 385–6.

[29] Further images are provided by Root (1979), plates XVII and XXVa, and Boardman (2000), figs. 4.13 and 4.16 for photographs; Kuhrt (2007), p. 536 (fig. 11.29) is a line drawing of one of the treasury relief panels. For line drawings see also Briant (2002), pp. 218–19 (figs. 20 and 21). Note that other relief sculptures from the palace at Persepolis show the king without the crown prince, and instead with attendants carrying parasols or flywhisks. See Root (1979), pp. 76–86 for detailed descriptions.

[30] Sancisi-Weerdenburg (1993), pp. 130–1 notes the absence of prostration before the king in Persian art (with the exception of the defeated rebel featured on the Behistun relief and identified as the impostor Gaumata); this has led scholars to suggest that *proskynēsis* did not involve such a gesture,

two attendants, one holding a towel and the other carrying an axe, bow and quiver. In these visual representations of the king and his heir the two royal figures are differentiated from those around them by their relative height and clothing (they wear the robe and strapless boots which set apart royal figures from non-royals in Achaemenid iconography), and are linked with one another by their close physical resemblance. Both carry a lotus flower in one hand;[31] the position of the crown prince's other arm, bent at the elbow in order to touch the king's throne in front of him, mirrors precisely that of the seated king (who holds in that hand the royal sceptre); and their long squared-off beards, hair, crowns and facial features are identical. It becomes clear that, as in the case of the DNb/XPl inscriptions, these visual representations of father and son were conceived not as lifelike portraits of the physical characteristics of individuals but rather as rigidly stylized depictions in which the royal figures served to personify the continuation of the Achaemenid dynasty from one generation to the next.

Whether the figures on these particular reliefs can be identified with absolute certainty as Darius and Xerxes is open to conjecture; some scholars have suggested the possibility that they represent Xerxes and *his* son, the younger Darius.[32] Often too the similarity of artistic representations of subsequent Persian kings renders the identification of individual rulers problematic.[33] Inscriptions labelling the sculptures are often our only means of a certain identification of the individual kings depicted on reliefs at Persepolis; on the door jambs of the palace of Darius at Persepolis the vertical folds of the kings' robes identify figures as 'Darius, the great king, son of Hystaspes, the Achaemenid' (DPb, on the west jamb of the southern doorway) and 'Xerxes, son of Darius the

but was perhaps the 'hand-before-mouth' gesture of the dignitary before the king seen on the Persepolis Treasury Relief. See also Frye (1972). Allen (2005) provides an iconographic analysis of audience scenes in Persian art and considers the way in which these are re-interpreted by Greek and Roman sources.

[31] Tuplin (1996), p. 91 (with n. 41) notes that the lotus flower held by the king is one of several such floral motifs in Achaemenid royal sculpture; it may relate to the association of Achaemenid kings with elaborate royal gardens.

[32] Root (1979), pp. 91–4 argues that the sculptures were planned during the reign of Darius, although her argument against Xerxes' appointment of his son Darius as his own crown prince uses Herodotus' novelistic account of Xerxes' affair with his son's wife as evidence that relations between the two could not have been congenial; this may be a flawed line of reasoning (Herodotus 9.107–8; see above pp. 70–1). Kuhrt (1997), p. 537 suggests the possibility that the panels 'were generic representations of king and designated successor', rather than being intended to represent individual kings.

[33] Note Briant (2002), p. 216: 'in every royal depiction, from Darius I to Artaxerxes I, the king wears the same robe with identical decoration'. See also Sancisi-Weerdenburg (1989), p. 558 on the difficulty of identifying specific Achaemenid rulers depicted on the reliefs: 'if individual kings are indeed portrayed, it is above all the unchanging traditional aspects of kingship that were emphasised and expressed'.

king, the Achaemenid' (XPk, on the garment of the corresponding figure of the east jamb).[34] Perhaps to seek such certain identification is, however, to overlook a key point about the symbolic function of the reliefs: the uniformity of the manner in which the kings are depicted, like the formulaic nature of many of the Achaemenid inscriptions, emphasizes above all the idea of continuity from one ruler to the next and the perpetuation of the dynasty.

A number of Xerxes' inscriptions also highlight very clearly the connection between father and son and the desire to project an image of the continuation of the Achaemenid royal line. One very simple way of stressing the familial link is for Xerxes to refer to himself explicitly as 'son of Darius' or to mention 'my father Darius'; these formulae are adopted in the majority of the surviving inscriptions.[35] One inscription in particular stands out as alluding explicitly to the issue of Xerxes' succession, however. Found in Old Persian and Babylonian versions serving as commemorative foundation stones for the building described as the 'harem' of Xerxes[36] – a structure whose sculptural decoration (reliefs showing the king followed by attendants; guards in Persian court dress; the figure of the 'royal hero' fighting lions in what might be a mythical allegory for the kings' military victories)[37] follows the style of that used on Darius' buildings – this inscription (XPf) advertises Xerxes' relationship with Ahuramazda and his credentials as king as well as outlining briefly the circumstances of his accession to the throne:[38]

> §1 A great god (is) Ahuramazda, who created this earth, who created yonder heaven, who created man, who created blissful happiness for man, who made Xerxes the king, one king of many, one lord of many.

> §2 I (am) Xerxes, the great king, king of kings, king of countries containing many peoples, king on this great earth far and wide, son of Darius, the king, an Achaemenid.

> §3 King Xerxes proclaims: My father (was) Darius; the father of Darius (was) Hystaspes by name; the father of Hystastpes (was) Arsames by name. Both Hystaspes and Arsames were living; nevertheless, thus was the desire of

---

[34] Root (1979), p. 83 suggests that by the time these robes were inscribed Xerxes had been formally selected as crown prince, although compare E. F. Schmidt (1953), p. 224, suggesting that Xerxes had his own name added after the death of Darius.

[35] Briant (2002), p. 524.

[36] On the dubious identification of the building in question as Xerxes' harem see p. 75 with n. 6.

[37] Root (1979), pp. 303–11.

[38] Kuhrt (2007), Ch. 7 no. 1 (p. 244).

Ahuramazda – Darius, who (was) my father, him he made king on this earth. When Darius had become king, much that (is) superior he built.

§4 King Xerxes proclaims: Darius had other sons also; (but) thus was the desire of Ahuramazda: Darius, my father, made me the greatest after himself. When my father Darius went to his (allotted) place, by the favour of Ahuramazda I became king in my father's place. When I became king, much that (is) superior I built. What had been built by my father, that I took into my care and other work I added. But what I have done and what my father has done, all that we have done by the favour of Ahuramazda.

§5 King Xerxes proclaims: Me may Ahuramazda protect and my kingdom! And what (has been) built by me and what (has been) built by my father, that also may Ahuramazda protect.

The detailed genealogical information which is given stresses Xerxes' connection with the past; the inscription also takes up Darius' practice of crediting the role of Ahuramazda in securing the king's position and protecting him as well as the buildings whose construction he has overseen.[39] The formulaic opening (an invocation of Ahuramazda and detailed genealogical information) mirrors that of DNa, on Darius' tomb; here, as elsewhere, Xerxes appropriates his father's wording as a way of affirming his connection with his predecessor.[40] The inscription also alludes to the unusual circumstances of his father's accession by noting that Darius' father and grandfather were both alive when he became king, and records the fact that Xerxes himself inherited the throne from his father, according to the will of Ahuramazda, despite there being other potential claimants (his brothers).[41] By stressing that he was his father's favourite Xerxes underlines the legitimacy of his own position. There is also perhaps here an implicit suggestion of a contrast between the peaceful transfer of power from father to son and the turbulent circumstances of Darius' accession; the passing of the kingship with relative ease from one generation to the next can be seen to cement the establishment of the dynasty.

It is significant too that in this inscription Xerxes refers to the building works undertaken both by his father and by himself. He is careful to stress that, just

---

[39] Cf, for example, DSf.

[40] Versions of the introductory formula are also used by Xerxes in, for example, XPa, XPb, XPc, XPd, XPh, XV.

[41] On Herodotus' account of the succession, see above, pp. 60–1. Briant (2002), p. 520 notes, by contrast with the Greek historiographical account, the absence of any reference to the influence of Atossa over the inheritance in the Persian inscription; this may reflect the Greek preoccupation with the domestic affairs of the Persian court (on which see further Ch. 5).

as Darius was responsible for much construction, he went on to add to these projects as well as taking care of those which his father created. This is a theme seen elsewhere in texts from Xerxes' reign which provide further evidence for the way in which buildings, as visible symbols of the king's power, might be used to promote an image of the Achaemenid dynasty. Many of Xerxes' other surviving inscriptions relate to his building works and as such they often note that the architectural projects with which they are associated are an extension of those initiated by Darius. So, for example, an inscription from the Persepolis Apadana (XPg) declares, 'Xerxes the great king proclaims: By the favour of Ahuramazda, much that is good did Darius the king, my father. And also by the favour of Ahuramazda, I added to that work and built more. Me may Ahuramazda protect, together with the gods, and my kingdom.' Similar texts, from other parts of the empire (XSd, from Susa; XV from Lake Van) as well as from Persepolis (XPa), announce that Xerxes continued the building programme which was initiated by his father. The notion of a seamless link between one king and the next is thus restated by way of the ongoing construction of structures which themselves bear witness to Xerxes' assumption of his father's role; this tradition was one which would be maintained too by Xerxes' own successors.[42] Whereas for subsequent kings this continuation of tradition may have seemed simply the natural thing to do, for Xerxes, however, the decision to adopt his father's architectural and iconographic programme must have been a more deliberate and conscious choice.

Alternative perspectives on Xerxes: The case of the *daiva*-inscription

Despite the overwhelming stress on the idea of continuity from father to son in the material evidence from Xerxes' reign, one inscription in particular has in the past been taken by some scholars to suggest that the king's actions represented a departure from those of his father where his tolerance of religious practices which did not involve the worship of Ahuramazda was concerned. The history of the interpretation of the so-called '*daiva*-inscription' (XPh) might indeed be seen as a case-study in the way in which the desire to seek confirmation of the impression given by Greek sources has coloured judgements on

---

[42] A¹Pa and A¹Pb, for example, assert that Artaxerxes completed Xerxes' building works at Persepolis, and an inscription of Darius II (D²Sb) indicates that he completed Artaxerxes' palace at Susa.

Persian texts;[43] the text has been used as a key piece of evidence in discussions concerning the contested scholarly territory of the nature of Xerxes' methods of rule. The original archaeological contexts of the limestone slabs bearing the inscription have not been determined, although multiple versions have been uncovered. Four texts of XPh – two in Old Persian, one in Akkadian and one in Elamite – were found at Persepolis in the 1930s, with a further Old Persian version excavated at Pasargadae in 1961.

The inscription opens (XPh §1–2) with familiar formulaic statements which are identical to those on Darius' tomb inscription (DNa), proclaiming the greatness of Ahuramazda and stating the king's lineage. There follows (§3) a country-list, the only such surviving list among Xerxes' inscriptions, as the text declares, 'By the favour of Ahuramazda, these are the countries of which I was king outside Persia; I ruled them; they bore me tribute.' Once again there is a clear link with DNa in which Darius too enumerated his subject nations; the language introducing Xerxes' list has one small but crucial difference, however. Where Darius' text states 'these are the countries which I seized', Xerxes' language is more passive, stating only that he 'ruled' over the lands record in the inscription;[44] this would seem to reinforce the impression which he creates elsewhere of the peaceful transfer of power by way of his rightful inheritance of the throne, unimpeded by the kind of apparently widespread resistance which Darius' Behistun inscription records. Xerxes' record of his imperial territories lists those detailed in DNa (cf. DSe §3) with the addition of two new names, the Dahae and Akaufaka; the text gives no supplementary explanation but there is perhaps a sense here that this king augmented the lands of his father, just as he built upon the works of palace construction which were initiated by Darius.[45]

It is the content of the text which follows that has been the subject of scholarly controversy, however:[46]

> §4a Xerxes the king proclaims: When I became king, there is among these countries which (are) inscribed above (one, which) was in turmoil. Afterwards Ahuramazda brought me aid; by the favour of Ahuramazda I defeated that country and put it in its proper place.

---

[43] As pointed out effectively by Sancisi-Weerdenburg (1989), pp. 557–8. Abdi (2010), pp. 279–83 details the chronology of the archaeological finds and provides a bibliographic survey of the history of scholarly interpretations of the inscriptions.

[44] Kuhrt (2007), p. 305; cf. Kent (1953), p. 138 (translation of DNa) and p. 151 (XPh).

[45] Briant (2002), pp. 553–4. Kuhrt (2007), p. 305 n. 5 also points out that the inscription is likely to have been carved after the Greek campaign but that it records no losses at the north-western fringe of Xerxes' empire: this reinforces the suggestion that the document is intended to create an idealized impression of Xerxes' flawless imperial power.

[46] Kuhrt (2007), Ch. 7 no. 88, p. 305.

§4b And among those countries there were (some) where formerly the *daiva*s ['false gods'] had been worshipped. Afterwards by the favour of Ahuramazda I destroyed that place of the *daiva*s, and I gave orders: 'The *daiva*s shall not be worshipped any longer!' Wherever formerly the *daiva*s have been worshipped, there I worshipped Ahuramazda at the proper time and with the proper ceremony.

§4c And there was something else, that had been done wrong, that too I put right. That which I have done, all that I have done by the favour of Ahuramazda. Ahuramazda brought me aid, until I had done the work.

§4d You, who shall be hereafter, if you shall think: 'Happy may I be (while) living and (when) dead may I be blessed', obey that law, which Ahuramazda has established! Worship Ahuramazda at the proper time and with the proper ritual! The man who obeys that law which Ahuramazda has established, and (who) worships Ahuramazda at the proper time and in the proper ceremonial style, he both becomes happy (while) living and blessed (when) dead.

§5 Xerxes the king proclaims: Me may Ahuramazda protect from evil, and my (royal) house and this land! This I pray of Ahuramazda; this may Ahuramazda grant me.

The lack of specific information concerning the country or countries to which Xerxes refers here makes interpretation difficult. Early publications of the text sought to pinpoint the exact date of the inscription as well as to identify territories to which it might relate.[47] Meanwhile Xerxes' assertions that he put down a rebellion, that he suppressed the worship of *daiva*s ('false gods')[48] and re-established the worship of Ahuramazda, and that he 'put right' another unspecified wrong, were used by historians to support a view of this king as an oppressive and intolerant despot, with a policy of persecuting followers of religions other than his own; in particular the hypothesis of Hartmann (1939) that the text referred to Xerxes' destruction of the temple of Bel-Marduk in Babylon alluded to by Herodotus (1.183) gained ground and became a cornerstone of this view. In more recent scholarship, however, doubt has been cast upon the historicity of the text, with some suggesting that Xerxes speaks here in general terms rather than about a specific occasion in the past.[49] Meanwhile the rereading of Kuhrt and Sherwin-White (1987) emphatically demonstrated that the interpretation

---

[47] Herzfeld (1936); Hartmann (1937); Lévy (1939); Kent (1943).

[48] See Herrenschmidt and Kellens (1993) and Lecoq (1997), pp. 154–5 for the linguistic history of the term *daiva*.

[49] Sancisi-Weerdenburg (1989), p. 551, p. 557; Wiesehöfer (1996), pp. 54–5; Briant (2002), pp. 552–3.

of the text as evidence for Xerxes' destruction of the Bel-Marduk temple was based on a misreading of Herodotus' description of Xerxes' actions in Babylonia and was built upon assumptions about the king's religious intolerance which themselves stemmed from Greek accounts of the Persians' destruction of sanctuaries during the campaign of 480 BC.[50]

The temptation to extrapolate from this one document a picture of Xerxes as oppressor and religious bigot, and in turn to suggest that his policies were less tolerant than those of Darius, owes more to preconceived ideas based on the Greek sources than to what can be derived from the Persian epigraphic record alone. The notion that Xerxes' behaviour was more extreme than that of his father might be traced to readings of Aeschylus' *Persians*, in which Xerxes' youthful rashness and the unfavourable comparison which is drawn between him and the deceased Darius are essential elements of the play's characterization of Xerxes (see pp. 26–30); meanwhile the burning of temples and sanctuaries met, unsurprisingly, with such outrage by the Herodotean Themistocles might readily serve to support a reading of the *daiva*-inscription which claims that Xerxes was in the habit of destroying all that was sacred. Yet if we remind ourselves that the inspiration for the creation of these Greek (or, more specifically, Athenian)[51] versions of the Xerxes-tradition was the momentous series of events surrounding the Persians' destruction of the Hellenic sanctuaries it becomes clear that to base our own views of Xerxes' actions on the emotional response to those events will almost inevitably lead to the formation of a negative judgement on their perpetrator. By way of comparison here we might think about the evidence from the Jewish tradition which sees Xerxes as far more tolerant of religious diversity; the biblical book of Esther and the writings of Josephus present the perspective of an ethnic group who had benefited from the benevolence of the Achaemenid kings and thus had no axe to grind with Xerxes (see pp. 141–8 on Esther and pp. 173–6 on Josephus).

One way of countering this interpretation of the *daiva*-inscription as a reflection of Xerxes' unequalled intolerance would be to look for evidence which helps to build a case for Xerxes as having simply followed precedents set by his father. In the first place it is worth bearing in mind that any argument *ex silentio* is problematic; given the fragmentary nature of the Persian evidence

---

[50] See also Kuhrt (2010) and Briant (2002), pp. 543–5.

[51] Note my analysis (above, pp. 46–7) of the way in which the character of Themistocles, as portrayed by Herodotus, voices the Athenian verdict on Xerxes; that is not to say that Herodotus' surrounding narrative necessarily upholds an Athenian viewpoint (and in fact, there are some indications that as narrator Herodotus cautions against some elements of Athenian behaviour: pp. 68–9).

which remains it is not possible to conclude with any certainty that Xerxes' inscription had no direct parallels in his father's epigraphic corpus. On the basis of what remains, however, we might suggest, for example, that the suppression of rebellion was in itself no radical new course of action, given that the very context of Darius' Behistun inscription was to report in particular the termination of various insurrections which threatened the stability of his rule in the early days. Meanwhile Xerxes' claim to uphold the worship of Ahuramazda in a place where *daiva*s had been worshipped makes no suggestion that he imposed his own religion upon subject peoples; the destruction of a place where *daiva*s had been worshipped might therefore be seen not as an act of religious persecution but rather as a form of response to unrest, and as a reassertion of the king's authority over unruly imperial subjects.[52] So too Xerxes' record of the destruction of places where *daiva* were worshipped and his institution there of the worship of Ahuramazda, although without a precise model, might be seen to follow on from Darius' own expression of his concern for maintaining adherence to the laws of Ahuramazda; in the Behistun inscription (DB col. V §72) Darius recorded a rebellion by the Elamites, asserting, 'Those Elamites were disloyal, and by them Ahuramazda was not worshipped. I worshipped Ahuramazda. By the favour of Ahuramazda, as (was) my desire, so I treated them.' While there is no mention of *daiva*s here, there is nonetheless a suggestion that an element of the Elamites' disloyalty was their rejection of Ahuramazda (and perhaps, by implication, his divinely ordained representative on earth) and that Darius sought to uphold the worship of Ahuramazda in their territory. It is equally possible to argue that the notion of a consistent Achaemenid 'policy' where religious matters are concerned is anachronistic, and that the actions of the imperial administration in any given situation were based on pragmatic considerations relating to how best to assert its authority – whether by toleration of diversity in some cases, or suppression where insubordination had been detected – on a case-by-case basis.[53]

To approach the document by trying to extract some absolute historical truth about the way in which Xerxes conducted himself might suggest, however, a conviction that we are able to use the inscription as concrete evidence for Xerxes' personal characteristics. An alternative approach to the *daiva*-inscription – and

---

[52] Brosius (2006), p. 68.
[53] Harrison (2011), pp. 82–3. Note too Georges (1994), pp. 56–8, suggesting that the burning of temples by the Persians was always politically motivated, and highlighting 'the Persians' consistency in making war only on the gods of their enemies, and giving cult status to those of their loyal friends'.

one which, in the context of the present study of ancient perspectives on Xerxes might prove more fruitful – would be to think of it not simply as providing us with evidence which might confirm or deny our view of Xerxes' personality or actions but instead as a carefully orchestrated projection of an image of his kingship which is no less selective in its inclusion of material than the texts written from a Greek perspective. As such the *daiva*-inscription, like other Persian sources – whether written, artistic or architectural – conveys an impression of Xerxes as, like his father, a mighty imperial ruler over the geographically diverse empire whose subject states are listed at the beginning of the inscription. The text reaffirms Xerxes' power, his royal virtues and his symbiotic relationship with Ahuramazda while making it clear that this king (again, like his father) will not tolerate rebellion of any sort and that states which revolt will suffer severe consequences.[54] We must acknowledge, therefore, that the impression of the king which is created – however we choose to interpret that impression – is one which Xerxes chose deliberately to project.

The omission of names of specific troublesome states here also suggests that the text – although perhaps originally conceived as a response to a particular incident – may have been constructed as a timeless and universal declaration of the king's will and ability to maintain order among subject peoples.[55] In this particular case the means by which Xerxes has chosen to assert his authority is to suppress the worship of gods other than Ahuramazda in places where such worship is deemed to be politically problematic. The emphasis which is placed upon his own worship of Ahuramazda is, meanwhile, entirely consistent with other Achaemenid epigraphic assertions of the king's reciprocal relationship with the supreme deity; in light of this it is also possible that the carving of the text was at least partially motivated by a desire to maintain the favour of Ahuramazda. The exhortation to obey Ahuramazda's laws, and the assertion that he who does so will be blessed in life and death, reaffirms the notion that the king is the god's representative on earth. Seen in this light, then, it becomes apparent that the *daiva*-inscription offers an insight into the creation of Xerxes' image from the Persian royal perspective; set within the context of the wider body of Achaemenid propaganda it can be seen to perform a similar ideological

---

[54] See also Sancisi-Weerdenburg (1999), pp. 96–8 and Briant (2002), pp. 552–3. Henkelman (2008), p. 10 also suggests that the *daiva*-inscription, as 'an ideological manifesto dealing with the eternal order', has parallels in earlier Neo-Elamite inscriptions.

[55] In the opening chapter of her doctoral dissertation Sancisi-Weerdenburg (1980), pp. 1–47, first set out the case against attempts to connect the inscription with specific historical events. Cf. Briant (2002), p. 553: 'In the *daivā* inscription Xerxes makes no allusion to a rebellious country or to royal activities specifically located in space and time. His inscription is instead intended to illustrate the permanence of his power and the transcendence of his virtues.'

function to that of other epigraphic and artistic representations of the character of the king and the nature of his rule.[56]

The Persian image of Xerxes – in the *daiva*-inscription as well as in every other extant Persian epigraphic and artistic source – is therefore a self-conscious vision of an idealized king and the authority which he commands. As part of an ongoing programme of Achaemenid royal propaganda this vision is the product of traditions cultivated during Darius' reign and perpetuated not only by Xerxes but also by successive Achaemenid kings. The Xerxes whom we find in his own homeland, his image adorning the royal palaces and his words carved on stone tablets, thus emerges as being as much an artificial construct as the character we encounter in the Greek literary texts; each of these retellings is shaped by the agenda – whether political, artistic, dramatic or personal – of its creator. Thus in the hands of an Athenian playwright whose intention is to create a dramatic spectacle for the entertainment of his audience and to celebrate a victory the protagonist becomes the epitome of emotional anguish; the contrast with the king described as calm in the face of adversity and able to control his impulses (XPl) could not be starker. If Aeschylus emphasizes the contrast between father and son as a way of highlighting Xerxes' inferiority compared with the virtues of Darius, Achaemenid sculpture and epigraphy stress instead the shared traits of the two kings and the seamless continuity of their reigns. Where in Greek accounts of Salamis designed to highlight the superior naval skills of the Athenians Xerxes' tactical aptitude is inferior to that of the shrewd Themistocles, the king's own records declare him to be a competent military strategist and one whose abilities enable him to suppress resistance effectively. Meanwhile the image of a vast empire of slave subjects, so effectively illustrated by Herodotus' catalogues of the king's troops and a source of such terror for Xerxes' Greek opponents, is displayed in the Persian texts as a cause for celebration; it is, the inscriptions declare, the divine will of Ahuramazda that the king should rule over so many. Even the sacking of sanctuaries, the cause of so much horror for the Greeks, is perhaps for Xerxes a sign of his ability to maintain order in the face of resistance to his power. Most significantly, however, where the Greek accounts of Xerxes are dominated by his role in the invasion of Greece,

---

[56] That the king was willing and able to manipulate this self-image in order to suit new contexts and audiences is also apparent in the Greek sources which bear the traces of the propaganda touted by Xerxes in the course of his invasion of Greece, in which he seems to have appropriated the narrative of the Trojan War as a means of garnering support from the Ionian Greeks; on this particular strand of Persian propaganda see Haubold (2007). Georges (1994), pp. 47–75 examines more broadly the way in which the Persians used the language and imagery of their subjects in order to define themselves to the diverse peoples of their empire.

there is no place for that campaign in the view left to posterity by the official Persian sources. The fact that this military campaign is not mentioned in the Persian sources acts as a powerful reminder that Greek perspectives on Xerxes – and those of the western inheritors of the traditions which they shaped – are overwhelmingly influenced by their response to that invasion.

5. *Xerxes rebuking the sea*. Based on a nineteenth-century Spanish lithograph illustrating *La Civilisación* (1881) by Don Pelegrin Casabó y Pagés

4

Pride, Panhellenism and Propaganda: Xerxes in the Fourth Century BC

The image of Xerxes as irascible tyrant, his anger provoked by the stormy sea which had thwarted his first attempt to bridge the Hellespont (Plate 5), is one which would doubtless be instantly recognizable to an Athenian audience of the fourth century BC. Although the story of the whipping of the sea originated with Herodotus (7.35; see above, p. 57) it is the traces of this aspect of the king's personality – the fearsome slave-master with an imperialist mission to conquer Greece – which form the dominant strand of traditions transmitted by later Athenian writers. A century after Xerxes' invasion of Greece the stories relating to his expedition were still common currency, as rhetoricians and historians continued to look back on the glorious moment of Greek history in which the might of Persia had been thwarted by the actions of their plucky forefathers. During this period the figure of Xerxes resurfaced in a variety of literary works; while no portrait as detailed as those crafted by Aeschylus or Herodotus survives from this period, it is nonetheless possible to detect the ongoing influence of the literary tradition, both in the use of explicit allusions to his role in the Persian Wars and, less directly, in the continuing presence of themes and motifs whose origins lie in the earlier narratives describing his invasion.

It is in the Athenian literary responses to Xerxes from the fourth century where we start to detect a more selective, and less subtle, approach by authors, as they begin to focus more closely only upon the few key elements of his image which best serve their immediate literary or rhetorical purposes. This shedding of some of the more nuanced aspects which we detected in particular in the historiographical work of Herodotus results in a slimmed-down literary portrait and a Xerxes who symbolizes the abhorrent enemy whom Athens could be proud to have resisted in the past. This was a brand of rhetoric which would be replayed countless times throughout the fourth century, as Athenians came to terms with a new set of political circumstances after the Peloponnesian War; in comparing the present with an idealized vision of a glorious bygone age some would advocate that the way to political harmony was for the Greeks to unite once more against Persia. The image of Xerxes as the great panhellenic foe was pressed into service in support of this cause. This chapter examines the fourth-century version of Xerxes, who occupies roles here as a reminder of the Athenians' celebrated past (seen particularly in Lysias' funeral oration of the early fourth century), as a focus for panhellenic sentiment (exemplified in the works of Isocrates spanning the years from around 380 to 340 BC), and as a key element in the propaganda campaigns of Alexander of Macedon, who sought to appropriate the anti-Persian panhellenic rhetoric as a means of garnering Greek support for himself as leader of a new campaign in the east. Prose writing from this period also offers us the possibility of a more positive model of Asiatic monarchy which differs from that exemplified by Xerxes, however. In particular Xenophon's portrait, in his *Cyropaedia*, of Cyrus the Great, will be used to illustrate this alternative perspective on the Persian kingship and to throw into relief the distinctive position occupied by Xerxes in the literary tradition.

Memories of a glorious past: Xerxes in Athenian rhetoric

With Persian support a decisive factor in bringing the Peloponnesian War to its eventual conclusion in 404 BC (the same year in which Artaxerxes II inherited the Persian throne from his father Darius II) and thereby securing Spartan ascendancy in Greece, the ongoing involvement of Persia in Greek political affairs in the decades which followed forms the backdrop to subsequent Athenian literary interest in the history of Greco-Persian relations.[1] As Sparta, under the leadership of Agesilaus, waged war against Persia in Asia Minor in the 390s BC, Artaxerxes II allied himself initially with Athens and other Greek states (the Boeotians led by Thebes, along with Corinth and Argos) against Sparta in the Corinthian War of 395–386 BC; this conflict too was concluded, however, by an agreement between Sparta and Persia which resulted in the King's Peace (also known as the Peace of Antalcidas).[2] Such shifting alliances were to set the pattern for Greek politics throughout the first half of the fourth century as

---

[1]   For a detailed analysis of Greco-Persian relations in the century after the Peloponnesian War see Hornblower (2004), pp. 64–95.

[2]   For a detailed discussion of the course of the Corinthian War and its eventual resolution see Seager (1994); the terms of the King's Peace are also discussed by Hornblower (2004), pp. 79–80.

Sparta, Athens and Thebes vied for dominance in Greece. It was this disunity which led some to look with nostalgia upon a past when Greek states had united in common cause against their eastern adversaries; the political situation also paved the way for the development of the panhellenic rhetoric which urged Greek states to set aside their differences and instead work once more against Persia, as the common enemy.

For the Athenian orators references to the past could act as an effective point of comparison with contemporary political affairs; the Persian Wars became something of a rhetorical commonplace in literature written in Athens during this period.[3] This was due at least in part to the fact that the fifth-century resistance to Persia had by now come to form a significant part of the catalogue of Athenian exploits, both mythical and historical, which is one of the key recurring elements of the *epitaphios*, or funeral oration.[4] Delivered at public funerals for the war dead, *epitaphioi* served both to honour those who had died in combat and to eulogize Athens and the Athenian past; in praising distant ancestors alongside recent casualties they created an idealized vision of Athenian history which could appeal to the audience's patriotic spirit and provide positive *exempla* which the contemporary audience might aspire to emulate.[5] It is in this context that the Persian Wars feature as the only historical example[6] alongside the genre's habitual use of a range of mythical themes (the defeat of the Amazons, Eumolpus' expulsion from Attica, the protection of the Heraclids, and Athenian intervention to ensure the lawful burial of the Seven who fought against Thebes) which served to emphasize Athens' self-styled role as civilized upholder of moral rectitude. In their selection of episodes for inclusion the authors of the *epitaphioi* can be seen to have played a key part in

---

[3] See, for example, Isocrates, *Panegyricus* 74 in which the speaker acknowledges that the theme has been spoken of many times before (cf. Isocrates, *To Philip* 147).

[4] The most detailed analysis of the genre of the *epitaphios* remains that of Loraux (1986); she discusses in detail the question of the origin of the Athenian collective eulogy at pp. 56–76, suggesting that it took on the form with which we are familiar during the 460s BC. Plato's *Menexenus*, a pastiche of the *epitaphios*, satirizes the tendency of the genre towards overuse of praise of the deeds of the ancestors, and accordingly contains a lengthy excursus on the Persian Wars (239d–241e). On the *Menexenus* as parody see Henderson (1975) and Pownall (2004), pp. 38–64, along with Loraux's analysis (1986, pp. 263–327).

[5] Epigraphic sources also illustrate use the of the Persian Wars tradition as a means of appealing to national pride in this period; Habicht (1961) identified a whole series of documents which purported to originate from the period of the Persian Wars yet which, he argued persuasively, were in reality produced in the fourth century and could be used to make a case for Athenian resistance to Macedon. Robertson (1976) also analyses the use of fifth-century history for the purposes of propaganda in fourth-century Athens. Cartledge (2013) is a comprehensive study of the 'Oath of Plataea'.

[6] See Kierdorf (1966), pp. 83–110, and Nouhaud (1982), pp. 135–77, for detailed analyses of the use of the Persian Wars theme in Attic oratory. Pearson (1941) and Perlman (1961) also discuss the oratorical use of historical examples.

influencing the way in which the Athenian version of history was preserved and transmitted.[7]

Of the extant examples of the genre it is Lysias' *Funeral Oration* which provides us with the most detailed insight into the way in which the traditions surrounding Xerxes' invasion could feature as a component of the catalogue of Athenian achievements. Lysias (c. 458–c. 380 BC), most of whose surviving speeches were written for delivery by litigants in the law courts at Athens in the early part of the fourth century, was of Sicilian descent and apparently studied rhetoric at the Greek colony of Thurii in southern Italy yet spent the majority of his career as a professional speech-writer at Athens;[8] his *epitaphios* was apparently delivered, like his other works, by a speaker other than himself and at some point during the Corinthian War of 395–386 BC.[9] During a war between the Greek states (and one in whose eventual outcome, like that of the Peloponnesian War, a Persian king would come to play a decisive part) Lysias' oration emphasized by way of contrast with contemporary circumstances the Athenians' role as saviours of Greece in the glorious wars of the past. After examining the mythical exempla (2.4–16), the speech turns its focus to the Persian Wars (2.20–47). While the account begins with Darius' campaign and the actions of the Athenians in repelling the Persian invaders at Marathon (2.20–6), little attention is paid to the Persian king himself in this section of the speech; Darius is left unnamed, being referred to only as the 'king of Asia' (ὁ τῆς Ἀσίας βασιλεύς, 2.21).[10] Lysias alludes here to the numbers of the troops which the king sent to Greece (giving a figure of five hundred thousand) and suggests that he was motivated by a desire to augment his wealth by enslaving Europe (2.21). The description of the first Persian invasion then allows for a lengthy reflection on Athens' role as saviour of Greece (2.22–6). By contrast with the lack of emphasis on Darius' role, however, the account of the second Persian campaign focuses closely upon the figure of Xerxes in order to provide an analysis of his motivation and actions. The portrait of the king seen here is the most comprehensive to be found in surviving Athenian oratory (2.27–9):

[7]   Thomas (1989), pp. 196–7.
[8]   Todd (2007), pp. 1–17 provides a comprehensive introduction to Lysias' life and work.
[9]   The precise date of Lysias' *epitaphios* is unknown, with some scholars suggesting that it was composed as a display piece rather than for delivery on a specific occasion. Todd (2007), pp. 157–64 summarizes the debate about its date and the context of its delivery.
[10] A similar omission of the king's name can be seen in Lycurgus' references to the Persian Wars in his *Against Leocrates*: here the speaker refers to Marathon without naming Darius (104), yet Xerxes' name is mentioned in passing several times in relation to occasions where Lycurgus praises the ancestors' actions against the Persians (68, 71, 80).

After this [Marathon] Xerxes, the king of Asia, was contemptuous of Greece, having been cheated of his hope, dishonoured by what had happened [the earlier Persian defeat], aggrieved by the disaster, and angry at those who were responsible for it; he was unused to disasters and unacquainted with honourable men. After making preparations he came in ten years' time with twelve hundred ships; and the number of the land army that he brought was immeasurable, so that to detail even the nations that followed him would be a lengthy task. But this is the best evidence of their numbers: although he had a thousand ships for taking his land army over the narrowest part of the Hellespont from Asia to Europe he did not want to do so, thinking it would be a great waste of time for him. So, showing contempt for principles of nature, the ways of the divine, and human inventions, he made a road across the sea and forced a passage for ships through the land. When he yoked the Hellespont and dug through Athos (ζεύξας μὲν τὸν Ἑλλήσποντον, διορύξας δὲ τὸν Ἄθω) no one stood in his way, for some submitted against their will and others were willing traitors.

In keeping with the demands of a genre in which brevity is essential in order for the speaker to communicate a message and to generate immediate impact upon his audience, Lysias' vision of Xerxes condenses key elements of the king's character and behaviour into this one short passage. Xerxes' motivation for the expedition of 480 BC is couched here as a set of emotionally driven responses to the failure of the earlier campaign, and is said to have been a combination of the king's desire to restore Persian honour and his need to vent his anger against the authors of the Greek victory. It is not made explicit anywhere in the text that it was in fact Xerxes' father who mounted the first invasion; in asserting that Xerxes himself was 'dishonoured' (ἀτιμαζόμενος) by the earlier defeat, as well as by omitting Darius' name in his reference to the campaign of 490 BC, Lysias blurs the distinction between the actions of the two kings and frames Xerxes' invasion as being, at least in part, a quest for personal revenge. There is no place in this version of events for the kind of detailed scrutiny of the reasons for Xerxes' expedition to Greece which is presented in the account of Herodotus, a key part of which is the notion of continuity of policy from the reign of the father to that of his son (see above, pp. 58–63). Xerxes is, however, credited with the angry response (ὀργιζόμενος) which does characterize several of his actions in Herodotus' account (see above, pp. 48–9); this irascibility becomes for Lysias a factor which apparently influenced the king's decision to prepare for a new expedition. At the same time the suggestion that Xerxes had no experience of honourable men (ἄπειρος ἀνδρῶν ἀγαθῶν, 2.27) draws an implicit distinction between the *andres agathoi*, who fought on Athens' behalf, and their contemptible Persian opponents.[11]

The description of the expedition led by Xerxes which follows focuses primarily – in line with earlier versions of the tradition – upon the size of the king's army;[12] Lysias' hyperbolic assertion that even listing the nations who accompanied him would be an arduous undertaking calls to mind the catalogue by means of which Herodotus performed precisely that task (Hdt. 7.59–99) while at the same time self-consciously drawing attention to the constraints imposed on the speaker by the genre within which he was working. In a context which is designed to highlight the courage and commitment of the Athenians' ancestors it is no surprise that the emphasis on the overwhelming size of the Persian force is so strong; this is clearly intended to reflect upon the scale of the achievement of those who defeated it. Coupled with the reference to Xerxes' vast army and navy is Lysias' description of the Hellespont crossing and the carving of the Athos canal. Here the two engineering feats by which Xerxes facilitated his army's journey to Greece are presented as being necessitated in part by the sheer size of Xerxes' force; Lysias' assertion that both projects were designed to save time is another indicator of the scale of the Persian army and navy, and foreshadows later oratorical treatments in which the crossing acted as shorthand for the king's arrogance. Once again the Hellespont bridge is conceived of as a 'yoking' (ζεύξας, 2.29)[13] which features as the key example of the king's contempt for nature and the ways of the gods, and hints too at Xerxes' intended enslavement of the Greeks.[14] The fact that Xerxes had spare transport ships yet still initiated this elaborate plan is taken here to be an indicator of his arrogance; the story of the crossings offers Lysias the opportunity here to condemn the king for his haughty (ὑπεριδών, 2.29) attitude to nature, the divine and mortals alike.

In providing this summary of Xerxes' role in the invasion of Greece Lysias' oration offers us an insight into the way in which the traditions relating to the king himself could, by the fourth century, be condensed into a concise and

---

[11] On the use of the term *andres agathoi* in praise of those who died in battle see Loraux (1986), pp. 98–101.

[12] Emphasis on the numbers of Xerxes' force in Aeschylus' *Persians*: see above, pp. 21–2; Herodotus: pp. 52–4.

[13] On the use of 'yoking' metaphors to refer to the bridge in earlier texts see pp. 15–16 (on Aeschylus) and p. 57 (on Herodotus).

[14] Lysias elaborates further on the fact that the Persians intended to enslave the Greeks at 2.33, where he also asserts that the Athenians chose freedom (ἐλευθερία) over servitude; references to the Greeks' ἐλευθερία occur frequently throughout the section of the speech relating to the Persian Wars (2.26, 34, 41, 42, 46, 47).

easily recognizable portrait which drew on familiar elements of the Persian campaign (the number of troops and the Hellespont/Athos crossings); when accompanied by an abridged assessment of Xerxes' character which suited the patriotic rhetoric of the funeral speech, this allowed the orator to create an image of the Persian king which was both striking and memorable. Here Xerxes is cast in the role of the arch-enemy of the Athenians who took a stand against him for the sake of their own freedom, and indeed that of the whole of Greece. It is this version of Xerxes – and the themes contained within it – which dominates many of the later accounts discussed in the present volume; the fourth-century sources might thus be seen to act as a bridge between the earlier and more detailed fifth-century depictions of Xerxes, which were formulated at a time when the Persian Wars were still within living memory, and his later literary incarnations. While it is not necessarily possible to pinpoint precisely the sources used by Lysias and later orators, we can nonetheless detect in their work a repertoire of recurring motifs which form key parts of the story as it had first been transmitted by the generation who themselves lived through the conflict with Xerxes.

For Lysias, the Athenians' role in the Persian Wars – and at Salamis in particular, where they are said to have been the chief contributors to the cause of Greek freedom (2.42; cf. 2.55)[15] – is also used as a justification for Athens' imperialist policy later in the fifth century.[16] As a result of their efforts, he tells his audience, the Athenians who confronted the Persians strengthened their allies as well as their own power; in doing so they 'displayed their own power in such a way that the Great King no longer desired what belonged to others, but surrendered some of his own possessions and feared for what remained; in that time no triremes sailed from Asia, nor did a tyrant rule over the Greeks, and no Greek city was enslaved by the barbarians' (2.56–7). It is for this reason, Lysias asserts, that the Athenians should now lead the Greek cities once more. This use of Athens' role in the Persian Wars as justification for a claim to the right to leadership of the Hellenes in a period when the Greek states were once again in conflict with one another is one which is often repeated by later orators. Here Xerxes is implicitly conflated with his fifth-century successors; Lysias' reference to a generic 'Great King' encompasses all kings who ruled Persia during the period when Athens' naval power was in the ascendancy. Meanwhile the present Persian king (Artaxerxes II – who ruled from 405/4 until his death in 359/8 BC

---

[15] On fourth-century claims by individual states to have fought in the Persian Wars for the good of Hellas as a whole see Marincola (2007), p. 115 with a list of textual references at n. 44.
[16] Cf. Thucydides 1.73.2–75.1: the Athenians' speech of 432 BC uses this same justification.

– although he is not named here by Lysias) has cause to be glad that Athens is no longer the leader of the Greeks; the misfortune of Greece in no longer having men such as those who fought in the Persian Wars is the good fortune of the king of Asia, and the Greeks are now enslaved (implicitly to the Spartans) while the Persian king emulates his ancestors' intentions (2.60: the implied suggestion here is that the king once again wishes to make the mainland Greeks subject to him). This emotionally charged reference to the recent actions of Sparta, and Artaxerxes II's negotiations with the Greek states (outlined in Lysias' synopsis of Greek history since the end of the Peloponnesian War at 2.58–9), reminds the audience once more of the contrast between the situation in which their noble ancestors defeated the external enemy and the current state of affairs in a Greece now beset by inter-state feuding. Such an assessment of the last century overlooks the unpopularity of Athens' imperial policy among some states in order to draw the contrast between what Lysias presents as Sparta's despicable behaviour in recent years and the purportedly noble intentions of the Athenians in maintaining their fifth-century empire.

Despite the fact that the chronological scope of Lysias' account of Athenian history encompasses the actions of several Persian kings, it is striking that Xerxes is the only king whose name is given and whose actions and character are drawn in any detail. In Lysias' version Salamis is afforded more attention than in other treatments of the Persian Wars in fourth-century oratory;[17] this, coupled with the emphasis on Athens' naval power, which is an essential component of the rhetorician's call for Athens to lead the Greeks once more, might go some way towards explaining the prominence of Xerxes in this section of the speech. No doubt, too, the fact that Xerxes was the one Persian king who had set foot on Athenian soil in the course of his invasion – a point which would later be explicitly acknowledged by Isocrates (see p. 108) – captured the imagination of the generations of Athenians for whom the Persian Wars had become assimilated into the encomiastic catalogue of Athens' fabled past exploits. The apparent appropriation of this king as the symbolic representative of all Persian kings – those both before and since his rule – also foreshadows the way in which Xerxes came to serve as shorthand for the Persian invasion in later literary

---

[17] Loraux (1986), p. 163, suggests that Lysias' political leanings as a 'fervent democrat' led him to give equal importance to Salamis, a naval victory fought by the masses, as to Marathon, the hoplite battle which was traditionally perceived as a more aristocratic undertaking. On the prominence of Marathon – which could be lauded as a purely Athenian victory – in the Persian Wars tradition as featured in other *epitaphioi* see also Loraux, pp. 155–71 and Thomas (1989), p. 226.

treatments of the theme, in which the mere mention of his name could call to mind an image of the archetypal barbarian oppressor.

Isocrates' rallying-cry: Xerxes as focus for panhellenic sentiment

The theme of Athens' resistance to Persia also looms large in later oratorical treatises, not least in fourth-century contexts where the idea of a new expedition against the Persians is advocated as a means of uniting disparate and warring Greek states in a collective mission against a common external enemy.[18] Nowhere is this appeal to the panhellenic ideal more apparent than in the writings of Isocrates. Born into a wealthy Athenian family, Isocrates (436–338 BC) began his career by producing law court speeches, yet later turned to writing political essays which were cast in the form of speeches; it is into this latter category that his works featuring Xerxes fall.[19] His *Panegyricus*, published in around 380 BC, differs from Lysias' funeral oration in both genre and intention yet in it his presentation of the Persian Wars theme, and of the figure of Xerxes, bears strong similarities to that of Lysias.[20] A piece of display oratory, probably intended by its author to be read by its audience rather than for actual delivery as a speech on a specific occasion, this 'festival oration' is a plea for the union of the Greek states, and for the launching of a panhellenic expedition against Persia under the joint hegemony of Athens and Sparta. By 380 BC Sparta, having exploited the terms of the King's Peace, was once again dominant in Greece; Isocrates' treatise appeals for an end to the ongoing conflict between Greek states. This lasting peace, he suggests, could be achieved if warring states were to desist from fighting one another and instead channel their energies into waging war on a common Persian enemy (4.173) in what is styled here as a war of vengeance for the earlier Persian Wars (4.185).[21] The presentation of Athens as the ideal leader for such an enterprise (4.20) means that, like Lysias' funeral oration, much of

---

[18] For a discussion of the origins of, and literary evidence for, panhellenism see M. A. Flower (2000b), who defines this as 'the idea that the various Greek city-states could solve their disputes and simultaneously enrich themselves by uniting in common cause and conquering all or part of the Persian empire' (pp. 65-6). On Isocrates' panhellenic agenda see also Perlman (1976), pp. 25–9.

[19] For an overview of the life and works of Isocrates see Papillon (2009).

[20] Loraux (1986), p. 91 goes so far as to describe Isocrates' use of Lysias' funeral oration as 'obvious plagiarism'.

[21] On the notion of 'war against the barbarian' as a panhellenic theme in Greek literature see Mitchell (2007), pp. 10–19.

Isocrates' speech – which incorporates elements of the *epitaphios* – is devoted to the justification of this claim to hegemony.

The *Panegyricus* is striking for its detailed portrayal of Artaxerxes II's alleged military ineffectiveness (4.140–9) and the way in which it articulates a stereotyped view of Persia by explicating the supposedly inferior nature and character of the Persians; here Isocrates attaches to them every conceivable negative characteristic – ill-discipline, servility, degenerate living, arrogance, treachery, impiety and effeminacy (4.150–6) – in a bid to justify his position and persuade his audience of the ease with which a Greek force might triumph over Persia.[22] As in Lysias' account, however, it is in Isocrates' catalogue of the Athenians' past achievements – in relation to Athens' role as champion against the barbarians – where we encounter the Persian kings of old. Once again it is in Isocrates' summary of Darius' invasion that the contrast between the vast number of Persian troops and the tiny Greek force is set up (4.86); in this case Darius' role in the first campaign is explicitly acknowledged, as he is named twice by the orator (4.71, 4.86). It is, however, Xerxes who is given the most detailed treatment in the account of the Persian Wars; Isocrates' stress (4.88) that the second expedition was led *in person* by Xerxes (αὐτὸς Ξέρξης ἤγαγεν), who himself acted as general (στρατηγός) on the campaign, supports the hypothesis suggested above (p. 106) that this may well be one of the reasons why this king in particular continued to attract the attention of Athenian writers. Isocrates' representation of Xerxes echoes elements of Lysias' version and similarly alludes to familiar aspects of the image of the king (4.89):

> Who, however eager to exaggerate in speaking about [Xerxes], has not fallen short of speaking the truth? For he reached such a level of arrogance (ὑπερηφανίας) that, thinking it a small task to subdue Hellas, and wishing to leave behind a memorial of one who was more than mortal, he did not stop until he had devised and carried out something which everyone talks about: so that he could sail his troops through the land and march them across the sea he yoked the Hellespont and dug through Athos (τὸν μὲν Ἑλλήσποντον ζεύξας, τὸν δ᾽ Ἄθω διορύξας).

Isocrates' recognition of the fact that this is a topic which has been dealt with by others before him gives rise to rhetorical reflection upon the difficulty of finding adequate ways of describing the extremes to which Xerxes' behaviour reached. While this summary of Xerxes' role in the second Persian invasion does not

---

[22] Isaac (2004), pp. 285–7 demonstrates that Isocrates' emphasis on Persian inferiority is designed to support the notion that the defeat of Persia would be an easy matter.

dwell on the king's motivation for launching the expedition, it nonetheless alludes both to his arrogance and to the fact that his actions might be deemed to go beyond the limits of ordinary mortal behaviour. Here the Hellespont/ Athos projects are referred to in terms almost identical to the Greek of Lysias' description; this suggests that the pairing of the two engineering feats had by then become firmly established as a formulaic element of the story. Isocrates' interpretation of the bridge and the canal as ostentatious displays designed to leave a lasting monument to Xerxes' achievement also echoes' Herodotus' reflection (Hdt. 7.24.1) that the passage through Athos was conceived of as a testimony of Xerxes' power, and the emphasis on this Persian king as a model of dubious morality foreshadows the later oratorical reuse of the theme in which Xerxes is a supreme example of the way in which decent humans ought not to behave (see in particular pp. 163–70 below on the use of this theme in Roman traditions).

Isocrates' description of Xerxes thus abbreviates the already concise version which featured in Lysias' account yet still retains the impression of excess, overweening pride and despotic power which are key features of the damning image of Xerxes preserved in the Athenian tradition. By sketching this portrait Isocrates is also able to draw a contrast between Xerxes – the haughty (μέγα φρονήσαντα)[23] author of such deeds, despot over so many people (4.90) – and the virtuous Greeks who fought against him to protect their homeland and their freedom. The ensuing narrative (4.90–8) highlights the deeds performed by the Greeks, with attention being drawn to the courageous actions of both Athenians and Spartans in order to promote the idea of panhellenic unity and to suggest that the two states would be ideal partners in any future military enterprise. Isocrates' summary of the king's character before his more detailed description of the events of the Persian Wars thus construes Xerxes as the common enemy against whom the Greeks once united in the past; this is a crucial element of his appeal for a new alliance of Greek states.

The issue of Greek relations with the Persian king, and the contrast between the present state of affairs and that during the Persian Wars, are also of fundamental importance for Isocrates' argument here. It is during his account of the battle of Salamis that the orator first hints of this contrast to his audience,

---

[23] Isocrates' phrasing echoes Herodotus' reference to Xerxes' *megalophrosunē* in relation to the digging of the Athos canal. For a discussion of the possible nuances (not all of which are negative) of Herodotus' use of the term, see above, pp. 56–7; Isocrates' phrasing in this context implies a wholly negative judgment on Xerxes' character. This is also in contrast with, for example, Alexander's use of the word to apply to Xerxes in Plutarch's account (see p. 122).

reminding them that, although the king then offered bribes to tempt the Athenians to ally with him, they remained impervious to such inducements despite the fact that other states had betrayed the Greek cause (4.94).[24] There is an implicit allusion here to the state of affairs in Greece a century later, in which the current Persian king was no longer being met with resistance but was now being actively courted by Greek states. This contrast is later made explicit as Isocrates compares the situation after the expulsion of the Persians, in which the Greeks had the upper hand over the Persian king, with that in his own day, when, he asserts, the king was able to dictate the actions of the Greeks and would have no reservations about destroying them (4.120–1).

When Isocrates' appeal for the joint leadership of Athens and Sparta met with no success he continued to advocate his panhellenic ideal but turned instead to the search for a powerful figurehead to lead a united Greece in an expedition against Persia; this is seen most clearly in his later appeal to Philip of Macedon to assume the mantle of leader of the Greeks. Composed in 346 BC, after the conclusion of the Peace of Philocrates between Athens and Philip following ten years of war, the *Philippus* again features the Persian Wars as part of the backdrop to a plea for a panhellenic expedition.[25] In making a case for the reconciliation of Greek states hostile to one another – an outcome believed by some to be impossible – Isocrates uses, among other examples, that of the Greeks' relationship with Persia as one which in the past changed from enmity to friendship (5.42): 'For what could be more extreme than the hatred of the Greeks for Xerxes? Yet everyone knows that we and the Spartans came to show to him more affection than to those who helped to establish our empires'. Here, by eliding the chronological space between Xerxes and more recent rulers of Persia[26] Isocrates creates one homogeneous Persian king in order to emphasize the contrast between past and present; the reference also conveniently allows him to register his disapproval of the fact that some Greek states (Athens included) would prefer to ally with Persia than with other Greeks. Once again

[24] Here Isocrates presents the Athenians as having stood alone at Salamis; this is in keeping with the tone of much of the *Panegyricus* in which, despite its purportedly panhellenic aims and some attempt to present the Spartans as displaying equal heroism in the past (for example at 4.90–2), he nonetheless stresses the prominence of Athens' role in the Persian Wars.

[25] Isocrates later reiterated this appeal in a letter to Philip (*Letter* 2) after the king received a wound in battle in Thrace. The letter advises Philip, who is again said to be the only man able to lead the Greeks in a united expedition against Persia, on preserving his own safety and supports this with the example of Xerxes who, although defeated by the Greeks, stayed alive in order to retain his empire and pass it on to his children; by contrast the younger Cyrus, after his defeat at Cunaxa, was unable to seize the Persian throne because of his premature death in battle (*Letter* 2.6–8).

[26] It is not clear whether he is referring here to Artaxerxes II or Artaxerxes III, both of whom were involved in negotiations with various Greek states in Isocrates' lifetime.

it is not Darius but Xerxes who serves as the representative of the archetypal hostile barbarian king here;[27] his name could by then be used as shorthand to provide an emotive reminder of the hatred which Greeks once felt for their then common enemy. Later in the speech Isocrates once again alludes to the Persian invasions of the fifth century in order to stir audience response, as he makes the point that, despite the barbarians' reputation among the Greeks for softness, luxurious living and lack of experience in war, there have been men among them who thought themselves fit to rule Greece; by contrast, no Greek has yet attempted to assert himself as master of Asia (5.124).

A similar conflation of Xerxes with his successors also occurs in Isocrates' *Panathenaicus*, an encomiastic piece focusing primarily on the deeds and constitution of Athens which was composed in around 340 BC in Isocrates' extreme old age (he was in his nineties at his death in 338 BC). In the account of the Athenians' role in the Persian Wars here Xerxes is given a brief mention, being characterized once again by the size of his force (12.49, where, by contrast with the *Panegyricus*, Isocrates gives precise numbers: thirteen hundred triremes and five million land-based troops including seven hundred thousand infantry); the effect here is to emphasize the great achievement of the Athenians in resisting Persia. It is later in the speech, however, where the notion of a composite Persian king reappears, as Isocrates once again registers his disapproval of the forging of treaties between Greek states and Persia. He asserts (12.156–7) that both Athens and Sparta did great service to the Greeks, yet, after Xerxes' expedition, they brought about great harm too, for while they displayed great virtue in opposing him they subsequently 'made peace with the man who marched against them and intended to destroy both cities entirely as well as to enslave the other Greeks'. Although it is unclear here to which treaty Isocrates is referring[28] the rhetorical technique of seamlessly identifying later Persian kings with the figure of Xerxes in order to stir up patriotic and anti-Persian feeling in the audience is not unusual.

Isocrates' contemporaries produced similar amalgamations of the Persian kings:[29] Xenophon presents the Spartan king Agesilaus as nurturing a hatred for Persia

---

[27] Cf. *Panathenaicus* 161 and 189 where the Persian Wars are described as 'the war against Xerxes'.

[28] Thompson (1983), pp. 77–9 makes the case that the passage relates to the purported 'Peace of Callias' (dated to around 449 BC) rather than, as some have argued, to the King's Peace of 386 BC.

[29] Llewellyn-Jones (2012), pp. 320–4 compares the notion of the composite Persian king as seen in literature with artistic representations of kings on vase paintings.

because in the old days he [the Persian king] marched out in order to enslave Greece but now allies himself with those who enable him to cause the greatest harm, gives gifts to those who he believes will injure the Greeks the most in return, and makes peace with those who will be most likely to cause war among us. (*Agesilaus* 7.7)[30]

Demosthenes' *On the Symmories* (354 BC) alludes to the Athenian victory at Salamis in suggesting that the present king (Artaxerxes III, although again he is not named)

knows that with two hundred triremes, of which we provided one hundred, our ancestors destroyed a thousand of his ships, and he will hear that we now have three hundred triremes ready – so even if he were completely mad he would not consider it a trivial matter to incur our city's hostility'. (14.29)

Later Aeschines' speech *Against Ctesiphon*, delivered in 330 BC, assimilates the traditions of Xerxes' invasion to the reign of Darius III in alluding to the reversal of fortunes of the Persian monarchy now that the Macedonian invasion of Persia, under the leadership of Alexander, had become a reality:

Is not the king of the Persians, who dug through Athos, who yoked the Hellespont, who demanded earth and water from the Greeks, and who dared to write in his letters that he was master of all men from the rising of the sun until its setting – is he not fighting now not merely for power over others, but for his life?[31] (3.132)

Once again the recognizable elements of Xerxes' invasion are selected as shorthand for the whole of the failed Persian mission, and Xerxes' actions are imagined as carrying ongoing resonance for the Persian kings of their own day.

Alternative models of Persian kingship? Xerxes and two Cyruses

The image of Xerxes which has been preserved in the Athenian rhetorical tradition is thus to a large extent a product of the aims of the orators whose desire either to appeal for Greek unity or to compare a morally inferior present

---

[30] Agesilaus' campaigns around Sardis led to the defeat of Persian forces there and ultimately to the removal from office and execution of the satrap Tissaphernes by the Persian king in 395 BC. On the presentation of Agesilaus' relationship with Persia see Hirsch (1985b), pp. 40–5.

[31] On Alexander's propaganda which presented his own campaign against Persia as one which would avenge the Greeks for the wrongs committed against them by Xerxes see below, pp. 119–25.

with the glorious past led to a focus on elements which allowed for succinct illustration of the wicked designs of a king whose mission was thwarted – against the odds – by the honourable actions of the Athenians' ancestors. Yet this model of Persian kingship – as enslaving, degenerate and malevolent – was by no means the only possible response to Asiatic monarchy which manifested itself in the Athenian literary tradition. By way of contrast, literature from the fourth century also provides us with a striking example of an alternative type of Persian king in the figure of Xerxes' maternal grandfather Cyrus the Great, whose characterization in the Athenian sources – most notably Xenophon's *Cyropaedia* – acts as a useful case-study against which we might compare that of Xerxes.

The changing political landscape at the end of the fifth and beginning of the fourth century seems to have stimulated debate at Athens on the possible alternatives to democratic government, with a series of writers in the fourth century exploring in particular the idea of one-man rule and how an individual's character and education might best prepare him to undertake this form of government. Discourses on kingship took a variety of forms, including literary portraits of monarchs (both Greek and non-Greek) designed to exemplify good practice, treatises exhorting existing monarchs to good behaviour and dialogues analysing what makes the ideal king.[32] This interest in the nature of kingship formed the cultural backdrop for Xenophon's admiring portrait of Cyrus the Great in his *Cyropaedia*,[33] a fictionalized biography probably written in the 360s BC which used the elder Cyrus as the focal point for a study of ideal leadership and as a vehicle for the expression of the author's views on education and military tactics.[34] The image of the king crafted here may well have been modelled on the figure of Cyrus the Younger, with whom the author

---

[32] Examples of such texts include Isocrates' *Evagoras*, in which he presents the virtues of the recently deceased king of Cyprus as a model for Evagoras' son and other statesmen, and his advice *To Nicocles*, which sets out for Evagoras' son the duties of a monarch toward his subjects. Both Plato's *Republic* and *Laws* discuss the phenomenon of monarchy in the context of dialogue on the government of an ideal state. Forsdyke (2009), pp. 241–5 summarizes the range of Athenian literary responses to tyranny in the fourth century.

[33] Xenophon also created a favourable portrait of the Spartan king Agesilaus, in a posthumous encomium in which he presented a direct point-by-point comparison between Agesilaus and the Persian king (*Agesilaus* 9.1–5), contrasting Agesilaus' openness, simple tastes and self-denial with the Persian's inaccessibility, luxury and self-indulgence. His *Agesilaus* seems to have been influenced by Isocrates' *Evagoras*: see Hirsch (1985b), p. 57–60.

[34] The *Cyropaedia* can be described as an early forerunner of what we might now term the 'historical novel': Drews (1973), p. 120. Stadter (1991) examines the way in which Xenophon constructs a fictional narrative in order to fulfil his didactic purpose. For a discussion of the precise nature and genre of the text, and a consideration of the evidence for earlier biographical works see also Gera (1993), pp. 1–13; she sets out the evidence for a date in the 360s at pp. 23–5. On fourth-century biographical writing see also Momigliano (1993), pp. 43–64.

had been personally acquainted, and whose character in his *Anabasis* bears close resemblances to that of his predecessor and namesake in the *Cyropaedia*.[35] Xenophon's eulogistic representation of Cyrus the Great – whose reported actions show him to be a model of military prowess, piety, justice, and moderation[36] – focuses not only upon his early life and education but also upon his kingship, conquests and the foundation and organization of the Achaemenid empire; throughout the work Cyrus is presented as a benevolent king who exercised his rule through the use of persuasion rather than by force.[37] In this respect he is contrasted in the final chapter of the *Cyropaedia* (8.8) with what Xenophon perceives as a decline in moral standards responsible for Persian degeneracy in his own day; this epilogue is a polemical denunciation of all that Xenophon sees as being wrong with the Persians' character and actions since the death of Cyrus.[38]

Xenophon's account is not the earliest literary work which pronounces a positive verdict upon Cyrus the Great; indeed, Herodotus' presentation of him as founder of the Achaemenid empire shows him – by contrast with other rulers – as having brought the Persians freedom from slavery and made them rulers rather than ruled (see, for example, Hdt. 1.210.2, 3.82.5).[39] Cyrus also has the last word in Herodotus' history, where he assumes the role of advisor to the Persians in drawing a correlation between the natural features of a territory and the character of its inhabitants ('soft lands breed soft men') and warning that if they wish to remain as valiant warriors, and as rulers of others rather than subjects, they ought not to undertake a migration elsewhere. [40] The implied contrast between this former hardiness and the allusions to Persian luxury

---

[35]   At *Anabasis* 1.9.1 Xenophon asserts that of all Persians who lived after Cyrus the Great, the younger Cyrus was the most kinglike and worthy to rule. For a comparison of Xenophon's presentation of the two Cyruses see Hirsch (1985b), pp. 72–6 and pp. 85–6.

[36]   See, for example, *Cyropaedia* 8.1.21–33, where Xenophon asserts that Cyrus himself intended to act as a positive example to his subordinates.

[37]   A similarly favourable verdict on Cyrus is pronounced in the Jewish tradition: Kuhrt 1983, p. 83.

[38]   See Tatum (1989), pp. 218–25. Opinions on the authorship of this final chapter vary: Hirsch (1985b), pp. 91–7, summarizes the discussion and argues against the authenticity of the epilogue. Due (1989), pp. 16–22 considers it to be part of the original text on the grounds that the subsequent degeneration of Persia which is outlined serves to highlight Cyrus' exceptional nature; for this view see also Gera (1993), pp. 299–300. Sancisi-Weerdenburg (1987b) demonstrates the ways in which the epilogue acts to create an orientalizing literary construction of Persia as the 'negative mirror-image of Greece' (p. 128).

[39]   On Herodotus' presentation of Cyrus see Avery (1972). Due (1989), pp. 117–35 compares Herodotus' and Xenophon's depictions of Cyrus. One major difference in the two versions is in the authors' accounts of his death: Herodotus places this on the battlefield during Cyrus' attempt to subdue the Massagatae (1.214), while in Xenophon's version Cyrus dies a peaceful death in old age at home (8.7).

[40]   For this interpretation of the close of the *Histories* see Flower and Marincola (2002), *ad* 9.122.

and degeneracy seen in the final book of the *Histories*,[41] although never stated explicitly by Herodotus, may also have planted the seeds of a literary tradition which suggested both the contrast between Cyrus and Xerxes and the idea that Xerxes' rule was the start of a period of decline for the Achaemenid empire.

Elsewhere in Athenian literature of the fourth century the positive exemplar offered by the figure of Cyrus the Great could be used to provide an explicit point of comparison with the negative image of Xerxes as a Persian king. This could be especially useful in the context of philosophical discussions of the nature of kingship and the exercise of rightful rule. In Plato's *Laws*, his last work (written perhaps in the 350s BC; Plato died in 347 BC) the philosopher gives to his Athenian speaker in the dialogue a concise exposition of Persian history which describes and attempts to explain Persia's perceived decadence and degeneracy (694a–696a). Here Cyrus – as in Herodotus' account and that of Xenophon[42] – is presented as having ruled in such a way as to allow his subjects both freedom and the ability to rule over others; his preoccupation with military matters is said, however, to have caused him to neglect the education of his children.[43] Plato's Athenian asserts that the influence on Cyrus' sons of the women and eunuchs of the court produced men who were decadent and lacking in the necessary self-discipline to rule successfully.[44] Cambyses is the first example of such a king; having killed his brother he went mad (this is attributed here to the consumption of alcohol as well as to the lack of an education) and lost his throne at the hands of the Medes. The same pattern is said to have been repeated once again with the father/son pairing of Darius and Xerxes; while Darius, not having been of royal birth, escaped the luxurious upbringing which blighted Cambyses' character, he made the same mistake as Cyrus in allowing Xerxes to be reared in the same manner with the result that Xerxes, 'having been a product of the same upbringing, ended up with almost the same misfortunes as Cambyses' (695e). This condensed version of Persian history, in pairing

---

[41] This is seen in, for example, Pausanias' comparison of a typical Persian banquet with a simple Spartan meal at 9.82, as well as in the final story relating to Xerxes at 9.108–113, discussed above at pp. 70–1.

[42] Hirsch (1985b), pp. 97–100 argues that the picture of Cyrus seen in the *Laws* derives ultimately from the *Cyropaedia*.

[43] Tatum (1989), pp. 215–39 provides an analysis which demonstrates the ways in which Plato's Athenian in the *Laws* engages with and critiques Xenophon's *Cyropaedia* by focusing on Cyrus' neglect of his sons' education.

[44] The emphasis on the influence of women and eunuchs here is reminiscent of Ctesias' portrayal of the Persian court: see below, p. 131, with n. 13. For Xenophon women and eunuchs feature most prominently not in the main narrative of the *Cyropaedia* but in the 'novellas', dramatic tales set in the East, such as that of Panthea and Abradatas (on which see Cartledge (1993), pp. 111–14). On the resemblances between these tales and those told by Ctesias see Gera (2003), pp. 199–201, and Llewellyn-Jones and Robson (2010), pp. 69–72.

Cyrus with Darius as good Persian kings, and Xerxes with Cambyses as their opposites, both draws upon earlier characterizations of Xerxes as the archetypal negative exemplar and explicitly makes the assertion that his rule was the start of a period of decline for Persia: 'Since then there has been scarcely a Persian king who has been truly "great", other than in name' (695e).[45] It is this brand of rhetoric – itself perhaps drawing on the contrast between Darius and Xerxes first seen in Aeschylus' *Persians* – which is at the root of a persistent view of Xerxes' reign as the starting-point for the deterioration of the Achaemenid empire.[46]

The images of both Xerxes as the model of a debased king and Cyrus the Great as his opposite might also be seen to filter indirectly into Xenophon's presentation of recent Persian history, of which he himself was a part, and which he related in his *Anabasis*. The text is an account of the advance and subsequent retreat of the Greek mercenaries in the service of Cyrus the Younger whose attempt to usurp the throne from his brother Artaxerxes II culminated in the battle of Cunaxa and Cyrus' death (401 BC).[47] Here we can detect motifs which seem to bear a relationship to elements of earlier historiographical narratives; the text contains echoes of the archetypal literary images of both good and bad Persian leaders. In this case it is the younger Cyrus who is marked out by Xenophon for special praise; the author's eulogy of Cyrus after his death at Cunaxa (1.9) highlights the positive qualities of this would-be Persian king in terms similar to those used in praise of his ancestor and namesake in the *Cyropaedia*,[48] focusing on his youth and education, his conduct as satrap and his treatment of cities and individuals in order to foster their loyalty. At the beginning of his obituary Xenophon makes the point that this Cyrus was the

[45] Later in the *Laws* (697c–698a) the theme of the broader decline of Persian morality is revisited; the emphasis here is on excessive despotism at the expense of the freedom of the masses. While Xerxes is unnamed here he is clearly identifiable in the ensuing discussion of the Athenian resistance to Persian invasion; in being described as 'young and impetuous' (698e) he is contrasted clearly with his father in a manner which echoes Aeschylus' emphasis on his youthfulness (on which see above, pp. 26–30). References to the Hellespont crossing, the Athos canal and the number of Persian forces (699a) leave us in no doubt as to which Persian king is being referred to here. For a detailed discussion of Plato's engagement with the broader Persian Wars traditions see Rowe (2007).

[46] See, for example, Sancisi-Weerdenburg (1987c), pp. xi–xii and Briant (2002), p. 517; on the broader theme of Persian decadence in the fourth-century sources see also Briant (1989).

[47] Lane Fox (2004), pp. 12–20 provides an overview of the historical background to events described in the *Anabasis*. The date of composition is uncertain: Cawkwell (2004), pp. 47–50 outlines the argument for a date of between 370 and 367 BC.

[48] Braun (2004), pp. 107–30 examines Xenophon's portrayal of Cyrus' character in the *Anabasis* and demonstrates that the account turns a blind eye to Cyrus' misdeeds, not least to the fact that his plan to usurp Artaxerxes II involved attempted fratricide. Note, however, M. A. Flower (2012), pp. 188–94, arguing that the younger Cyrus is not depicted by Xenophon as a perfect leader – the virtue of piety is notably absent from his characterization here – but that instead 'the reader is meant to notice that Cyrus is an imperfect replica of his famous namesake' (p. 189).

'most kingly and worthy to rule of all those Persians born since the elder Cyrus' (*Anabasis* 1.9.1). The statement clearly implies a negative judgement upon all Persian monarchs since the reign of Cyrus the Great down to Xenophon's own day, and while the text makes very little explicit reference to individual Persian kings it is nonetheless telling that Xerxes features – if only briefly – at key points in the narrative.[49]

The first of these references occurs early on in the *Anabasis*, at the beginning of Xenophon's narrative of Cyrus' expedition. When Cyrus holds a review of the Greek troops under his command at Celaenae (1.2.9), Xenophon comments that this is the spot where Xerxes built a palace and an acropolis on his retreat from Greece. In the light of the nature of the Greeks' expedition alongside Cyrus with the aim of toppling a Persian monarch from his throne it is possible that the reference at this point in the narrative is intended to draw attention to the contrast between past and present events. Neither the comparison nor the Greek/Persian dichotomy here is, however, straightforward: these Greek soldiers are led by a Persian (who in fact initially misleads them as to the true purpose of his expedition), and there is no way in which their mission – as mercenary soldiers serving the self-interested political motives of their leader – could be framed as comparable to their ancestors' fight for their own freedom. Yet at the same time there are references throughout the narrative of their march from Sardis to Cunaxa which echo motifs seen in the Herodotean narrative of Xerxes' invasion of Greece. Cyrus crosses the Maeander which is 'yoked' (ἐζευγμένη) by means of a bridge of boats (1.2.5),[50] and at Celaenae (shortly after Xenophon has referred to the palace built by Xerxes there) he holds a review of the number of Greeks with him (Xenophon gives the numbers as 11,000 hoplites and 2,000 peltasts: 1.2.9). This review, and that which is later carried out by Cyrus for the benefit of the Cilician queen (1.2.14–16), is reminiscent of the attention which is given by Xerxes to enumerating his troops in Herodotus' narrative (7.44, 7.59,

---

[49] While we do not encounter Artaxerxes face-to-face in Xenophon's narrative, it is his representative, the unscrupulous satrap Tissaphernes, who exhibits many of the negative characteristics associated with Persians in the Greek literary tradition. This is seen most clearly in his treatment of the Greek generals after Cunaxa when, having promised them safe conduct back to Greece (2.3) he tricks Clearchus into bringing the generals to him and has them killed and beheaded (2.5–6). On Xenophon's presentation of Tissaphernes' character see Danzig (2007); note too Hirsch (1985b), p. 22, pointing out that, although it may have contributed to a stereotypical Greek view of Persians as cunning and treacherous, the negative image does not for Xenophon apply to all Persian rulers, as the satrap Pharnabazus is, by contrast, presented as both courageous and trustworthy.

[50] See also 2.4.13 and 2.4.24 for references to the boat bridges across the Tigris used by the Greeks on the homeward march. Tuplin (2004b), p. 173–4 refers to such descriptions as 'direct attestation of an everyday version of the famous bridges which Darius and Xerxes built over the Bosporus and the Hellespont'.

7.100: see also p. 53 above). On the second occasion Cyrus conducts his review from his chariot (παρελαύνων ἐφ᾽ ἅρματος, 1.2.16) just as Xerxes is said by Herodotus to have done at Doriscus (διεξελαύνων ἐπὶ ἅρματος, 7.100.1). The beheading of Cyrus' corpse after his death at Cunaxa (1.10.1) might also call to mind the posthumous treatment which was inflicted on Xerxes' orders upon Leonidas at Thermopylae (Hdt. 7.238.1). Although it is not possible to state with complete certainty that such echoes reflect a conscious intention on Xenophon's part to allude to the work of his best-known literary predecessor, we might suggest that the use of such familiar motifs at least hints at the kind of influence which the account of Xerxes' invasion might have exercised upon subsequent historical narratives.

The second of Xenophon's two explicit references to Xerxes in the *Anabasis* draws upon the brand of rhetoric used by the Athenian orators. Having assumed the role of leader of the stranded Greek force after the death of Cyrus, Xenophon gives a speech which is designed to inspire in the Greeks confidence that they will survive the journey home. In outlining the reasons for optimism he refers to the role of their ancestors in the Persian Wars (3.2.11–14).[51] His summary of the wars touches briefly upon the courage of the Athenians in standing alone against the Persians at Marathon, and their subsequent annual sacrifice to Artemis. Xerxes is then described as having gathered 'an army which could not be counted' for his attack on Greece; the prize for the Greeks' victory over the Persians on that occasion was the freedom which they still enjoy. Here Xenophon's reference to the glorious deeds of the past is firmly situated within the oratorical tradition which draws on the Persian Wars as a way of inspiring listeners to strive to emulate the actions and character of their ancestors; it also serves to make the point that even a seemingly impossible task can become possible.[52]

---

[51] Rood (2004), pp. 313–19 looks at the use of motifs from the Persian Wars elsewhere in the *Anabasis*, and examines the relationship between these allusions and the situation among Xenophon's Greek troops. He suggests (p. 319) that 'Xenophon's Greek mercenaries move from relative unity in the face of common danger to disunity and squabbling, and allusions to the Persian Wars are replaced by references to the Peloponnesian War. The journey of the Ten Thousand begins to seem like a mirror of the experience of the Greeks at large over the previous few generations.'

[52] Some have also read into Xenophon's account an endorsement of panhellenist ideology and seen it as a demonstration that a Greek expedition to Persia was in fact possible: see Cawkwell (2004), pp. 63–7 and M. A. Flower (2012), pp. 170–88.

Alexander and Xerxes: Panhellenist rhetoric revisited

It was not only the Athenian descendants of those who had fought against Xerxes who recognized that the rhetorical alignment of a new military mission with the successes of the past could be a powerful persuasive tool. Isocrates' vision that Philip of Macedon might lead a new alliance of Greeks to Asia (see above, pp. 110–11) was realized when, at the head of a confederation of Greek states known as the League of Corinth, Philip sent an advance force to Persia in 336 BC; he seems to have exploited panhellenist sentiment in order to gain support (Polybius 3.6.12–13; Diodorus 16.89.2, cf. 17.4.9).[53] The notion of a new campaign against Persia as a quest for vengeance for the Persians' fifth-century onslaught upon Greek territory would, after Philip's death, gain increasing momentum under the leadership of his son Alexander. As leader of Macedon Alexander, a masterful manipulator of his own image, presented his own expansionist expedition to Persia as a means of seeking retribution for the Persian invasion of Greece 150 years before (Diodorus 17.4.9; Arrian 2.14.4). By advertising his own military action in this way Alexander could rebrand Macedon (which had in fact been subject to Persia in 480–479 BC) as being on the same side as the Greeks and thereby secure support both for the campaign, and for himself as leader of a Hellenic alliance, from hitherto reluctant Greek states.[54] Despite his insistence on having records made of his Persian campaign as it was taking place, no contemporary account survives, yet later texts bear the traces of the propaganda which packaged the expedition as a means of punishing the Persians for the sins of their ancestors.

For Alexander the memory of Xerxes' invasion became a central element of his own propaganda campaign. The launch of his invasion of Asia in 334 BC with the crossing the Hellespont was accompanied by the performance of rituals – including a sacrifice at the tomb of the hero Protesilaus, the first of the Greeks to be killed at Troy (Arrian, *Anabasis* 1.10.5) – which may have been intended both to align his own mission with the Trojan War and to portray his actions as revenge for Xerxes' invasion of Greece.[55] There is evidence which suggests too

---

[53] M. A. Flower (2000a), pp. 98–9. Faraguna (2003), pp. 99–102 summarizes Philip's relations with Greek states and the formation of the League of Corinth prior to the declaration of war on Persia. See also Worthington (2003).

[54] On Alexander's use of propaganda, particularly in relation to his Persian campaign, see Spencer (2002), pp. 5–9. M. A. Flower (2000a) explores Alexander's manipulation of panhellenist discourse; see also Faraguna (2003), pp. 107–15.

[55] Georges (1994), p. 64, and Faraguna (2003), p. 108; see Zahrnt (1996) for detailed discussion of the sources relating to Alexander's actions at the Hellespont. Note, however, Lane Fox (1973), pp.

that Alexander carried out other actions which were contrived in order to style himself as seeking recompense for the wrongs committed by Xerxes. Arrian's *Anabasis* – written in the second century AD but derived from sources written by Alexander's officers which were favourable to their leader[56] – relates, for example (3.16.4; cf. 7.17.2–3), that in Babylon he declared that the sanctuaries which Xerxes had destroyed should be rebuilt; these are said to have included the shrine of Bel, the god most sacred to the Babylonians.[57] Similarly, after the capture of Susa in 331 BC Alexander is said to have undertaken to send back to Athens the bronze statues of Harmodius and Aristogeiton which Xerxes had removed (*Anabasis* 3.16.7; cf. 7.19.2); such anecdotes may well account for the characterization of Xerxes as wilful hooligan and destroyer of sanctuaries in later sources. Alexander's policy of reprisal might extend also to the punishment of those associated with Xerxes: later in his Persian campaign Alexander is said to have come across a town inhabited by the Branchidae, whose ancestors betrayed the temple of Apollo at Didyma to Xerxes. Alexander took revenge for the ancestral crime by destroying the town and massacring its inhabitants (Quintus Curtius 7.5.28–35; Strabo 11.11.4).

Nowhere in the sources is the recollection of Xerxes' actions against the Greeks more prominent, however, than in the accounts of Alexander's burning of Persepolis.[58] While the ancient authors disagree as to whether the act was premeditated, all surviving versions of the story carry some suggestion that the conflagration could be perceived as an act of vengeance for the damage which Xerxes inflicted upon the Greeks. Arrian (*Anabasis* 3.18.11–12) says little about the burning of Persepolis other than to relate that, despite being urged by his general Parmenio to spare Persepolis for political reasons, Alexander vowed to destroy it as punishment for the Persians' destruction of Athens, their burning

---

109–15, describing the rituals performed by Alexander but suggesting that he was motivated more by a desire to align himself with Achilles than to call to mind Xerxes' precedent.

[56] Arrian states in the preface to his *Anabasis* that his sources are the writings of Ptolemy and Aristobulus (both of whom accompanied Alexander on his Persian campaign). On Arrian's use of sources see Bosworth (1988), pp. 38–60.

[57] On the erroneous allegation that Xerxes destroyed the temple of Bel see Kuhrt and Sherwin-White (1987), p. 77: 'One should not … take the evidence of Arrian that the temples in Babylon to be rebuilt were those destroyed by Xerxes as hard and fast evidence for any real destruction by him but regard it as reflecting a specific Greek version of Persian behaviour, of which Xerxes was the prime example.' See also Briant (2002), p. 545, suggesting that the emphasis placed by Hellenistic authors on Xerxes' sacrileges derives ultimately from Alexander's propaganda.

[58] Balcer (1978) summarizes the sources for the burning of Persepolis. See also Sancisi-Weerdenburg (1993a), summarizing the archaeological evidence for the destruction of the city (as detailed in Schmidt's 1953 excavation reports); she suggests that, aside from the symbolic interpretation of his actions, one of Alexander's reasons for burning Persepolis may have been that 'he did not want to leave behind a supply of items that could be used to propagate various forms of political power, at various echelons' (p. 185).

of sanctuaries 'and all the other wrongs which they had done to the Greeks' (cf. Strabo 15.3.6). A dedication by the Thespians recorded in the *Palatine Anthology* (6.344) suggests too that this propaganda was successful; the text reports that the citizens of Thespiae dedicated an altar to Zeus in thanks for their success in sacking of Persian cities with Alexander 'to avenge the ancestors' who had fought and fallen alongside Leonidas and the Spartans at Thermopylae. For the Alexander of both Diodorus (writing in Greek in the first century BC) and Quintus Curtius (whose Latin account was compiled in the first century AD) Persepolis is a seat of Persian menace: Diodorus' Alexander describes it as 'most hateful of the cities in Asia' (17.70.1), and Curtius' account has the Macedonian recall that it was from there that, with their vast armies, both Darius and Xerxes 'waged impious war on Europe' (5.6.1). Yet their accounts – which originate in traditions less favourable to Alexander and may derive from the late fourth-century BC version of Cleitarchus[59] – give far more detail than that of Arrian, and elaborate upon the story with the additional sensational detail that amid a drunken revel Alexander was incited by an Athenian courtesan named Thaïs to torch the palace at Persepolis (Curtius 5.7.3–7; Diodorus 17.72). Diodorus' version of the story concludes with a summary in which the action is portrayed as the final humiliation of Xerxes, bringing closure for the Greeks who still remembered his offences against their ancestors: 'It was most incredible that the impiety of Xerxes, king of the Persians, against the acropolis of Athens, should, many years later, be repaid in the same way by one woman, a citizen of the wronged city, as entertainment' (17.72.6).

It is in Plutarch's second-century AD retelling of the burning of Persepolis, however, where we see the clearest intersection between the story of Alexander and that of Xerxes.[60] His *Life* of Alexander, compiled from a range of sources,[61] was composed with a moral function in mind; like the other biographies in his series of parallel lives it explored of the virtues and vices of his subject (*Alexander* 1.2). Plutarch's account of Alexander's sojourn at Persepolis (*Alexander* 37–8) provides details not recorded in other extant sources. He begins by referring to the slaughter of prisoners and the vast amount of wealth found by Alexander at Persepolis, then goes on to record a story in which Alexander comes face-to-face with a likeness of Xerxes (37.3):

---

[59] Bosworth (1988), pp. 1–15 and Baynham (2003) provide overviews of the sources for Alexander. On Diodorus' use of sources see Drews (1962).The fullest exploration of Curtius' account is that of Baynham (1998).

[60] For a discussion of the way in which the Xerxes-tradition manifests itself elsewhere in Plutarch's work see pp. 182–7.

[61] Hammond (1993), pp. 149–51 compiles a list of sources for the *Life*.

On seeing a great statue of Xerxes which had been carelessly overturned by a mob that had forced its way into the palace, Alexander stopped before it and, addressing it as though it were alive, said, 'Should I pass by and leave you lying there because of your expedition against the Greeks or, because of your magnanimity and virtue in other ways (διὰ τὴν ἄλλην μεγαλοφροσύνην καὶ ἀρετὴν), should I raise you up again?' But finally, after communing with himself a long time in silence, he moved on.

Alexander's ambivalence to the figure of Xerxes here is apparently at odds with his avowed intention of seeking vengeance for the Greeks for the Persian king's past offences; his statement that Xerxes, despite his wrongs against Greece, had positive qualities, is similarly enigmatic as Plutarch does not specify what the 'other ways' in which these manifested themselves might be. The use of the potentially ambiguous word μεγαλοφροσύνη to describe Xerxes' actions echoes the use of the term in Herodotus' account of Xerxes (see above, pp. 56–7), in which it can connote 'arrogance' as well as the more positive 'magnanimity' which, when paired with ἀρετή ('virtue') seems to be the sense in which Plutarch's Alexander uses it here.[62]

It is in what comes next, however, that the incident takes on particular significance within the context of Alexander's life. Immediately after relating the story of Alexander and Xerxes' statue Plutarch goes on to relate that it was here that the Macedonian sat for the first time upon the royal throne beneath a golden canopy. The vivid visual image is reminiscent of Herodotus' descriptions of Xerxes as seated upon a throne or beneath a gold canopy; this connection is not made explicit by Plutarch yet the idea of Alexander seated on the Persian throne immediately after the mention of the most notorious occupant of that throne might well raise questions about Alexander's own character and motives. Demaratus the Corinthian is then reported as commenting that Greeks who died before seeing Alexander seated upon the throne of Darius (that is, Darius III, who had fled Persepolis) had been deprived of great pleasure. The flattery of Alexander here and Demaratus' praise of his success in defeating the Persian king do not disguise the fact that the sight of a leader who had aligned himself with the Greeks and was now emulating the ruler of Persia also had the potential to be perceived by a Greek audience – even centuries after the event – as deeply troubling. Alexander's adoption of a version of Persian dress and customs is well-documented in the surviving sources, and while his assumption of the

---

[62] Mossman (1988), pp. 92–3 suggests that the episode with Xerxes' statue is one of several deliberately Herodotean elements in this *Life*.

trappings of Achaemenid kingship might project a favourable image to his new Persian subjects,[63] the reminders here of the Greeks' ancient enemy might suggest not merely that Alexander was the embodiment of Xerxes' nemesis but that in fact he too was behaving in ways which could be perceived as uncomfortably akin to those of the most notorious of Persian despots.

There follows Plutarch's own account of the burning of Persepolis (38); although he judiciously reports that some say the deed was premeditated (38.4), in the version upon which he elaborates it is an impulsive action set, like those of Diodorus and Quintus Curtius, amid a scene of drunken debauchery. Again the idea is attributed to the Athenian Thaïs, courtesan of Alexander's general (and later his successor) Ptolemy (38.2):

> For she said that, as she luxuriated in the magnificent palace of the Persians, she was on that day being rewarded for the hardship she had endured by wandering through Asia; but that it would be a still greater pleasure to set fire in revelry to the house of the Xerxes who burned Athens to the ground, she herself starting the fire as the king watched. For thus there would arise a story among men that the women accompanying Alexander inflicted upon the Persians on behalf of Greece a greater punishment than that meted out by Greece's generals and naval commanders.

The emphasis placed in Plutarch's account upon the role of a woman in carrying out the final revenge upon Xerxes echoes that of Diodorus; here, in the context of an elucidation of Alexander's character, however, the story also performs another function. The juxtaposition of the burning of Persepolis with the story of Alexander's response to Xerxes' statue and the image of him sitting upon the Persian king's throne begins to raise questions in the reader's mind as to the character and motivation of this conqueror of Persia. Despite the allusions to these events as representing the eventual settling of an old score against Xerxes there are nonetheless indications here that Alexander's actions bore more than a passing resemblance to those of the Greeks' arch-enemy. Ultimately, in torching Persepolis, Plutarch's Alexander begins to resemble the hooligan Xerxes against whom he was allegedly seeking revenge. Plutarch goes on to say that Alexander's Macedonian troops participated with enthusiasm as they thought it indicated that Alexander now intended to return home rather than to live among the

---

[63] Plutarch observes this at *Alexander* 45.1–3, but suggests too that Alexander's assumption of Persian dress may have been part of a gradual attempt to induce his Macedonian followers to perform *proskynēsis* before him. On the issue of Alexander's alignment of himself with the Achaemenid kings see Fredricksmeyer (2000) and Lane Fox (2007). Brosius (2003), pp. 173–9 explores the ambiguity of Alexander's attitude towards the Persians.

'barbarians' (38.4). The unspoken irony here is that these events did not mark the end of Alexander's foray into Persia; and in Plutarch's account it is from this point that the reader begins to see gradual changes in Alexander's personality which align him more closely with the contemptuous behaviour traditionally associated with Persian kings. This is perhaps seen most clearly in his shameful attempt to introduce the practice of *proskynēsis* – a gesture which, for the Greeks, was suggestive of divine worship[64] – among his companions (54); other indications include his developing tendency towards cruelty and relentlessness when dealing with those who criticized him (42.2) and the fear which he came to inspire among his troops (57.2). Plutarch's Macedonian avenger thus gradually begins to seem more like the barbarian king whom the Greeks despised.[65]

The engagement of Alexander and his later chroniclers with the Xerxes-tradition demonstrates, then, that to draw attention to a comparison between Xerxes and another ruler could work in two very different ways. For Alexander the memory of Xerxes – or, more specifically, of his destructive tendencies – could be the focal point for a propaganda campaign in which he positioned himself as the righteous champion of a moral crusade to seek vengeance for past wrongs done by the Persians to the Greeks. In this respect he seems to have appropriated for himself the brand of rhetoric which we saw being used by Isocrates, in which a campaign against Persia could be a means of uniting Greek states in a common cause; Xerxes' descendants were thus the inheritors of the crimes of their ancestor. Yet, as Plutarch's *Life* shows, to draw such a comparison could also be potentially subversive; in the final reckoning there may be as many parallels as differences between Xerxes and any other supremely powerful ruler or military commander.[66] This realization was one which would inform many of the literary treatments of Xerxes created, like Plutarch's texts, during the period when Roman domination of the Mediterranean had furnished commentators with a plentiful supply of new examples whose actions might be compared with those of the Persian

---

[64] See above, p. 25, with n. 42.

[65] For Mossman (1991), pp. 117–18 Alexander's encounter with the statue of Xerxes comes at a point when the Macedonian conqueror is becoming more autocratic. She considers the reference in relation to an episode related by Plutarch in his *On the Fortune or Virtue of Alexander the Great* (335c–e) in which Alexander refuses to have his own statue carved into Mount Athos, asserting that it is enough that the mountain should remain as a memorial to the arrogance of one king (that is, Xerxes). By contrast in the *Life of Alexander* (72.4) Plutarch once again relates Alexander's rejection of this proposal but reports that subsequently he engaged in far more elaborate artistic projects. There is perhaps here another implied suggestion that Alexander was becoming even more overweening than Xerxes.

[66] Alexander himself later became a point of comparison for Roman writers in evaluations (whether favourable or unfavourable) of their own rulers: Spencer (2002), p. 3.

aggressor; these reworkings of the Xerxes-tradition will be discussed in Chapter 6. First, however, we turn to an alternative theme which developed concurrently with the motifs which were highlighted by the rhetoricians and statesmen: that of the king's court.

6. *Esther at the court of Xerxes*. Based on an illustration from Harold Copping's *Women of the Bible* (1937)

5

The King at Court: Alternative (Hi)Stories of Xerxes

To step inside the court of the Persian king was, for the Greek writers who evoked the scene in their work, to enter an exotic and decadent realm, richly decorated and populated by influential courtiers, eunuchs and powerful women; this world, to which only a few outsiders could gain access, was imagined as a place where domestic scandal and political treachery could flourish. The biblical Esther's vantage point in the accompanying image (Plate 6) is that of the voyeur; her view of the interior of Xerxes' palace affords her the opportunity to observe the king's court, with all its richness and luxury, at close quarters. This is the view which a series of ancient authors – over a wide chronological span, and from a range of different historical and cultural vantage points – sought to reconstruct for their readers. The closing chapters of Herodotus' narrative, in which the historian looked beyond Xerxes' invasion of Greece in order to conjure a vision of the king's court as a setting for intrigue (see above, pp. 70–1), were the forerunner to a series of literary accounts whose focus was the life of the king's court. These diverse texts, many of which sit at the intersection between historiography and romantic fiction, are united by the insight which they offer into the continuing fascination exercised by the image of the king's household; they offer us, as readers, the opportunity to become voyeurs of this world behind closed doors.[1]

Our starting-point for this chapter is the fourth-century BC work of Ctesias, whose position as a Greek doctor at the court of Artaxerxes II afforded him the rare opportunity for access to the king's palace. The theme of court life is one which also arises in a series of fourth-century visual depictions of Persians by

---

[1] The pseudo-Aristotelian text *On the Cosmos* (398a10–398a19) highlights the Persian king's 'invisibility' and inaccessibility to outsiders, imagining him as ensconced within the magnificent palace which sets him apart from other people. See Allen (2005), pp. 39–40.

Greeks – although none of these explicitly focuses on Xerxes, there is a sense in which these images are the product of curiosity sparked by the Persian invasions of Greece. There is also one particular story – that of the exiled Themistocles' adventures in Persia – which allowed authors, including Diodorus (in the first century BC) – to use the king's palace as a backdrop for their writing. Yet it was not only Greeks whose interest was piqued by this setting; the biblical book of Esther, written from a Jewish perspective, shares a similar preoccupation with the goings-on inside the palace of Xerxes (named Ahasuerus in the biblical version), which proves to be a colourful venue for domestic affairs as well as political plotting. These varied texts share narrative strands which continued to fascinate authors for centuries, and which also inspired new kinds of imagined narratives long after the archetypal accounts were set down: the chapter will close with a consideration of the ways in which two types of later literature – Greek novels of the first and second century AD, and the *ekphrasis*-writing of Philostratus in the third century AD – bear traces of the motifs first found in depictions of the court of Xerxes.

Behind closed doors: Ctesias' view of Xerxes' court

Originally from Cnidus on the coast of Asia Minor, Ctesias was court physician to Artaxerxes II at the beginning of the fourth century; Diodorus Siculus (2.32.4) suggests that he arrived in Persia as a prisoner of war and spent 17 years there, although the details of his biography are the subject of some speculation.[2] His *Persica* in twenty-three books dealt with Near Eastern history from the reign of Ninus to that of Artaxerxes II[3] and seems to have been based on a combination of personal observation and information obtained from oral traditions which he heard at the Persian court, although Diodorus' testimony also suggests that Ctesias claimed to have had access to Persian royal records. One major problem for our interpretation of his work is that we must always deal with it at one

---

[2] Stevenson (1997), pp. 3–9 summarizes the details and outlines the main points of contention; see also Llewellyn-Jones and Robson (2010), pp. 11–18. For the testimonia relating to Ctesias' life see Jacoby (1958) *FGrHist* 688 T 1–19, translated by Llewellyn-Jones and Robson (2010), pp. 95–110. Stronk (2010) provides a comprehensive survey of the sources for Ctesias' life and works, along with Greek text and English translation.

[3] Ctesias also wrote an *Indica* and a *Periodos*, although, like the *Persica*, neither of these has survived in its entirety. He was not the only fourth-century historian to have written a *Persica*, although no others mentioning Xerxes have been left to us. Llewellyn-Jones and Robson (2010), pp. 45–55 provide a summary of the evidence for other historiographical writing about Persia before and after Ctesias. See also Drews (1973), pp. 97–132 and Stevenson (1997), pp. 9–21.

remove; the original does not survive and so we are wholly reliant upon citations or summaries by later authors. For information regarding Ctesias' account of Xerxes the most important source is the epitome of the ninth-century Byzantine scholar, Photius, which summarizes books 7–23 of Ctesias' work. Clearly this cannot reveal to us the entire content of the original, and we are left to rely on Photius' selection of the elements which he deemed worthy of inclusion in his synopsis.[4] It is possible to deduce, however, that as a writer of Persian history Ctesias appears to have set himself up as competing with Herodotus; Photius describes his account from Cambyses to Xerxes as differing almost entirely from that of Herodotus and suggests that Ctesias described Herodotus as a 'tale-teller' (λογοποιός) as contrasted with his own position as an 'eyewitness' (αὐτόπτης) and 'earwitness' (αὐτήκοος) to the stories which he tells.[5] It was perhaps in part this desire to distance himself from his best-known predecessor which resulted in a difference of emphasis in Ctesias' work; he seems to have overlooked, or treated only cursorily, much of what had already been dealt with by Herodotus. It may well be the case that Photius' selection of material for his summary of Ctesias' work was also influenced by the later scholar's intention to highlight the differences between Ctesias and Herodotus.[6]

Many scholarly critics of Ctesias' account have focused on its apparent inaccuracies and its tendency to contradict Herodotus (in relation to, for example, the chronology and order of events or the numbers of the Persian forces during the invasion of Greece).[7] In the context of a study of the ideological construction of the figure of Xerxes himself, however, the question of the imprecision of the historical detail is of less interest than a consideration of the elements of the king's rule upon which Ctesias' account apparently focused.[8] Despite discrepancies concerning chronology many of the memorable *topoi* of the Persian campaign against Greece, familiar from Herodotus' version, remain in place in

---

[4] For an overview of the life and works of Photius see Stronk (2010), pp. 107–45.

[5] Note that such agonistic criticism of predecessors is part of the rhetoric of early historiographers, seen most famously at Thucydides 1.22.4 where the writer implicitly criticizes others by saying that his own work lacks elements of the 'fabulous' (τὸ μυθῶδες) but that as a result it will be a 'possession for all time' (κτῆμα ἐς αἰεί).

[6] Stronk (2007), p. 27 and p. 35.

[7] Drews (1973), p. 106 is a typical example – he characterizes Ctesias' account of the Persian Wars as 'merely a woeful "correction" of Herodotus'. On the subject of Ctesias' questionable reliability see also Bigwood (1978) and Burn (1984), pp. 11–12. Note also Georges (1994), p. 51, pointing out that, despite Ctesias' apparent claims to privileged access to information, he was nonetheless 'only a foreign servant in a great oriental palace'; this, Georges suggests, may account for the texture of his work, which often reads like 'harem gossip'.

[8] Xerxes' reign is dealt with in Photius' epitome at Jacoby, *FGrHist* 688 F 13.24–33, translated by Llewellyn-Jones and Robson (2010), pp. 182–5 and by Stronk (2010), p. 330–9. For a discussion see Lenfant (2004), pp. lxxxvi–c.

abbreviated form in Ctesias' account: here we find the vast force mustered by Xerxes, and the Hellespontine bridge described as a 'yoke'; the claim that one of Xerxes' motives for entering Greece was in revenge for the Calchedonians' attempted destruction of his father's bridge echoes the Herodotean construction of Xerxes' campaign as following on from Darius' actions; and we are given a recognizable picture of a despot who rules over slave subjects, as Xerxes' troops at Thermopylae are said to have been whipped as they went into battle. Later Ctesias also offers examples of the destruction inflicted by Xerxes' forces. For example, the king is said to have ordered Mardonius to sack the temple of Apollo at Delphi after the battle of Plataea; here Ctesias diverges from Herodotus' account by adding the detail that the general died there following a heavy hailstorm.[9] Xerxes is also seen here (in this case *after* Plataea, again in contrast with Herodotus' version) capturing and burning Athens itself; later, after his own departure from Greece, the king is said to have sent the eunuch Matacas to plunder the temple at Delphi. One other story told by Ctesias also seems to deal with the subject of Xerxes' impiety: Photius' summary refers to an incident in Babylon at the tomb of the god Belitanes, where apparently Xerxes 'was unable to fill the vessel with oil, as had been written'. The cursory reference suggests that this was perhaps a well-known anecdote either at the time Ctesias was writing or when Photius summarized the work: Aelian's late second-/early third-century AD *Varia Historia* (13.3) fills in the details.[10] There Aelian writes that, having opened the sarcophagus of the god, the king found the body lying in olive oil and an inscription to the effect that things would turn out badly for one unable to fill up the sarcophagus with more oil. No matter how much oil Xerxes had poured in by his men the level in the tomb never rose. The story thus combines an idea of the king as one who violated sacred spaces with imagery related to that familiar from Aeschylus' *Persians* in which he is repeatedly seen – both metaphorically and literally – as wasting and emptying.[11]

Such elements of the presentation of Xerxes, while they may diverge from Herodotus' account in specific points of detail, can be seen to relate to some of the broader themes identifiable in earlier Greek depictions of Xerxes' invasion. Where Ctesias' account of Persian affairs differs from that of Herodotus, however, is in its concentration throughout on events of a more intimate nature connected with the personal lives of those at the centre of the Persian

---

[9]   Hdt. 9.63–4 records that Mardonius was killed at Plataea.
[10] On Xerxes' actions in Babylonia and the way in which these have been misrepresented on the basis of Herodotus' text see Kuhrt and Sherwin-White (1987), discussed above, p. 75.
[11] See above, p. 25 and p. 34, and Harrison (2000), pp. 66–75.

court. Ctesias – perhaps as a result of his own close association with the royal household and his desire to present himself as having privileged access to Persian tradition[12] – seems to have been at pains to give details of the family relations and influential individuals at the heart of the lives of the Persian rulers. This is a feature of his writing which is by no means peculiar to his account of Xerxes: the summaries of his work suggests that he took particular interest in the influence of royal women and eunuchs as well as in the details of court intrigues.[13] Photius' synopsis of Ctesias' account of Xerxes' reign opens with a list of key individuals at the Persian court: Artapanus[14] and Mardonius are said to have had particular influence over Xerxes; Natacas is described as the most influential eunuch;[15] and Xerxes' family members (his wife Amestris, his sons Darius, Hystaspes and Artaxerxes, and his daughters Amytis and Rhodogyne) are named. Thus Ctesias' text appears to have provided an overview of key relationships within the king's court. These might be categorized as both personal and political, since the named family members and their relationship with the king had a bearing on the continuation of the Achaemenid dynasty. Meanwhile the power wielded by other associates and advisors outside the family sphere could also influence the actions and policies of the king.[16]

It is at the end of Photius' summary of the account of Xerxes' life, however, that we are given a brief insight (one which was no doubt more detailed in the original text) into the role ascribed by Ctesias to these individuals in the king's downfall. First comes a brief reference to the alleged adultery of Xerxes'

---

[12] See Sancisi-Weerdenburg (1983), p. 32, arguing that, despite his claims to having had access to royal documents, most of Ctesias' sources were oral and that this has a particular effect on the type of history which he writes. On the nature of his sources see also Stronk (2007), pp. 37–40.

[13] On eunuchs in Ctesias' work see Lenfant (2012). For a broader survey on the role of eunuchs (both real and perceived) as well as their relationship with royal women at the Achaemenid court see Llewellyn-Jones (2002). Note that in Herodotus' work eunuchs rarely have a significant role to play. One exception in Xerxes' case is his chief eunuch Hermotimus, who is entrusted with escorting the king's children after Salamis. Herodotus relates the story of how Hermotimus eventually exacted revenge upon Panionius, the man who had had him castrated, by forcing him to castrate his four sons and the sons to do the same to their father (Hdt. 8.104–6).

On the political influence of royal women at the Achaemenid court as presented by Ctesias and other Greek writers, see Brosius (1996), pp. 105–19. Such influential women are a recurring feature of Ctesias' Persica; Sancisi-Weerdenburg (1987a), pp. 40–2 looks at the involvement of royal women in acts of revenge and punishment and highlights a parallel between Ctesias' stories and that of Masistes' wife in Herodotus' account.

[14] This Artapanus – who later participates in Xerxes' assassination – is named as son of Artasyras, whom Ctesias records as having participated in the assassination of the pretender to the throne prior to Darius' reign (*FGrHist* 688 F13 (16)). He is not to be confused with Herodotus' Artabanus, Xerxes' uncle and the son of Hystaspes (Kuhrt 2007, p. 309 n. 1).

[15] This would appear to be the 'Matacas' referred to as having plundered Delphi later in Ctesias' account.

[16] The book of Esther (discussed below, pp. 141–8) provides an insight into the way in which a text might elaborate upon the interplay of personal and political relationships at Xerxes' court.

daughter Amytis, denounced by her husband Megabyzus; Xerxes extracts from her a promise that in future she will show more self-control. There follows a description of the plot to kill Xerxes, carried out by Artapanus and the eunuch Aspamistres. The conspirators are said to have persuaded his son Artaxerxes that Darius, another of Xerxes' sons, had killed the king, with the result that this Darius was put to death. This is the earliest surviving literary account of the king's death and even Photius' brief synopsis conveys some sense of Ctesias' particular interest in the nature of the court intrigues which surround the Persian kings throughout his work. The hint of a pernicious female presence in the character of Amytis, the figure of the conspiring eunuch and the sinister character of the double-crossing advisor Artapanus all combine to create a dramatic tale of the king's demise which is part of the broader picture of the Persian court drawn by Ctesias throughout his *Persica*.[17]

The emphasis placed on private affairs at the king's court in this version of Xerxes' reign, taken within the context of Ctesias' wider preoccupation with stories relating to sexual politics, influential eunuchs and conspiracies, offers a tantalizing glimpse at an alternative version of the Persian king which looks beyond the story of his invasion of Greece and sets elements of his story close to home in Persian surroundings. Xerxes in this context is not a unique character, singled out for posterity because of his expedition to Greece, but is instead presented as one of a long line of eastern monarchs whose stories were chronicled by a Greek observer for the delectation of a Greek audience.[18] This raises the important issue of the extent to which Ctesias chose his material in order to cater for the tastes and expectations of his readers; his focus on 'harem politics' may well tap into Greek curiosity about the exoticism of the Persian court. This world behind closed doors and the character-types seen there proved to be a source of fascination for later writers and subsequently became the setting for imagined narratives which were magnetically attracted to the kinds of stories first outlined by Ctesias; in this sense his work prefigures what has now come to be described as the 'historical novel' and thus shares common literary ground with Xenophon's presentation of the Persian court in his *Cyropaedia*,[19] as well as with later texts which sought inspiration in the palace setting.

[17] Sancisi-Weerdenburg (1987a) identified Ctesias' account as being largely responsible for the perception, held until relatively recently by many scholars, of the Achaemenid empire as 'decadent' and in decline in the period beginning with Xerxes' murder. See also Briant (2002), p. 7. Llewellyn-Jones and Robson (2010), pp. 25–31 critique this view, offering a summary of the scholarly debate.

[18] On the notion that Ctesias is more concerned to present an image of the life of the Persian court as a whole rather than to differentiate between Persian kings, see Lenfant (2004), pp. cxxxiii–cxxxvii.

[19] See, for example, Gera (1993), pp. 199–206 (with particular emphasis on the role of women and eunuchs in the stories or 'novellas' of Xenophon and Ctesias). Stronk (2007) offers a reading of

Visual images: Persian kings in art

It is perhaps surprising, given the highly visual nature of Greek theatre and the vivid images of Xerxes drawn in Aeschylus' dramatic *Persians* (and presumably in other tragedies on similar themes),[20] that no Greek works of art featuring Xerxes himself survive, yet we can detect in Attic vase painting elements of a broader interest in the private world of Persian royalty which might be linked with a developing Greek interest in the king's court following the invasion of 480 BC. Prior to this period there is little evidence of artistic interest in Persian subjects,[21] although from the century after the Persian Wars vase painters seem to have developed a wider repertoire of Persian themes,[22] with images of Greek warriors fighting Persians on drinking vessels dating from the 470s onwards.[23] Persian soldiers often carry bows and arrows and are identifiable by their clothing – fabric headdress, trousers, patterned tunic and shoes with turned-up toes – which distinguishes them clearly from Greek hoplites, who are depicted as fighting naked.[24] Perhaps the best-known early artistic response to the Greek defeat of the Persians is an Attic red-figure oinochoe which features a caricature in which a man in Persian dress bends over, about to be sodomized by a Greek; the inscriptions on the vase – in a reference to the Athenian Cimon's defeat of the Persians in 465 BC – translate as 'I am Eurymedon. I stand bent over.'[25]

Stereotyped Persian royal figures depicted on Greek painted pottery are given more dignified postures, however, and are cast in surroundings associated with the Persian court. Examples of Attic red-figure pottery from later in the fifth century include a pelike dating to around 440 BC depicting a Persian king and queen who are labelled as such (βασιλεύς and βασιλίς).[26] Other vases provide a version of the royal 'audience scene' familiar to us from the Persian

---

Ctesias which considers his work as – like Xenophon's *Cyropaedia* – a combination of historical fact with fictitious elements and which demonstrates that the notion of a generic distinction between 'history' and 'novel' is anachronistic and unhelpful in relation to our reading of the *Persica*.

[20] Taplin (2007) provides an extensive exploration of fourth-century vase-paintings which bear a relationship to tragedies of the fifth century.

[21] Shapiro (2009), pp. 58–62 describes the few examples which show an interest in Persian subjects.

[22] Raeck (1981), pp. 101–63 traces the development of Persian imagery in Athenian art between the Persian Wars and the beginning of the fourth century.

[23] For example, an oinochoe by the Chicago Painter (Boston 13.196); see Boardman (1989), p. 29 fig. 29.

[24] Bovon (1963) discusses relevant examples.

[25] Hamburg, Museum für Kunst und Gewerbe 1981.173. See Smith (1999) for a discussion of the vase's use of 'political personification'. Miller (2010) provides a detailed analysis of the image on the vase.

[26] Rome, Vatican 16.536{1} = Raeck (1981), fig. 58. The image is similar to that found on another oinochoe from the same period (Louvre, Campana collection 11164); see Shapiro (2009), p. 75.

palace reliefs, with royal figures seated and surrounded by attendants,[27] and elsewhere we find images of Persian rulers (whether they are kings or satraps is not made clear) being entertained by scenes of dancing.[28] One vase, a lekythos from c. 380 BC by the Athenian artist Xenophantos,[29] is particularly interesting in that it names some of the Persian figures which it depicts. The body of the vase shows a hunting scene, with Persian participants named, among others, as Darius and Cyrus;[30] for Greeks of the fourth century these names would call to mind well-known Persian rulers of both the recent and distant past.[31]

Perhaps the most striking artistic image of Persian royalty, however, is the so-called 'Darius vase',[32] an elaborately decorated volute-krater fashioned in a Greek workshop in Apulia in around 340 BC. In the central register sits a Persian king, wearing a sumptuous robe and tiara and holding a sceptre, and named as Darius by the Greek inscription above him. He is addressed by a messenger and surrounded by advisors. Below him is a scene in which Persian officials receive what appear to be tribute-offerings; above, in the divine plane, are personifications of Asia, Hellas and Apatē ('Deception'), along with the Olympian gods. The pedestal on which the messenger stands bears the word *PERSAI*, which may suggest a link to a tragic play on the theme of the Persian Wars, although given the central position of Darius and his direct engagement with the messenger here this could not be Aeschylus' *Persians*; some have suggested perhaps a fourth-century revival of Phrynichus' *Persians* or an altogether different fourth-century play.[33] By the fourth century relations between Greeks and Persians may have changed but the fact that the vase – from a location far away from Athens, and well over a century after the Persian Wars – depicts a view of the Persian court from a Greek perspective demonstrates the depth to which the fascination with

---

[27] Istanbul, Archaeological Museum 7501 and Stockholm, Historical Museum V294; see Shapiro (2009), figs. 3.14–3.15. On the audience scene in Achaemenid sculpture see above, pp. 85–6 with figure 2; vase-painters in Greece may have become aware of such scenes on portable objects such as royal seals which might feature on communications between the king and states outside his empire. For a discussion of the audience scene on Persian seals see also Allen (2005), pp. 46–52.

[28] Vienna, Kunsthistorisches Museum 158 is a fourth-century volute krater depicting a seated king at the centre, attended by a fan-bearer as he watches a dance; cf. British Museum E695, a lekythos on which a Persian ruler, seated on a camel, observes the entertainment.

[29] St. Petersburg, State Hermitage Museum P 1837.2 = Beazley record 217907.

[30] For a detailed analysis of the vase which situates it in its historical and artistic context see M. C. Miller (2003).

[31] Llewellyn-Jones (2012), pp. 322–3, pointing out that the blurring of the distinction of past and present Persian rulers is similar to that seen in some fourth-century oratorical texts. On the latter, see above, pp. 110–12.

[32] Naples, Museo Archeologico Nazionale 3253; see Hall (1996), p. 29 (fig. 1) and the detailed description of Llewellyn-Jones (2012), pp. 332–4.

[33] Anti (1952) suggests that the Darius vase relates to a revival of Phrynichus; see also Trendall and Webster (1971), p. 112. Hall (1996), p. 8 suggests that it might relate to a new play on the theme of the Persian Wars.

the Great King and his surroundings had penetrated the Greek consciousness. The image thus forms part of a tradition which relates to Aeschylus' vision of the response in Susa to the invasion of Xerxes, to Herodotus' tales of events at the Persian court, and to the many related strands of the Xerxes-narrative which focus on the world of his royal palaces. While, then, the lack of any explicit reference to Xerxes on any of the examples of artwork featuring Persian royal figures is in stark contrast to his ubiquity in the written texts relating to the history of Greek encounters with Persia, the ongoing resonances of Greece's earliest conflict with Persia might nonetheless be detected in these painted images of Persian royalty.

Diodorus: Alternative strands of the Xerxes-tradition

The interest which Ctesias displayed in examining events within Xerxes' court beyond his invasion of Greece is also apparent in a much later historiographical text. Diodorus Siculus' *Bibliothēke*, a 'universal history' written in the first century BC, attempted to document events from mythological times (beginning with the Trojan War) down to his own time. Having grown up in the Sicilian town of Agyrium, Diodorus spent time in Egypt before moving to Rome, where he lived until around 30 BC. It was during this time, in the turbulent last years of the Roman republic, that he researched and wrote his work, the only one of its kind from this era of which anything has survived although only fifteen of the original forty books are extant. Diodorus seems to have relied heavily on earlier sources for much of his material, although many of the histories which he is thought to have used are now themselves lost, and much scholarly effort has been devoted to attempts to identify his sources.[34] Books 11–16 deal mainly with Greek history from the early fifth century to 340 BC and include (in Book 11) material on the Persian Wars; this section is thought to derive primarily from the work of the fourth-century historian Ephorus of Cyme.[35] In what follows I shall refer to the work of Diodorus although this is not necessarily to imply that the strands of the Xerxes-tradition preserved in his work are necessarily the product of his own era. Rather, because of his reliance on a fourth-century source for the Persian Wars, it is possible that the images of Xerxes seen here originated in a much earlier period. At the same time, however, the selection

---

[34] See, for example, Drews (1962). Sacks (1994) argues that Diodorus did not simply plagiarize material from earlier historians but that he also had subjective input of his own.
[35] Hornblower (1994), pp. 36–7.

and organization of material can be seen to reflect Diodorus' own preoccupations as a writer of history.

Much of Diodorus' account of Xerxes' invasion of Greece (11.1–19; 11.27–39)
bears clear parallels with the story as told by Herodotus: emphasis is placed
throughout upon the size of the king's armament (at, for example, 11.3.7;
11.5.2–3; cf. 2.5.5 and 8.1.3) and the fact that this also worked against him,
with heavy losses sustained at Thermopylae (11.12.2) and the defeat at Salamis
effected by the strategy of Themistocles, by which the Persian fleet was forced
to fight in the narrow strait. Key episodes featuring Xerxes also appear here,
although in a version which provides far less detail than that of Herodotus.[36]
One result of the compression of the story into a shorter space is that we find
in Diodorus' version no development of a portrait of Xerxes, his character or
his motivation such as that seen in Herodotus' account. Diodorus makes little
attempt to consider the Persian king's temperament or to understand the reasons
behind his actions: the author rarely alludes to elements of Xerxes' psychology
or emotions. Minor exceptions include the description of his response to
Demaratus' assessment of Greek valour, where Xerxes is said to have laughed
scornfully (11.6.2: the Greek has καταγελάσας, here also echoing his response
to Leonidas' message via the Persian envoys at 11.6.1)[37] and the king's reaction
to the offer of help from a treacherous Greek at Thermopylae, when he is said
to be 'delighted' (περιχαρής, 11.8.5). The same adjective is also used to describe
Xerxes' response at 11.57.6 when Themistocles is acquitted of wrongdoing by a
Persian jury (see further below, p. 138).[38] Only on one occasion is the king given
any direct speech by Diodorus, when he asks Demaratus 'Will the Greeks flee
faster than my horses, or will they dare to face such forces in battle?' (11.6.1)
These few brief instances of characterization aside, this Xerxes is merely the
figurehead of the expedition to Greece and, while we see some instances of his

---

[36] The following examples of significant episodes involving the Persian king stand out: Xerxes is said
   to have been influenced by pressure from Mardonius to undertake the expedition (11.1.2–3; cf. Hdt.
   7.5); the Hellespont bridge and Athos canal are described early in the account (11.2.4; 11.3.6); we
   see, in condensed form, Xerxes' conversation with Demaratus prior to the battle of Thermopylae
   (11.6.102; cf. Hdt. 7.101–105) and his victory in that battle as a result of the treachery of a Greek
   (11.8.4, although note that the traitor here is said to be a Trachinian; Herodotus tells us at 7.213.1
   that he was a Malian, and names him as Ephialtes); at Salamis Xerxes is taken in by the false message
   from Themistocles pretending that the Greeks are about to flee (11.17.1–3; cf. Hdt. 8.75–6); after
   Salamis he delegates responsibility to Mardonius for the remainder of the campaign so that he can
   return to Asia (11.19.6; cf. Hdt. 8.113–115).
[37] Cf. Herodotus' account of the exchange between Xerxes and Demaratus, discussed above (p. 66).
[38] Diodorus' lack of interest in the characterization of Xerxes prefigures that seen in Plutarch's *Life
   of Themistocles*, which also focused upon Themistocles' sojourn at the Persian court (see below, p.
   182–7, for a discussion which suggests that Plutarch may have had political reasons for his decision
   not to dwell too long upon the figure of Xerxes).

tendencies towards cruelty and destruction (for example, at 11.8.1 when he tells his troops at Thermopylae that the punishment for fleeing will be death; 11.14 where he and his troops sack Delphi, Thespiae, Plataea and Athens; and 11.19.4 when the Phoenicians who instigate the flight from Salamis are put to death), the main source of interest here is not the man himself but the actions which he instigates against the Greeks.

That Diodorus (or Ephorus) was interested in the delineation of character is, however, apparent elsewhere in the account of the Persian Wars and their aftermath. The version of events preserved in Diodorus' account places particular emphasis on the figure of Themistocles, his role as strategist in the Greek resistance to the Persian invasion and his subsequent adventures when exiled.[39] This strand of Diodorus' narrative also preserves a tradition which is of particular interest in the context of a study of the reception of the figure of Xerxes. Where other sources claim that Themistocles, after his ostracism from Athens, was eventually received in Persia by Xerxes' son Artaxerxes,[40] Diodorus' story (11.56–8) instead brings him face-to-face with the king who led the expedition against Greece. The notion that Themistocles and Xerxes actually met seems likely to be a dramatic invention;[41] its purpose here is in enabling Diodorus to explore further Themistocles' character, yet it also provides us with another perspective on the atmosphere at the Persian court as envisaged in the Greek imagination and as seen earlier in the account of Ctesias. The ruse by which Themistocles is first brought before Xerxes hints at the luxury and sexual liaisons characteristic of accounts of life at the Persian court: he is concealed in a wagon like one of Xerxes' courtesans (11.56.7). After working his charm upon Xerxes he is allowed to remain there unpunished; the remarkable notion that the victor of Salamis was able to build a relationship with his once arch-enemy provides the starting-point for an extraordinary pseudo-biographical tale in a Persian setting.

Themistocles, once ensconced in Persia, becomes involved in a story with thematic elements which resemble those in Ctesias' account where a powerful

---

[39] Themistocles' role at Salamis 11.15–17; ruse to hasten Xerxes' departure from Greece with a message that the Greeks were about to destroy the Hellespont bridges 11.18.5–6; role in fortifying Athens and the Piraeus 11.39.4–43.3; ostracism and subsequent adventures ending with his eventual death in Persia 11.54–58.

[40] See Thucydides 1.137–8. Plutarch (*Themistocles* 27.1) writes that Charon of Lampsacus agreed with Thucydides in bringing Themistocles before Artaxerxes but is unable to say with conviction which account he believes to be true; in his own narrative he therefore avoids the use of a name, referring simply to 'the king' throughout. On Plutarch's *Themistocles* and its treatment of Xerxes see further below, pp. 183–5. Keaveney (2003), pp. 24–5 (with pp. 138–9, nn. 147–56) surveys the evidence relating to whether Themistocles visited Xerxes or Artaxerxes.

[41] So Lenardon (1978), p. 137; see also Rhodes (1970), p. 394.

feminine influence is felt at the Persian court (11.57): Xerxes' sister Mandane, whose sons had been killed at Salamis, begs Xerxes to take vengeance upon Themistocles, but when the king pays her no attention she persuades the Persian nobles and masses to call for Themistocles' punishment. Xerxes decides to form a jury of the noblest Persians to decide his fate. Here an apparently Greek, democratic aspect has found its way into the tradition; we remember that Themistocles had been ostracized as part of the Athenian democratic process, and perhaps it was natural for a Greek writer to assume that he would be tried by a similar process at the Persian court. The incident, according to Diodorus, precipitates Themistocles' learning of the Persian language;[42] by the time the trial comes around he is able to defend himself and secure his acquittal. Diodorus' report of the king's delight at this outcome is followed by an account of the way in which he subsequently plied Themistocles with gifts, including a Persian wife and cities to provide for his every need (11.57.6–7).

The episode in which Themistocles builds a favourable relationship with Xerxes is one which, although the characters it features are historical, seems likely to be an invented narrative which formed part of the traditions surrounding the figure of Themistocles. The question arises as to why Xerxes may have been keen to court the architect of the Persians' naval defeat at Salamis; Diodorus' version offers the possible motivation that the king hoped that Themistocles would assist in another attack on Greece. Such Greek treachery was not unprecedented, and was doubtless a feature of Greco-Persian relations during the Persian Wars period and beyond; Diodorus' narrative features too the demise of the Spartan Pausanias (11.44–6) who, as part of a secret agreement with Xerxes, planned to marry the king's daughter and betray the Greeks, though the Spartans ultimately punished him for his emulation of Persian luxury and tyrannical treatment of his subordinates.[43] Diodorus' account also relates one report (11.58.2–3) of Themistocles' own demise in which Xerxes invited him to take command of a further expedition to Greece; Themistocles made the king swear under oath that he would not march against the Greeks without him. Themistocles, despite his dubious dalliance with Xerxes, is redeemed here as the ultimate patriot, sacrificing himself for the good of his country when, in a

---

[42] Thucydides' version of Themistocles' story has him learning Persian *before* his arrival at the court of Artaxerxes (1.138.1); Gera (2007) offers an analysis of the variant versions of this detail in the Themistocles-tradition.

[43] Diodorus 11.44–6. The story of Pausanias is also told by Thucydides (1.128–34), who relates an exchange of letters between the Spartan and Xerxes, and who also emphasizes Pausanias' love of Persian luxury as a factor in bringing about his demise. See Rhodes (1970), pp. 387–92 for an analysis.

final act of loyalty to his homeland, he safeguards Greece against a future attack by committing suicide once Xerxes' oath is sworn. The tale, which contradicts other versions of Themistocles' death,[44] forms an appropriate ending to the story of the wily commander – famed above all for his winning strategy at Salamis – who remains a master of cunning to the end.

One reason for the focus on the character of Themistocles rather than that of Xerxes in this episode may be detected in Diodorus' particular agenda as a writer of history. A feature of his work is the emphasis which it places upon his own Sicilian homeland; in Book 11 this is particularly apparent in his excursus on Sicilian history (11.20–26) in which he describes the victory of the Sicilians, led by Gelon, over the invading Carthaginians (under the generalship of Hamilcar) at the battle of Himera. Diodorus places this battle on the same day as that at Thermopylae (11.24.1), 'as if by divine design the finest victory and the most honourable defeat took place at the same time'. The contrast here allows him to emphasize the success of the Sicilians;[45] this is a theme which recurs throughout the excursus, in which he also asserts that the victory of the Sicilians spurred the Greeks on to victory against the Persians (11.23.2). Of particular significance here is the comparison which Diodorus draws between Gelon's achievement and that of the Greek leaders, Pausanias and Themistocles. He declares the Sicilian victory to be superior to that of the Greeks, because in the case of Xerxes' invasion the king survived with many of his troops intact, while the Carthaginian general was slain along with every member of his force. Furthermore, Gelon himself was held in high esteem by the Syracusans and retained the kingship until his death; by contrast Pausanias was put to death for his treachery and hunger for power, while Themistocles 'was exiled from the whole of Greece and fled for refuge to the most hated Xerxes, and resided with him until his death' (11.23.3). It is therefore possible to suggest that the entire episode between Xerxes and Themistocles is set up in order to facilitate the portrayal of Gelon as superior – both as a tactician and in moral terms – to the Greek commander.

The emphasis in Diodorus' account on the fact that Xerxes survived his expedition to Greece, by contrast with the defeated Hamilcar, is also useful in explaining the presence of another episode relating to the king which does not feature in any earlier extant sources on the Persian invasion. The course of the battle of Thermopylae is described in much the same way as in Herodotus'

---

[44] See Marr (1995) for an analysis of the various traditions.
[45] Herodotus (7.166) puts the battle of Himera on the same day as the Greek victory at Salamis.

account, although with one significant additional incident. Diodorus records a direct attack there at night upon the Persian camp by the Spartans (11.10).[46] Describing the general chaos among the Persians during the incident, he writes that many of the barbarians were slain, although Xerxes himself managed to evade capture by escaping from his tent amid the confusion; the Spartan troops searched the camp for him in vain. Had the Spartans captured and killed Xerxes at this point, the course of the invasion might have been very different; as it was, the king lived on to proceed with his expedition. By contrast, the Carthaginian general Hamilcar was, according to Diodorus, slain inside his own camp (11.22.1). In light of the emphasis which Diodorus then places upon the Sicilian victory at Himera as having taken place on the very same day as Thermopylae (11.24.1) the survival of Xerxes after the incursion into his camp takes on particular significance in relation to the comparison which Diodorus draws between Sicilian and Greek achievements. Thus the manipulation of the story of Xerxes can perhaps be seen to be motivated here by Diodorus' own patriotic pro-Sicilian agenda; his interest in the king's story becomes subordinated to the wider purpose of his historical record.

Xerxes' eventual death in 465 BC is later recounted by Diodorus (11.69); the story follows a pattern similar to that seen in Ctesias' work, as the king is killed as the result of a plot formulated by some of his closest associates (11.69).[47] As in Ctesias' version Artabanus attempts to usurp the kingship by assassinating Xerxes; he plots with a eunuch who is highly trusted by the king (named in Diodorus' account as Mithridates; Ctesias called him Aspamistres), then slays Xerxes and sets out after the dead king's sons, trying to convince Artaxerxes that it was his brother Darius who was responsible for the murder. In this account further details are offered: Artabanus attempts to murder Artaxerxes, who retaliates and kills the would-be usurper in revenge for Xerxes' death, and finally Artaxerxes goes on to assume the kingship.[48] The emphasis here on political subterfuge and scandal, with the figures of the conspiring eunuch and the duplicitous Artabanus, mirrors Ctesias' interest in the atmosphere at the Persian court, yet for Diodorus the story takes on particular resonance in the light of

---

[46] M. A. Flower (1998) compares the accounts of Herodotus and Diodorus/Ephorus and suggests that the poetry of Simonides may have been the original source for the story of the night attack. Plutarch also followed the tradition recorded by Diodorus (*De malignitate Herodoti* 866a), using the night attack as an example of the heroism of Leonidas' men at Thermopylae. See also Green (2006), pp. 61–2 n. 43.

[47] For Ctesias' account of the death of Xerxes, see *FGrHist* 688 F 13.33 (29). See above, pp. 131–2, for an analysis.

[48] At 11.71.1 Diodorus also notes that Artaxerxes punished those who had participated in his father's murder.

the fact that the king had evaded capture at Thermopylae 15 years earlier. For Diodorus' Xerxes, who escaped even the valorous Spartans' mission to kill him, the risk of death on foreign soil in the field of battle ultimately proved to be less of a threat than that of a conspiracy far closer to home.

Esther and the king: Xerxes in the biblical tradition

A rare insight into the presentation of Xerxes in a source originating from beyond the Greek-speaking world has been transmitted to us in the form of the Old Testament book of Esther, whose setting and plot display an interest in Persian court life similar to that seen in what remains of Ctesias' accounts. The text, which might best be described as a historical novel or novella in a Persian setting,[49] is also an aetiological tale which narrates the origin of the Jewish festival of Purim; at the same time it has also been viewed as an exploration, albeit one which is at times humorous in tone, of the challenges faced by Jews living in a diaspora setting.[50] As with much of the Old Testament it has been preserved in several forms; the Hebrew version of the text (the Masoretic Text) is accepted as authoritative by Jews and most Christians but the Greek (Septuagint) translation, although mostly close in sense to the Hebrew, contains several extended additions.[51] Those variations which have a direct bearing on the characterization of Xerxes in the story will be discussed below. The date of the original composition of the Hebrew text remains open to question, with some suggesting a date as early as the late fifth/early fourth century BC – while the Achaemenid empire was still in existence – on the basis of the presence of the author's familiarity with details concerning Persian court life and bureaucracy as well as the frequent occurrence of Persian names and words.[52] Others, however, noting apparent historical inaccuracies which might suggest that the text was first written after the decline of the Achaemenid empire (for example, the claim at 1.1 and 9.30 that the Persian king ruled over 127 provinces, or the divergence from the Herodotean tradition in which Xerxes' wife is named as Amestris), argue for a date in the Hellenistic period.[53]

---

[49] For a discussion of how we might categorize the genre(s) of the book of Esther see Fox (2001), pp. 141–52. Wills (1994), and (1995), pp. 16–28 explores Jewish 'novelistic' literature and its relationship with the ancient Greek novel.

[50] Gruen (2002), pp. 137–48.

[51] Clines (1984) examines in detail the variant versions of the text.

[52] Moore (1971), pp. lvii–lx; Baldwin (1984), p. 49. On the book's use of Persian words see Gehman (1924); see Millard (1977) on the Persian names.

[53] See Fox (2001), pp. 131–40. Berg (1979), pp. 169–73 discusses the evidence regarding the book's date.

The Persian king named in the Hebrew text as Ahasuerus has for the last century been positively identified with Xerxes on the basis of Achaemenid inscriptions in which he is named as the Persian equivalent *Xšayāršā*, anglicized via Greek as 'Xerxes'.[54] Prior to the discovery of the Persian texts, however, confusion was caused by the fact that the Greek version of Esther translates Ahasuerus as 'Artaxerxes', presumably on the basis of the phonetic similarity of the names.[55] To identify the king as Xerxes is not, however, to suggest that the story is necessarily based on any real historical events; rather the text provides us with an example of how an imagined narrative concerning the vicissitudes of Persian court life might find this particular king an appealing figure upon which to focus attention.[56] The book is remarkable in that it provides us with the most detailed extant depiction of an imagined Xerxes-character within the court setting, and, while precise sources for the text cannot be securely identified,[57] elements of the portrayal of Xerxes can be compared with those seen in our Greek texts; its preservation of the perspective of a Jewish writer upon the Persian royal household makes this unique among surviving Xerxes-narratives. The story, set in Susa and beginning in the third year of Xerxes' reign but unfolding over several years, takes place as follows:

> 1.1–22: Xerxes holds rich feasts for the nobles of his kingdom and the people of Susa; meanwhile his queen, Vashti, entertains the women. Xerxes, angered at his queen's refusal to come to him so that he might display her to his people, deposes her on the advice of his councillors and issues a decree enforcing the submission of wives to their husbands throughout his empire.

> 2.1–23: Xerxes has the most beautiful virgins from throughout his kingdom brought to Susa, to be overseen by Hegai, his chief eunuch, so that he may choose a new queen. Among them is Esther (also known in Hebrew as Hadassah), niece of Mordecai; she is of Jewish descent but has been instructed by her uncle not to reveal this fact. Esther is chosen as the new queen. Mordecai

---

[54] Paton (1908), pp. 53–4 sets out the Persian evidence used to confirm the identification of Ahasuerus as Xerxes. See also Fox (2001), p. 14 and Yamauchi (1990), p. 187. The only other mention of Ahasuerus/Xerxes in the Bible is in the book of Ezra (4.6) which refers to an accusation lodged against the Jews during his reign.

[55] Josephus (*Jewish Antiquities* 11.6) also makes this erroneous connection, placing Esther's story in Artaxerxes' reign: Wills (1995), p. 222. See below, p. 174.

[56] Levenson's statement (1997, p. 25) that 'the author borrowed Xerxes's name but little else about him in order to create the novella' highlights the fact that the story may not be based upon objective historical detail but does not take into account that – as discussed here – much in the text is based upon broader traditions surrounding Xerxes' court and his behaviour.

[57] On the problematic question of sources for the story see Clines (1984), pp. 115–138.

learns of a plot by two eunuchs to assassinate Xerxes, and Esther reveals this to the king.

3.1–15: Mordecai (who is now a royal official)[58] refuses to do obeisance to Haman, Xerxes' right-hand man. Angered, Haman resolves to take revenge by destroying all Jews in Xerxes' kingdom; he tells the king with deliberate obliqueness that a 'certain people' throughout the empire is failing to observe the laws, and thereby persuades Xerxes to give him the power to issue an edict for their destruction.

4.1–17: Esther learns of Haman's plan from the anguished Mordecai and resolves to intervene.

5.1–14: Esther gains an audience with the king and invites Xerxes and Haman to a feast. Haman prepares a stake for Mordecai's impalement.

6.1–14: The king is unable to sleep so has the royal chronicles read to him; these reveal that it was Mordecai who had uncovered the conspiracy against him, and the king learns that Mordecai was not rewarded for his actions. He asks Haman how a faithful subject should be honoured and Haman (thinking that Xerxes intends to honour him) suggests that such a man should be paraded on horseback wearing royal attire. To Haman's humiliation, he is instructed by the king to arrange this honour for Mordecai.

7.1–10: At her feast with the king Esther asks for her people to be spared, and reveals that Haman is to blame for the plot to massacre the Jews. In his anger Xerxes also accuses Haman of intending to rape Esther and has him impaled in Mordecai's place.

8.1–17: Mordecai takes Haman's place in Xerxes' court and the king authorizes him and Esther to issue a new decree reversing that which authorized the killing of the Jews. The edict also gives the Jews permission to take vengeance by killing those who attack them.

9.1–32: On the given day in the month of Adar the Jews gather to retaliate against those who harm them. Xerxes grants Esther's requests that the slaughter of their enemies is allowed to continue on the following day and that the bodies of Haman's ten sons are impaled. A day of respite and feasting follows (this is the explanation for the origin and date of Purim, which Mordecai decrees will henceforth be observed every year).

---

[58] See Gordis (1976), pp. 47–8 for the interpretation of the phrase 'at the king's gate' to refer to the holding of office in the king's administration.

10.1–3: Xerxes imposes a tribute upon his subjects. Mordecai is greatly esteemed by the Jews.

The story, which explores the machinations of the royal court, is thus based on a pair of reversals of fortune in which the promotion of Mordecai – courageous and loyal both to his king and his people – along with his salvation of the Jews is counterbalanced by the downfall of the corrupt and vindictive Haman and the vengeance which the Jews take upon those who had intended to destroy them.[59] Esther, despite her passive role at the start of the story, comes to occupy the role of protagonist.[60] Within this framework there are several elements in the presentation of Xerxes and his world which are particularly prominent and which might be compared with versions of the Persian king's story seen elsewhere. For example, details such as the reference to *proskynēsis* (with Mordecai's refusal to perform this before Haman as the catalyst for Haman's malicious plot: 3.1–6), and the presence of capital punishment in the form of impalement (5.14; 7.9–10; 8.7; 9.13) are familiar from our study of the Greek texts relating to Persian kingship. Perhaps most striking from the outset, however, is the image of the ostentatious luxury and wealth of Xerxes' court. The prolonged and lavish feasting which takes place at the start of the story (for 187 days in total) is presented as a display of the king's power and riches (1.4–5), and detailed visual descriptions are given of the luxurious adornments of his palace (fine colourful cloth hangings, couches of gold and silver and a mosaic pavement of marble and precious stones: 1.6–7);[61] these descriptions call to mind Herodotus' account of Xerxes' lavish dining arrangements even while on campaign in Greece (Hdt. 7.119; cf. 9.82). Feasting at court is also a recurring motif at key points in the book; another banquet is held when Esther is appointed queen (2.18) and the revelation of Haman's plot takes place at the banquet arranged by Esther (5.4–6; 6.14–7.8).[62]

Meanwhile the text's interest in the royal harem is reminiscent of Ctesias' focus on the role of women and eunuchs in Persian court life. The description of the procedure by which Xerxes finds a replacement queen is rich in detail which lends an insight into the perceived image of the king's domestic arrangements;

---

[59] Bickerman (1967), pp. 172–84 examines the way in which the book uses traditional story patterns or themes seen elsewhere in folklore.

[60] On the character of Esther and the ways in which this relates to the book's presentation of women see Fox (2001), pp. 196–211.

[61] Fox (2001), p. 18 notes that the level of descriptive detail in the opening scene is unusual for a biblical text and suggests that the author may have imitated the techniques of authors of Hellenistic romance.

[62] Berg (1979), pp. 31–57 examines the use of the feasting motif (and the related motif of fasting) in the text.

the selection of beautiful virgin women who are to be at the king's disposal sexually (2.2; cf. 2.14) is overseen by the eunuch Hegai who is in charge of the harem and whose favour Esther wins (2.8–9; cf. 2.15), and the candidates are prepared for their presentation to the king by undergoing elaborate beauty treatments for twelve months (2.3; 2.9; 2.12).[63] Eunuchs also feature elsewhere as figures in the story, sometimes with a key role in the plot: the names of seven eunuchs who serve the king are given at 1.10; at 2.14 Shaashgaz is named as being guardian of the concubines; Bigthan and Teresh are responsible for conspiring against Xerxes at 2.21 (this part of the story is perhaps related to the strand of the tradition, seen in Ctesias' account, in which a eunuch was involved in the conspiracy which killed Xerxes); Esther is attended by eunuchs at 4.4–5; Xerxes' eunuchs summon him to Esther's banquet at 6.14; and it is Harbona, one of the king's eunuchs, who tells him of the stake which Haman has prepared for Mordecai's impalement.[64]

This, then, is the domestic backdrop for the biblical portrayal of the character of Xerxes. The influence wielded by several of these figures is symptomatic of an atmosphere in which the king himself is imagined as a somewhat passive character throughout the story. The occasional flashes of anger – stereotyped elements of the characterization of an absolute ruler[65] – which he displays (at 1.12, after Vashti's disobedience; and 7.7, after his discovery of Haman's underhand plot to kill the Jews) belie the dispassionate figure seen elsewhere in the book. Despite the geographical extent of his authority (1.1; 9.30) and the riches he possesses he exercises surprisingly little control over the events which take place in the story. Thus even at the outset the policy which is initiated in response to the disobedience of Vashti is that suggested by one of his advisors, Memuchan (1.16–21). Later it is Xerxes' delegation of authority to Haman which enables his subordinate to issue an edict for the massacre of the Jews; the king's failure to enquire as to the precise identity of the people whom Haman condemns, and his authorization for Haman simply to do as he pleases, result in Haman's publication of the deadly edict (3.8–14).[66] This, then, is represented by

---

[63] De Troyer (1995) analyses this element of the selection process in the variant versions and considers its significance in relation to how the book presents the role of women in the king's court.

[64] See p. 131 n. 13 on the role of eunuchs in other literature relating to Xerxes.

[65] On the anger of the Herodotean Xerxes see pp. 48–9. In Aeschylus' *Persians* the pitiful figure of the defeated Xerxes once he appears onstage contrasts sharply with the 'raging' leader imagined by the Chorus at the start of the play (see above, p. 31).

[66] The revocation of the edict is carried out in a similar manner, as Xerxes authorizes Esther and Mordecai to write a new decree as they see fit (8.8). Fox (2001), pp. 173–6 attributes these actions to Xerxes' 'laziness', yet this is perhaps to overlook the practicalities of administering a vast empire and the need to delegate responsibility to appointed officials. Nonetheless, Xerxes' lack of interest in the details allows Haman to proceed with his malicious plan: Talmon (1963), pp. 441–2.

the author of the book as a court in which corruption and self-interest are able to flourish as it is not the will of the king but that of his courtiers which dictates the law. The king's indifference is highlighted by the fact that he and Haman are shown as sitting down to drink together at the very point at which the news of the impending massacre causes consternation throughout Susa (3.15).

The eventual salvation of the Jews is brought about when Esther extracts from the king an unconditional promise that he will do whatever she asks (5.2; 5.5; 7.1); this is another story-pattern which reminds us of one used by Herodotus, in which Xerxes is tricked by his mistress, Artaÿnte, into giving her the robe made by his wife (Hdt. 9.108–10; see p. 70). Thus, although Xerxes himself is not represented as harbouring any prejudice against the Jews or as being personally responsible for the plot to do them harm, nor can he claim the credit for saving them from destruction.[67] It is worth noting too that, although the Jews are saved, a brutal massacre still ultimately takes place on Xerxes' watch; only the recipients of the violence have changed, as we are told that the Jews killed 300 of their enemies in Susa and a further 75,000 throughout the empire (9.15–16).

Xerxes' character in the Hebrew text thus bears several resemblances to the Xerxes seen in the traditions which originated from Greece in the fifth and fourth centuries BC. Some of the later additions to the text found in the Greek version of Esther also have a bearing on the book's portrayal of the Persian king.[68] There are six such supplements in total (A–F); these include the text of documents (Haman's original edict and a later proclamation by the king which rescinds it) as well as episodes which allow the writer to introduce the presence of God into the story (there is no mention of a divine presence in the Hebrew text; in Additions A and F, however, Mordecai is said to have had a dream which revealed the intentions of God).[69] In Addition D the imagination of the writer takes us into the royal chambers and allows us to view Esther's audience with the king in an intimate scene as she prepares to intercede on behalf of her people.[70] Having put on rich clothing she enters the throne room where we are

---

[67] Fox (2001), pp. 176–7 suggests that in these respects the author portrays (and satirizes) Xerxes as the epitome of the gentile king upon whom Jews must depend for their precarious existence.

[68] While the Greek text erroneously names him as Artaxerxes (see p. 142) the content of the additions nonetheless builds upon the picture of the king which is seen in the Hebrew version.

[69] Baldwin (1984), pp. 45–8 summarizes the additions; she gives a translation at pp. 119–26. See also Fox (2001), pp. 265–9. In English versions of the Bible the additions are regularly included in the Old Testament Apocrypha. The date of the additions – which are not all thought to have been composed at the same time, nor in the same language (some were composed in Greek, others in Hebrew or Aramaic) – is not known, although a note at the end of the Greek text suggests that it was brought to Alexandria in 78 BC, which gives us a *terminus ante quem*.

[70] Day (1995), pp. 101–3 considers the effects of the Greek version of this episode.

presented with a vivid image of the king in his royal splendour: seated on his throne he is dressed in robes adorned with gold and precious stones. When he looks up in anger Esther faints in fear; God turns the king's anger to gentleness and he takes her in his arms to reassures her that she is not under threat of danger, describing himself as her 'brother' before touching her with his royal sceptre and then embracing her. The monarch's characteristic irascibility is thus used here by the writer to introduce an element of divine agency in which it is God who is responsible for taming human emotions and inspiring benevolence. As a result the scene becomes one which conveys an element of tenderness in the relationship of the royal couple; the addition to the text which demonstrates the ruler's affection for his wife could have been conceived of too as a way of explaining the king's willingness to grant Esther her request. The words of Esther which follow allow her to flatter the king so as to gain his ear: she explains her earlier fear by telling the king that his appearance called to mind that of a 'messenger (angel, Greek ἄγγελος) of God', before fainting once more. In this way the scene uses as its setting the motif of an audience with the king, at the same time playing upon a perception of the king as inspiring awe and fear in those who look upon him. The tableau calls to mind the royal 'audience scenes' familiar from Persian material culture and echoed in Greek art (see pp. 85–6 and 133–4).

The second addition which lends an insight into the Greek text's representation of the king is rather different in tone. Addition E imagines his words in the form of a proclamation reversing Haman's edict. Here the king rails against those who scheme against their benefactors, accusing such men of arrogance; he absolves himself of responsibility for Haman's crime by asserting that, despite his own benevolence, he has been taken in by a deceiver and then promises to pay no heed in future to slanderers. The text also offers an explanation of Haman's motives, suggesting that by killing both Mordecai and Esther he would have weakened the king's authority and transferred power to Haman's own people, the Macedonians. Here, then, is a more direct analysis of the politics of the king's court than we see elsewhere in the book; it is one which acknowledges the possibility for manipulation and exploitation by malicious or ambitious courtiers whose power is allowed to remain unchecked. This is the closest which the text comes to an explicit critique of the nature of Xerxes' royal power. The document goes on to relate the punishment of Haman and to declare that the Jews shall be allowed to live under their own laws; his subjects are to allow them to do so on pain of death, and Persians as well as Jews are to celebrate this day. The inclusion of this document gives the reader an impression of the way in which the king is seen to exercise his authority. In terms of characterization, however, it also serves to reinforce the image of this fictional Xerxes – seen in the earlier Hebrew text – as having allowed corruption to flourish because of his inability to exercise control over his subordinates when necessary.

The fictional construction of Xerxes in the book of Esther thus offers an alternative perspective on the king, from the point of view of a Jewish writer, which sits outside the traditions which originated in tales of his invasion of Greece. Yet despite its non-Greek origins the text shares features with other narratives which focus on 'harem politics', political intrigue and the exotic world of the royal household. That such detail – of the king's eunuchs, the women of the harem, and the lavish surroundings of his court – captured the imagination of the composer(s) of this text too reminds us that an interest in these royal themes was not the sole preserve of those for whom Xerxes was the archetypal enemy. Just as Ctesias was fascinated by the world inhabited by the Persian king and his closest associates, so too the author of Esther could use the court setting to create a richly detailed backdrop for his story. Here was a fantastical setting which could transport the reader far beyond the realm of familiar everyday experience. By contrast with the fifth-century Greek traditions – and the later texts which were shaped by them – the Xerxes imagined in the Esther-narrative is by no means culpable of destruction on a grand scale like the Xerxes seen in the Greek-derived tradition; his errors stem from his apathy and ultimately his actions work for the good of the Jews whose traditions are represented in Esther's story. In this respect the biblical narrative anticipates too the stories of Xerxes' benevolence which would later be recorded by Josephus (see pp. 173–6).

The Persian peacock: King and court in later literature

The continuing literary influence of the strands of the Xerxes-tradition which focused not upon his military actions but upon the exotic and – for Greek writers – perennially fascinating world of his court, and the political intrigue which took place within it, can be detected long after Herodotus and Ctesias sought to take their readers behind the doors of the king's palace. While later re-imaginings of the Persian royal household may not necessarily make explicit reference to Xerxes himself, fictional narratives far removed in time from the events of the fifth century BC nonetheless bear the traces of the archetypal story-patterns and images first associated with Xerxes in the Greek imagination.

Two such literary genres in which the ongoing influence of these traditions can be clearly detected in a much later period are Greek prose fiction and *ekphrasis*-writing.

The Greek novel – narrative fiction written in prose, of which several complete examples and many more fragmentary texts have survived – is a creation of the late Hellenistic or early imperial Roman period; romantic love forms the basis of its plots, in which the protagonists usually undergo a series of trials and adventures, often set in far-flung locations in a largely imagined Greek past, before their eventual reunion.[71] The earliest extant work in this genre, Chariton's *Chaereas and Callirhoe*, dates probably to the late first or early second century AD.[72] Its geographical starting-point is Syracuse in the late fifth century BC, but the action takes the protagonists to Miletus and from there to Babylon and the court of the Persian king Artaxerxes; it is here that royal power and sexual passion are combined in a manner reminiscent of the stories of Xerxes' romantic intrigues which were told by Herodotus. The king, called upon to arbitrate in a dispute between the beautiful Callirhoe's rival suitors, falls in love with her himself and contrives to make her his own; the chaste Callirhoe, however, fends off his advances. War intervenes in his romantic plans when he is forced to mobilize his troops to put down a rebellion among his Egyptian subjects. The king's overwhelming desire for Callirhoe is a key focus of the reader's attention in the latter part of the novel; he lies awake at night thinking of her (6.1.8, 6.7.1), contrives to visit the women's quarters more often than usual so that he might see her (5.9.7, 6.1.7) and weeps when he confesses his desires to his trusted advisor (6.3.3), whom he charges with attempting to bring Callirhoe to him.

While in Chariton's novel the image of the all-powerful Great King brought to his knees by the power of Eros plays upon a stereotyped view of the Persian monarch as being driven by his desire for pleasure,[73] the incidental details concerning the Persian court are also the literary descendants of earlier narratives which focus on the king's household. The king's most trusted

---

[71] Reardon (1989), pp. 1–16 provides an introduction to the genre; see also Swain (1996), pp. 101–31 for a discussion of the ways in which novels relate to the wider preoccupations of Greek society and culture during the Second Sophistic. On the novels' use of exotic locations see Bowersock (1994), pp. 29–53. Romm (2008), pp. 112–14 looks at the use of the Achaemenid Persian empire as a setting for the action in some of the stories.

[72] On the dating of the novels, and for bibliographic details of scholarly discussions, see Swain (1996), pp. 423–4.

[73] The novel also places a stress more generally on the cultural superiority of Greeks over barbarians: see E. L. Bowie (1991), pp. 188–92 and Bowersock (1994), pp. 41–2. On the way in which Chariton's novel reflects a popular image of Persia (rather than precise historical 'reality') and the range of sources which can be seen to have inspired this see Baslez (1992).

advisor, Artaxates, is a eunuch; he acts as Artaxerxes' confidante and is entrusted with the task of communicating with Callirhoe on the king's behalf (5.2.2–6; 5.3.10; 6.2.2–3; 6.3.1; 6.4–8; 8.5.6–9).[74] The suggestion that Greeks are naturally superior to non-Greeks is also highlighted when Artaxates' mistaken assumption that persuading Callirhoe to accede to the king's requests will be an easy matter is explained on the grounds that he thinks 'like a eunuch, like a slave, like a barbarian' (6.4.10; cf. 6.5.10 where Artaxates, having been brought up under a powerful tyranny, is said to be unable to conceive of the fact that there is anything which is impossible either for the king or for himself). The king's wife, Stateira, also features in the story, although she bears little resemblance to the scheming and powerful females seen in the accounts of Ctesias.[75] Initially scornful of claims about Callirhoe's superior beauty (5.3.1–3) she comes to realize the irony of her position as her husband too becomes smitten with Callirhoe. Elsewhere in the novel, however, descriptive elements apparently draw upon the Greek vision of the Persian royal household. At the court scene, for example, we see Artaxerxes enthroned in a large and beautiful room, flanked by his friends (5.4.5); although elements of the trial relate more closely to the Roman world in which the novel was produced[76] the scene itself is reminiscent of the royal audience scenes familiar to us from Greek vase paintings and their counterparts in Persian sculpture. Meanwhile the Persian king's wealth and luxurious lifestyle are apparent throughout this part of the story. Artaxates, in attempting to console his master in his distress at being unable to woo Callirhoe, reminds him that, as king, he already has many beautiful things – gold, silver, clothing, horses, cities, peoples, and countless beautiful women, chief among them his wife Stateira – at his disposal, and that such power is worth more than love (6.3.4).[77] Subsequently, in an attempt to distract the king from his lovesickness, Artaxates persuades him to arrange a hunt; this affords the author another opportunity to draw a picture of the king's lavish lifestyle as we see him dressed in a cloak of Tyrian purple and a tiara dyed the colour of hyacinths, carrying a sword of gold, a costly bow and

---

[74] See also 5.9.10 where it is clear that he is one of several eunuchs; it is the eunuchs who bring Callirhoe to the queen in the women's quarters.

[75] We might compare here the character of Arsace, sister of the Persian king and wife of the satrap Oroondates in Heliodorus' *Aethiopica* (*Theagenes and Charicleia*). She fits the profile of the stereotyped scheming and powerful oriental female more closely; lustful and conniving she desires the novel's hero Theagenes and plots ruthlessly against his beloved, the chaste Charicleia. See Hägg (1983), pp. 54–73 for a discussion of the *Aethiopica*. Anderson (1984), p. 48 notes the Herodotean texture of this novel; see also Romm (2008), p. 114.

[76] Schwartz (2003), pp. 382–5.

[77] In language characteristic of Greek representations of the Persian king the Greek text here describes Artaxerxes as one 'to whom all beautiful things are enslaved' (ᾧ τὰ καλὰ πάντα δουλεύει).

quiver, and mounted on a magnificent horse whose trappings are also made of gold. In a list which calls to mind the insights which Herodotus provides into Xerxes' extravagant lifestyle even while conducting military action we are also given a glimpse of the elaborate royal entourage which accompanies the king in his campaign against the Egyptians, as our narrator tells us that the custom for Persian king and nobles is to take with them 'wives and children and gold and silver and clothing and eunuchs and concubines and tables and costly wealth and luxury' (6.9.6).

That Chariton, despite his novel's focus on a king other than Xerxes, was conscious of the broader tradition of Greek resistance to Persia in the now-distant past, is clear from his fictional hero's deployment of that tradition. Chaereas, in joining the Egyptian forces fighting the Persian king, distinguishes himself as the Egyptians lay siege to Tyre. He seeks out 300 Greek mercenaries among the Egyptian king's army and, in order to inspire them with courage, addresses them in words reminiscent of Xenophon's speech to the Greek mercenaries in his *Anabasis* (see p. 118). Despite the fact that they are only 300 in number, Chaereas says, 'the same number of Greeks resisted Xerxes at Thermopylae' (7.3.9); and yet there are far fewer Tyrians than there were soldiers in Xerxes' army.[78] Thus the Persian Wars tradition continues to resonate as a rhetorical theme, yet Chariton's novel as a whole, in its creation of an imaginative and escapist fantasy, is concerned more with the domestic arrangements of the Persian royal household than with the details of the military campaign.

These images of the Persian court also find their way into a later imagined narrative of a different genre, yet one which shares with the ancient novel an interest in the exotic and unusual.[79] Philostratus' *Imagines*, dating from the first half of the third century AD[80] and drawing on a long literary tradition of *ekphrasis*-writing, are a series of 65 vivid descriptions in Greek of paintings supposedly in a gallery near Naples.[81] Composed in an era when Greek writers working under the Roman empire chose to assert their Hellenic identity

---

[78] Cf. 6.7.10 where Callirhoe, in defending Chaereas' honour, asserts that he is the foremost man in Syracuse, a city which even the Athenians – who 'defeated your Great King at Marathon and Salamis' – could not defeat. The conflation of all Persian kings into one single transhistorical Great King here is similar to that seen in some of the Athenian oratory of the fourth century BC; see above, pp. 105–6 and 110–11.

[79] Note Reardon (1974) on the relationship of the Greek novel to 'sophistic' literature.

[80] E. L. Bowie (2009) summarizes the evidence for Philostratus' life and the corpus of work attributed to him; on Philostratus and Hellenism see also Swain (1996), pp. 380–400.

[81] On the *Imagines* and literary *ekphrasis* see Anderson (1986), pp. 259–82 Webb (2009), pp. 187–90. Anderson (1986), pp. 277–8 n. 4 has a summary of the bibliography relating to the debate concerning whether the paintings described are real or imaginary.

through recourse to the themes and stylistic literary conventions of the past,[82] the *Imagines* draw upon a range of subjects taken from Greek history and myth, and include among their number one whose subject is an imagined picture of Themistocles at the Persian court (2.31). During the period in which Philostratus was writing, topics relating to the Persian Wars were a favourite theme for declamatory oratory,[83] so much so that Lucian, in his *Rhetorum Praeceptor* (18), was able to satirize the overuse of the Persian Wars traditions in declamation and to mock those speakers who employed clichéd hyperbole regarding episodes from this period of history.[84] Elsewhere, in his *Lives of the Sophists*, Philostratus' own work bears witness to his familiarity with the rhetorical use of the Persian Wars. For example, he mentions Scopelian of Clazomenae's enactment of speeches involving Darius and Xerxes, and his ability to convey 'the character of the barbarians' (*VS* 519–20); he later cites Polemo as saying that it is impossible for one who lives on a cheap diet to convey accurately the pride of Darius and Xerxes (*VS* 541);[85] and in listing the oratorical roles spoken by Alexander Peloplaton he includes that of the man who advised Darius to bridge the Danube and the part of Artabazus (i.e. Artabanus) trying to dissuade Xerxes from making a second expedition against Greece (*VS* 575).[86]

That Philostratus chose the image of Themistocles at the court of the Persian king as the subject of one of his descriptions perhaps attests to his familiarity with the broader theme of Greek-Persian relations, yet the tableau he describes is also particularly well-suited to a genre in which visual description is a crucial

---

[82] On Greek writers' recourse to the past during the 'Second Sophistic' (itself a term coined by Philostratus in his *Lives of the Sophists*) see especially E. L. Bowie (1974), Swain (1996), pp. 65–100 and Anderson (1993), pp. 101–32. Whitmarsh (2005), pp. 1–22 provides an introduction to the Second Sophistic.

[83] See Swain (1993), pp. 92–4 on historical themes in oratory of the Second Sophistic.

[84] The most extensive surviving Greek oratorical use of the theme from the period is that seen in Aelius Aristides' second-century AD *Panathenaicus*, a consciously archaizing piece of rhetorical panegyric in praise of Athens which takes elements of the rhetorical traditions of fourth-century BC Athens (on which see pp. 100–112). Here Aristides gives an extended narrative of the Persian Wars which features a well-worn image of Xerxes which focuses on his excesses and his *hybris* (*Panathenaicus* 115–124). See Oliver (1968) for a discussion of the text.

[85] Schmitz (1999) explores this theatrical aspect of sophistic declamations.

[86] The Persian Wars were also a theme for declamatory oratory in Latin, on which see pp. 164–70. The longevity of the Xerxes-theme in Greek oratory is attested by an oration attributed to Himerius (*Oration* 5) as late as the fourth century AD, which imagines a situation after the Persian Wars in which the Athenians vote for a war against the barbarians. The king promises to restore the damage of his earlier invasion if they put a stop to this; the text, which features references to Xerxes' bridge of boats and Athos canal, imagines a debate among the Athenians and plays with the idea that Xerxes tries to undermine what he failed to conquer during his expedition by dividing opinion among the Athenians. See Anderson (1993), pp. 61–2.

element.[87] While the question of precisely which king Themistocles visited is disputed by the ancient evidence (see p. 137 with n. 40), and elsewhere Philostratus suggests that it was Artaxerxes rather than Xerxes to whom he fled after his expulsion from Athens (*Life of Apollonius* 1.29), this particular *ekphrasis* nonetheless draws upon elements of the literary vision of the royal court seen in the Xerxes-tradition too.[88] His Themistocles is conceived of as a virtuous Greek among barbarians, 'a man among those who are not men', and the imagery employed draws a contrast between the simple appearance of the Athenian exile and the luxurious surroundings in which the king is ensconced. The setting of the Persian court affords Philostratus the opportunity to create a feast for the senses as he imagines the king, seated upon a golden throne and tattooed, 'like a peacock'(οἷον ταώς), perhaps the most ostentatious and colourful of birds.[89] Wearing a tiara and fine clothing embroidered with images of wild animals and golden thread, the king is attended by eunuchs in a palace rendered by the painter as being made of gold.[90] The description not only plays with the visual impact of the scene but also appeals to our sense of smell, as the air is heavy with the scent of frankincense and myrrh with which the barbarians 'pollute the freedom of the air'; the choice of phrasing here is suggestive of a rhetorical tradition in which Persians continue to be envisaged as enslavers and oppressors. Meanwhile Themistocles – while being admired by the king's spearmen – remains unmoved by his surroundings and, in the Median language which he has recently learned, speaks to the king of his services to Xerxes while he was in command of the Greek forces;[91] the reference perhaps harks back to the story told by Herodotus (8.109–110) that Themistocles – with a view to his

---

[87] We might also compare here Philostratus' *Life of Apollonius* (1.25) in which the sage Apollonius visits the king of Babylon, whose palace is richly decorated and adorned with tapestries featuring scenes from Greek mythology and the Persian Wars, including Xerxes' Hellespont bridge and the Athos canal. After a dream in which he imagined himself as Artaxerxes the king declares that his visitor is a latter-day Themistocles (1.29).

[88] Elsewhere Philostratus chose another Persian theme for one of his paintings: *Imagines* 2.9 focuses on the figure of Panthea, whose story features in Xenophon's *Cyropaedia* (see p. 115 n. 44).

[89] Dubel (2009) p. 314, with n. 18 notes that rich colouring, here and elsewhere in the *Imagines*, is associated with oriental exoticism.

[90] The association of the Persian king with gold can be traced as far back as Aeschylus' and Herodotus' depictions of Xerxes; see above, p. 55, with n. 26.

[91] See Gera (2007) pp. 455–6 on the relationship of Philostratus' text to Thucydides' report of Themistocles' acquisition of the Persian language; she suggests that Philostratus reworks the story in such a way that his Themistocles uses the language as a way of conveying his superior Greek values to the Persians. We might compare here Diodorus' version (see above, pp. 137–9) and that in Plutarch's *Life of Themistocles*, in which the exiled Athenian is redeemed as a patriot by his suicide after extracting a promise from the Persian king that he will not invade Greece without him (see below, pp. 183–5 for further discussion of Plutarch's text).

own future exile at the king's court – persuaded the Athenians not to destroy Xerxes' bridges but to allow the Persian fleet to make their escape after Salamis.

Philostratus' image of Themistocles' audience with the Persian king thus crystallizes into one concise description a long-enduring tradition in which the focus is not upon the king's military action but instead upon the atmosphere and appearance of the royal court.[92] The resulting tableau combines a series of familiar elements associated with the king's palace and audience scenes in both literature and art to create a vision of his surroundings which are colourful both literally and metaphorically. Meanwhile the vision of Persian extravagance is contrasted with Greek simplicity, as represented here by the person of Themistocles.[93] Philostratus' text bears witness to a continuing fascination with the apparently outlandish nature of the Achaemenid court long after Ctesias first sought to examine the political machinations of that court for the entertainment of his own Greek audience. In doing so it provides Philostratus' readers with the opportunity to view – like Themistocles – the interior of the royal palace and allows us voyeuristic access to the exotic and intriguing world which had fired the imagination of so many writers. While these strands of the Xerxes-tradition were enjoying their own varied afterlife, however, tales associated with events outside the court setting, and relating to the invasion of Greece, were still going strong; my final chapter will explore the diverse directions in which both Greek and Roman writers would take the theme of Xerxes' military expedition.

---

[92] A different type of prose (fiction/text), the 'epistolary novel', also took as its inspiration Themistocles' relationship with the Persian monarchy. The *Letters of Themistocles*, a historical novel consisting of the exiled Athenian's imaginary correspondence, survives only in a manuscript dating from the ninth or tenth century AD but may have been composed in the first or second century. See Lenardon (1978), pp. 154–93 and the edition of Doenges (1981).

[93] See Allen (2005), p. 56, suggesting too that 'the conventional themes of Greek austerity and cleverness are contrasted with Persian luxury and complacency'.

7. *Xerxes' return to Persia.* Adapted from a lithograph illustrating Jacob Abbott's *History of Xerxes the Great* (1878)

6

The Past as a Paradigm: Xerxes in a World Ruled by Rome

The return of Xerxes from Greece, bereft of his massive army and with only the feeble remnants of his navy to escort him (Plate 7), offers a view of his mission which contrasts starkly with the impression created by the stories of his magnificent advance across the Hellespont at the beginning of his expedition. In literature of the Roman period, however, the image of the terrifying despot who invaded Greece could coexist with that of the vanquished enemy who was driven back to Persia humiliated and stripped of his grandeur. A whole swathe of texts written in both Greek and Latin during the era when Rome was now the dominant power in the Mediterranean world demonstrate the continuing appeal of the Xerxes-tradition; these works of literature, despite their differences in genre and authorial perspective, their geographically disparate origins and the broad chronological span across which they were created, are united by an awareness that the stories surrounding the Persian king from the now-distant past could continue to be used to draw lessons which were applicable in their own societies. In a world ruled by Rome the elasticity of the theme of Xerxes' invasion – overtly acknowledged by some writers of the period to be a literary commonplace – thus became more apparent than ever before.

The reuse of the figure of Xerxes as an exemplum in this period sits within the broader context of the Romans' appropriation of the Persian Wars traditions in the service of their own political propaganda. This chapter will consider the literary and political context of allusions to Xerxes in the Roman world before examining in detail the Persian king's role as a moral paradigm. This use of Xerxes' image is seen most clearly in texts originating in the rhetorical schools at Rome, and particularly in the works of the Elder Seneca which incorporate familiar aspects of the king's persona as fearsome invader alongside reflections upon the elements of his story which draw attention to the theme of

the mutability of human fortune. These two elements of the Xerxes-tradition
are also recurring features in the anecdotes and moral exempla collected by
Valerius Maximus. From writers' extraction of these more general lessons we
move to thinking about the way in which Xerxes could be used as a point of
comparison for specific individuals, most notably the emperor Caligula, who
would himself come to be seen as a stereotypical tyrant in the hostile historiographical tradition. The Roman period also brings us a reminder, however, that
the dominant negative view of Xerxes was not one which held true from the
viewpoint of every commentator; the work of Josephus, written from a Jewish
perspective, casts the king instead in a favourable light, as pious and respectful
of the Jewish people. Nonetheless, the prevailing verdict on Xerxes remains a
disparaging one; this is seen too in the writing of subject Greeks, whose texts
show that the memory of their ancestors' glorious victory had not yet faded.
Indeed the Xerxes-image could be put to politically subversive use; some writers,
such as Pausanias, would use it as a point of comparison for the behaviour of
their contemporary Roman masters. An awareness of this subversive potential
seems to have informed Plutarch's cautious treatment of the Xerxes-traditions;
wary of using allusions to the Persian Wars in contexts which might inflame
anti-Roman sentiment, he emerges as having taken a more considered approach
to the recollection of this era of the Greeks' past. This chapter will conclude with
a discussion of Juvenal's satirical take on the Persian king, which – as one of the
latest ancient literary treatments discussed in the volume – encapsulates neatly
some of the manifold ways in which Xerxes was appropriated in the Roman
period.

Xerxes' invasion as a literary commonplace

Just as in the fourth century BC the Athenian orators had come to realize that
Xerxes needed no introduction, and that his exploits against the Greeks were an
easily employable theme for their rhetoric (see pp. 100–112), so too texts written
in Latin demonstrate a recognition that the Persian king was a well-known, and
for some overused, subject for literature. By the first century BC Propertius,
outlining to Maecenas his reasons for writing love poetry, could comment
that if his Muse would let him sing of wars he would choose as his subject
Caesar's glory rather than any of the stock themes for such poetry – Titans
fighting gods, tales of Thebes and Troy, 'two seas joined at Xerxes' command',
Remus or Carthage (*Elegy* 2.1.17–26). Similarly, early in the first century AD

the writer Manilius, in explaining the choice of theme for his didactic poem on the stars, wrote that he would not base his work on familiar subjects such as the Trojan War, the Seven against Thebes, Oedipus or Alexander the Great. Nor, he wrote, would he tell of 'the Persian declaration of war upon the deep, when the sea was hidden by a vast fleet, a channel was let into the land, and a road made on the waves of the sea' (*Astronomica* 3.19–21).[1] The throwaway allusions to the bridging of the Hellespont or the Athos canal in lists of what the poets deem to be literary commonplaces, with the attendant assumption that their readers needed no further explanation of the context, indicates that the stories relating to Xerxes' invasion of Greece had by this time penetrated the consciousness of a society far removed from the historical events themselves.[2] Although the political landscape of the Mediterranean had been transformed by the progression of Roman domination, traditions relating to Xerxes' invasion of Greece would endure in literature written in Rome itself as well as in works penned by Greek writers in the Hellenic portion of the empire.

Roman familiarity with the events of the Persian Wars formed part of a broader trend in which Rome's territorial expansion into the eastern Mediterranean – and the cultural contacts forged through war and systems of patronage – had brought with it an increasing awareness of Greek history, literature and culture.[3] It was in this context that Xerxes' expedition to Greece came to find its way into the Roman psyche as one of the many themes (along with, for example, the Trojan War and the exploits of Alexander the Great) of the literature which learned Romans assimilated into their own culture. Though it might serve as a source of inspiration for students of oratory or composers of biography, however, the theme of Greece's moment of glory in resisting the Persian onslaught could never carry for Romans the same emotional resonance which it continued to hold for the Greeks; Propertius' comment to Maecenas suggested that Roman military excellence was a subject more worthy of attention than anything which the Greeks had achieved in this field, and the fact that Rome had conquered Greece rendered redundant any possibility

---

[1] The Latin authors' reflections upon Xerxes' invasion as a hackneyed topic had a parallel in the Greek work of Lucian: see above, p. 152. The recognition of the triteness of the Persian Wars as a theme for Latin literature had surprising longevity: as late as the fifth century AD the Gallo-Roman poet Sidonius, in his poem *To Felix* (9.38–49), asserted that he intended to avoid the old clichés, including tales of Marathon as well as Xerxes' vast army which drank rivers dry, his crossing of the Hellespont and the Athos canal.

[2] Allusions to Persians in Roman literature often assume that the reader knows something of the background to the reference, without needing further explanation: Rosivach (1984) examines several such examples.

[3] The influence of Greek culture upon Rome is examined in depth by Wardman (1976); see in particular Chapter 4 on Greek history and historians at Rome. See also Gruen (1992).

that Greece might still lay claim to pre-eminent military prowess. While the Romans assimilated Greek culture and literary style it seems that the tendency to vaunt Rome's military superiority in this way was an enduring one. In his second-century AD *Epitome* of Roman history, for example, Florus pointed out that the Athenians need not be too boastful about their own past, reminding his readers of the Romans' Syrian war against king Antiochus and declaring that this conflict was more formidable than those of the Greeks against Darius and Xerxes, when 'impassable mountains were said to have been dug through and the sea covered with sails' (1.24.2–3); he asserts that in Antiochus the Romans had defeated their Xerxes and declares that at Ephesus the Romans fought their own Salamis (1.24.13).[4]

Roman political propaganda and the Persian Wars tradition

Despite such belittlement of the achievements which Greeks still perceived as representing their finest hour, Romans were able to recognize the potential of the story of Greek resistance to Persia as a theme for their own political propaganda. Even in the early stages of Rome's domination of Greece an awareness of Greek historical sensitivities had been necessary on the part of the ruling power. Flamininus, after his victory over the Macedonians under Philip V at Cynoscephalae in 197 BC – an event which was decisive in the Romans' conquest of Greece[5] – had announced at the Isthmian Games of 196 BC that the Greeks were now to be 'free, ungarrisoned, without tribute and free to govern themselves in accordance with their own ancestral laws' (Polybius 18.46.5).[6] Such appeals to Greek freedom echoed the propaganda touted by Hellenistic rulers in the struggles for power following the death of Alexander,[7] yet the origins of the emotional weight of such rhetoric can be traced back to the

---

[4] The fact that one of the battles in which the Romans defeated Antiochus, after his invasion of Greece, took place at Thermopylae (in 191 BC) might naturally suggest a comparison with the Persian Wars. The comparison of the naval engagement at Ephesus with Salamis is hyperbolic, however. Appian's version of events presents this as a defeat for the Roman force (*Syrian Wars* 24); see Spawforth (1994), p. 243.

[5] For an overview of Rome's political relationship with Greece in the Republican period see Gruen (2004).

[6] The event is also described by Plutarch in his *Life of Flamininus*, 10.3–5. For the view that during the second Macedonian War Flamininus sought to compare the Macedonian threat to Greek freedom with that posed earlier by Persia see Ferrary (1988), p. 86.

[7] Gruen (1984), pp. 132–57 charts the diplomatic use of slogans relating to the 'freedom of the Greeks' in the Hellenistic and Roman period. For a broader survey which traces the use of these slogans back to the fifth century BC see Dmitriev (2011).

Persian Wars in their status as struggles to retain Hellenic liberty in the face of the threat of Persian enslavement. Such a connection seems to have been made by Alcaeus of Messene in an epigram which contrasted Flamininus, as liberator of the Greeks from the Macedonian threat, with Xerxes, the enslaver of the past (*Anth. Pal.* 16.5).[8]

It was in relation to one aspect of Roman foreign policy in particular, however, that the theme of the Persian Wars acquired particular contemporary resonance. During the later republican and imperial periods the monarchy of Parthia, homeland of the ancient Persians, continued to resist Roman domination; in the Roman imagination Parthian resistance came to be equated with the fifth-century BC Achaemenid invasions of Greece.[9] As early as 57 BC Cicero had referred to the Parthians as *Persae* (*De domo sua* 60); the comparison continued to be made in Latin literature, with Horace in particular repeatedly referring in his *Odes* to anti-Parthian campaigns and describing the enemy as 'Medes' or 'Persians' rather than as Parthians.[10] The theme of Greek resistance to Persia also provided the Roman imperial administration with the opportunity for some spectacular re-enactments of key events from the historical narrative. In 2 BC, for example, Augustus staged a *naumachia*, a mock naval battle, in a specially excavated site by the Tiber; Cassius Dio (55.10.7–8) writes that the opposing sides were called 'Athenians' and 'Persians' and that, as in the past, on this occasion too the Athenians were victorious.[11] In light of Augustus' propaganda relating to his recovery, by diplomacy in 19 BC, of the Roman legionary standards captured by the Parthians at the battle of Carrhae in 53 BC,[12] the *naumachia* might well have been staged as a means of asserting on a grand scale the link between the Parthian enemy and the Persians against whom the Greeks fought in the past; Ovid (*Ars Amatoria* 1.171–84) relates the show to his own panegyric of Gaius Caesar, grandson and adopted son of Augustus, on the eve of his departure for a new eastern expedition, and warns that the Romans

---

[8] Dmitriev (2011), p. 159 suggests that Alcaeus' epigram may have been composed in response to Greeks who thought of Flamininus and the Romans as 'just another group of foreign invaders'.

[9] Spawforth (1994), pp. 238–40 documents the instances for which there is evidence of occasions upon which Parthians were apparently presented in imperial propaganda as the reincarnation of Persians. He includes in the list Caligula's bridge of boats in the Bay of Naples in AD 39; this is discussed in more detail below (pp. 171–3).

[10] As noted by Campbell (1924), p. 104 and p. 110. Hardie (2007), pp. 139–41 discusses Horace's equations of Parthians with barbarians, listing the relevant textual references at n. 45. For a list of references to other authors who refer to Parthians as 'Persians' see Rosivach (1984), p. 3 n. 2.

[11] Coleman (1993) discusses the use of elaborate aquatic spectacles, which were themed upon a variety of historical and mythological topics, as a part of imperial propaganda.

[12] See H. I. Flower (2000), pp. 56–8.

will conquer the east and thereby be avenged against the Parthians.[13] The theme
was later reused by Nero in his own *naumachia* of AD 57 or 58 when, Cassius
Dio writes (61.9.5), this emperor flooded a theatre and stocked it with fish
and other marine creatures; he then enacted a naval battle of 'Athenians versus
Persians'; this too coincided with the launching of a war in the east, this time in
Armenia.[14]

While on one level such dramatic spectacles were staged as a form of entertainment for Roman citizens, the messages which they carried also performed
an important role in a programme of imperial propaganda. The association of
the Parthians with the Greeks' historic enemies not only provided the Romans
with an illustrious model for their contemporary military exploits – one
which they might strive to emulate and indeed outdo – but could also act as
a powerful tool in forging and cementing a relationship with the Greeks who
were now their subjects. By reusing the symbolism of the Persian Wars in order
to align the Parthians with the Persians, Rome could implicitly style herself
not as Greece's conqueror but as her defender against a new eastern threat.[15] It
seems that some Greeks at least accepted this official rhetoric; in AD 61/2, while
his generals were still waging war with Parthia over control of Armenia, the
emperor Nero was honoured at Athens with an inscription on the Parthenon,[16]
itself a monument to Athens' resistance to Persia (as well as being a reminder
of the Persians' sacrilege on the site) and surrounded on the Acropolis with
trophies relating to the Athenians' historic victory.[17] That a Roman emperor
could be publicly commemorated in this way by a Greek state suggests that the
Athenians too had bought in to the Romans' casting of themselves in the role of
protectors of Greece against the contemporary threat from the east.[18]

---

[13] See Bowersock (1990), p. 175, Spawforth (1994), pp. 240–1 and Hardie (2007), p. 129, the latter
noting that although the official propaganda presented this as a military campaign of conquest,
'the reality was a far less heroic diplomatic settlement'. Zanker (1988), p. 84 suggests that the
spectacle was intended to draw a parallel between Actium – Augustus' own naval victory over the
eastern threat represented by Antony and Cleopatra – and the Athenian victory over the Persians at
Salamis. Pelling (1988), p. 282 and p. 305 suggests that Plutarch drew attention to parallels between
the two battles in his *Life* of Antony.

[14] Spawforth (1994), p. 238.

[15] The Roman image of Parthia as the external enemy should also be seen within the broader context
of the way in which the notion of 'barbarism' came to be constructed in Roman society. This is
explored in depth by Dauge (1981).

[16] *IG* II² 3277 = Sherk (1988), no. 78. The inscription is analysed in detail by Carroll (1982).

[17] See Carroll (1982), pp. 65–74 for an analysis of the associations between the Acropolis and the
resistance to the Persian threat. His assertion that the dedication to Nero drew a clear link between
the emperor's eastern campaign and the fifth-century Persian Wars is also discussed and endorsed
by Spawforth (1994), pp. 234–7.

[18] An Athenian inscription hailing Julius Nicanor as the 'new Themistocles' when he bought back
the island of Salamis for Athens demonstrates too that it was possible for Romans to be viewed as
'honorary Greeks'; it was a high honour to be associated with the hero of Salamis. On the identity

Xerxes as exemplum

The inclination to draw comparisons between events from the past and those of the present was related to the far-reaching assumption in Roman thought that historical actions and individuals could provide educative moral paradigms.[19] By examining the deeds of those who had gone before, and by arriving at ethical judgements on their actions, it was understood to be possible to provide models for good behaviour which Romans might aspire to emulate as well as examples of the kind of conduct which ought to be avoided.[20] As represented in the Latin tradition by the surviving works of Cornelius Nepos, written in the first century BC, this type of exemplary discourse was perhaps most evident in the genre of biography, by means of which the lives of famous individuals from the past could be used as a way of exploring questions of contemporary relevance.[21] Although his corpus as a whole included many more Roman examples, the extant text of Nepos' work, which is based upon Greek sources including Thucydides,[22] deals primarily with Greek leaders from the fifth and fourth centuries BC, including those famed for their role in the Persian Wars: Aristides, Themistocles and Pausanias. Apparently for Nepos Xerxes himself was of little intrinsic interest, however, and the biographer of illustrious Greeks saw no need to embellish or manipulate the stories which he had inherited from his sources, yet the texts are of interest for the way in which they demonstrate how a somewhat static picture of the king had filtered through to Roman writers. In a manner not dissimilar to that of the Athenian orators Nepos' accounts abridge the traditions into the

---

of Nicanor and the circumstances of the dedication, see Jones (1978), pp. 222–8. The date of the episode is disputed, its having taken place either during the reign of Augustus (preferred by Jones), or in AD 61/2.

[19] The sentiment that the provision of moral examples is the primary function of historical writing is one expressed by Tacitus at *Annals* 3.65. Note that exemplarity was not a mode of thought which had been invented by the Romans (see, for example, Skidmore (1996), pp. 3–12 on the Greeks' use of examples – *paradeigmata* – for moral instruction); its pervasive influence upon Roman literature is, however, unparalleled in Greek texts.

[20] It is in Livy's narrative of Roman history that we see the most self-conscious attention to exemplarity in a historiographical text: see Champlin (2000), pp. 1–31 for a discussion of his articulation of exempla. Roller (2004) sets out a clear theoretical framework for the way in which exemplary discourse functions in Roman culture. See also Bell (2008) and Barchiesi (2009). Kraus (2005), pp. 191–8 examines the way in which, under the imperial regime, the notion of continuous historical narrative as a way of constructing exempla gave way to more disjointed collections of anecdotes – such as those gathered by Valerius Maximus – which could be combined and interpreted in different ways.

[21] Dionisotti (1988) suggests that Nepos used his lives of famous figures from the past as a way of commenting on contemporary politics, in particular in order to consider the issue of the way in which successful military leaders might acquire power. Nepos also wrote a collection of *Exempla*, which is now lost: Wiseman (1979), p. 38 with n. 60. The most recent comprehensive discussion of Nepos' corpus is that of Rex Stem (2012).

[22] Jenkinson (1973), pp. 713–14, drawing attention to the historical inaccuracies of Nepos' accounts.

concise format which his genre demands; there is no place here, for example, for elaborate analysis of Xerxes' decision-making process, or of the course of the invasion, such as that given by Herodotus. Xerxes appears in Nepos' *Life of Themistocles* with a military force described as being larger than any seen before or since – the author briefly gives numbers for his land and sea forces[23] – and, in an abbreviated assessment of his motivation, is said to have attacked Athens 'because of the battle of Marathon' (2.2.4–66). After Thermopylae the king marches upon an empty Athens, massacres the priests on the Acropolis and sets fire to the city (2.3.1); Nepos then outlines Themistocles' execution of his plan to force Xerxes' fleet to fight in the narrows at Salamis and the scheme by which he subsequently tricked Xerxes into believing that his Hellespont bridge was about to be destroyed and thereby convinced him to flee from Greece (2.4.3–2.5.2).[24] Ultimately the story of the invasion is used here – as in Plutarch's later Greek biography of Themistocles (see pp. 183–5) – as a means of emphasizing the Athenian naval commander's own intelligence and the significance of his actions in freeing Greece from the Persian threat (2.5.3).[25] The treatment of Xerxes in Nepos' brief *Life of Pausanias*, meanwhile, is incidental to the focus of the biography, which features a straightforward abridgement of Thucydides' account of Pausanias' approach to the king requesting a personal alliance (4.2.2–6; cf. Thuc. 1.128–9, with p. 137 n. 40 above).

If Roman biography was more interested in the exposition of positive role models than in elaborating upon the image of a villain from a bygone era, it is to the rhetorical schools at Rome where we might turn for insight into the ways in which stories from the past concerning bad behaviour could be used to provide moral guidance. Writers of practice declamations might seek inspiration in historical events and adapt these as a way for speakers to hone their oratorical skills; at the same time lessons could be derived not only from the virtuous exempla provided by the heroes of the past but also from the immoral acts of those renowned more for their villainy than their virtue. That the Persian Wars could act as a suitable backdrop for such exercises is apparent from the

---

[23] Cf. Nepos' *Life of Miltiades*, in which he emphasizes the contrast between the size of the Persian force and that of the Athenians at Marathon (1.4.1, 1.4.5, 1.5. 3–5).

[24] Cf. Herodotus 8.60, 8.75. In Herodotus' account Themistocles actually sends a message to Xerxes to the effect that he has persuaded the Greeks *not* to destroy the Hellespont bridges in order to allow the Persians a safe passage home: Herodotus cites as Themistocles' motive his desire to gain Xerxes' favour so that he could flee to Persia in future (8.109–110). Stories of Themistocles' tactical aptitude – by which he is shown to have defeated Xerxes' superior military might – also feature in Frontinus' first-century AD manual on Greek and Roman military stratagems (2.2.14, 2.6.8).

[25] Nepos follows Thucydides in having Themistocles flee later to the court of Artaxerxes, rather than to the court of Xerxes as in Diodorus' account (see above, pp. 137–9).

writings of the elder Seneca (c. 55 BC–c. AD 40).[26] Two of his seven surviving
suasoriae – exercises in deliberative oratory – use fictitious scenarios relating
to Xerxes' invasion of Greece. One (*Suas.* 2) imagines a debate among the 300
Spartans at Thermopylae as to whether they should retreat or stand up and
fight; another (*Suas.* 5) envisages a situation in which Xerxes has threatened to
return to Greece unless the Athenians take down the trophies commemorating
their victory over the Persians. These oratorical reworkings feature a Xerxes
described as *insolens barbarus* ('arrogant barbarian', 2.7, 2.22) and select familiar
elements of the king's image such as the size of his army (2.1, 2.7–8, 5.1), or the
Hellespont bridge and Athos canal and his attempt to enslave the sea (2.3, 5.4,
5.7).

Among the familiar symbols and themes of Seneca's rhetorical descriptions
of Xerxes and his invasion of Greece it is also possible to identify moralizing
strands which can be related to the tradition of exemplarity at Rome. While
these reflections on the moral issues raised by Xerxes' actions are not developed
at length and appear as being incidental to the main function of Seneca's
declamatory exercises the texts nonetheless offer an insight into some of the
ways in which this king, as the negative exemplum *par excellence*, might be used
by Romans as a means of thinking about questions of contemporary concern.
For example, Seneca's comments on the second *Suasoria* (2.17) highlight
one particular example of the way in which Xerxes might be used as a moral
yardstick. Here he relates the story of another Seneca (appropriately nicknamed
Seneca Grandio) who loved large things, and was mocked for his acquisition
of all things outsized, from his slaves and his silverware to his mistress. This
lover of excess is said to have enthused at the thought of declaiming on the
activities of Xerxes, whose fleet covered the ocean and who rearranged land
and sea; the unstated implication is one which equates moral overreaching with
self-indulgence. This particular theme was instrumental in shaping the way in
which Xerxes' actions came to be used as a point of comparison for the morally
questionable acts of notorious individuals in the Latin tradition (for specific
examples see below, pp. 170–3).

Meanwhile, Seneca's second *Suasoria* also touches upon the issue – a
favourite in the declamatory tradition, whose remote origins might be traced
in the Herodotean treatment of the theme (see pp. 64–6) – of the mutability of

---

[26] The Persian Wars seem to have been a common source of inspiration for such pieces: Cicero (*De
officiis* 1.61) commented that in his day the teachers of rhetoric drew upon Marathon, Salamis,
Plataea, Thermopylae and Leuctra for their exercises. On the use of historical themes (Roman as
well as Greek) in declamation at Rome see Bonner (1977), pp. 277–87.

human fortune, and illustrates the way in which references to Xerxes' actions might illuminate this moral theme. Here (2.3) one speaker, Triarius, argues that, despite the king's impressive feats of engineering (alluding to the Hellespont bridge and Athos canal), arrogant good fortune (*superba felicitas*) has no firm foundation, and that even great empires fall since humans are fallible; there is a suggestion here too that human prosperity arouses the envy of the gods. In the fifth *Suasoria*, in which the speakers debate whether to take down the Persian Wars trophies in order to prevent Xerxes from returning to Greece, the orator Arellius Fuscus emphasizes the king's dramatic reversal of fortune and the reduction of his vast army to a force barely able to escort him home,[27] recalling the heavy losses which he sustained during his invasion and contrasting his former arrogance with his imagined fearfulness and distress after his defeat by the Greeks (5.1–2, 5.5–6); the envisaging of Xerxes' reaction to the disaster at Salamis is part of a tradition stretching back to Aeschylus' *Persians*.[28] The notion of a contrast between Xerxes' ostentatious display and his demise was one upon which other Roman writers touched too; for Lucretius in his *De rerum natura* this formed part of a reflection not upon the failure of the expedition to Greece but instead upon the inevitability of death, even for powerful and famous men (3.1029–33). There is also evidence to suggest that this take on Xerxes' defeat was one which penetrated society beyond literary circles; an anonymous Greek drinking-song of the first century AD (*P.Oxy.* 15.795), whose stanzas begin with each successive letter of the alphabet, has for the stanza beginning with the letter 'xi' an arrogant Xerxes, 'the king who said he shared all things with Zeus' but who returned to Greece 'with a single rudder' (that is, with only one ship of his vast navy). The mention of Xerxes inspires a reflection on the transience of all worldly goods and a reminder that no one goes to Hades with more than an obol to his name.[29] The motif of the mutability of human fortune is one which perhaps has at its root Herodotus' exchange between Xerxes and Artabanus in

---

[27] This observation also surfaces in Justin's abridgement (of uncertain date) of Trogus' universal history (2.3.10) and was later adopted by Orosius in his early fifth-century AD *History Against the Pagans*; his description of Xerxes' invasion (2.10–8.10) appears to have relied heavily on Justin's account. A Greek version of the *topos* appears in Dio Chrysostom's discourse on covetousness (17.14).

[28] Hardie (2007), p. 135 considers ways in which the contrast between extravagant military ambition and the ignominy of defeat manifests itself in relation to other commanders in Roman literature.

[29] I am grateful to Bloomsbury's anonymous referee for bringing this text to my attention. See Page (1950), pp. 508–13 for the fragments and a translation. Note too that here Xerxes is also juxtaposed with a reference to Midas as a paradigmatic wealthy king; we see a similar juxtaposition of Midas and Xerxes in the exempla on wealth recorded by Valerius Maximus (1.6 ext. 1–3). The rhetorical motif of Xerxes' return from Greece with only a single ship is one which also appears in Josephus' work (*Jewish War* 2.358; see p. 174) and the *Satires* of Juvenal (10.185; see pp. 188–9).

which the king, having counted his troops at Abydus, weeps as he reflects upon the brevity of human life (7.45–7; see pp. 64–6). For the younger Pliny, writing a letter of condolence in the early second century AD, this story came to mind as a means of consoling its bereaved recipient with the reminder that death comes to all men (*Letters* 3.7.13).[30]

It is through the work of Valerius Maximus, a collection of anecdotes compiled in the first half of the first century AD,[31] that we gain an insight into the means by which such traditions might find their way into the texts of other writers. In his *Facta et dicta memorabilia* (*Memorable deeds and sayings*) he uses the episode of Xerxes' weeping for the transience of human existence in a section of his work designed to illustrate that the desire for death is sometimes both braver and wiser than the desire for life (9.13 pref.). Valerius asserts that, while the king appeared to weep for the situation of others, he was in fact lamenting his own lot; the writer suggests that this indicated that despite his great power Xerxes lacked sense, 'for what reasonably prudent person would weep that he was born mortal?' (9.13 ext. 1). This concise extraction of a moral point from a condensed version of a well-known story demonstrates the way in which, for Valerius, the habitual Roman use of exemplary discourse was instrumental in shaping his choice of material relating to Xerxes. His compilation of deeds and sayings functioned as both a handbook of anecdotes which could be used by rhetoricians and – as the preface announces – a set of exempla for the encouragement of virtue and the censure of vice, which might function as a means of moral instruction for Valerius' readers.[32] Organized thematically, each of the nine books features both Roman and 'foreign' (*externus*) examples.[33] Xerxes appears on several occasions in the 'foreign' sections and the text thus illustrates the range of themes upon which this negative paradigm might be

---

[30] For a discussion of the later presentation of the theme in the poetry of Juvenal, see pp. 188–9. In a much later Latin reference to Xerxes' weeping for the brevity of human life a letter of consolation written by Saint Jerome in AD 396 adduces the story as a reminder that all men must die (*Letters* 60.18).

[31] Little is known of Valerius' life. He dedicated his handbook of illustrative examples of 'memorable deeds and sayings' to the emperor Tiberius, and there are indications in the text that it was completed after the fall of the conspirator Sejanus in AD 31.

[32] On the use of Valerius' work as a source for declamation see Bloomer (1992), pp. 1–10; Skidmore (1996), pp. 53–82 critiques Bloomer's approach and argues that the true purpose of the text – as a means of inspiring virtuous conduct and moral excellence (*virtus*) and discouraging reprehensible behaviour (*vita*) in his readers – is obscured if we assume that it was merely a 'handbook' for rhetoricians. Note also Roller (2004), p. 32, suggesting that by 'grouping his narratives under ethical rubrics [Valerius makes it] clear that his work's concerns are, above all, moral'.

[33] See Lobur (2008), pp. 177–85 on Valerius' use of exempla and the organization of his material. Wardle (1998), p. 212 notes that the foreign examples seem to have been included for the sake of variety and the provision of material less familiar to the audience; see also Skidmore (1996), pp. 89–92 on the use of foreign examples.

used to shed light, as well as highlighting the continuing appeal, as a form of entertainment, of some of the more unusual anecdotes attached to the figure of the king. In his section on prodigies, for example, two Xerxes-related examples are given, one in which a mare gave birth to a hare while his army was en route to Greece (1.6 ext. 1a; cf. Herodotus 7.57) and a second in which wine turned into blood, interpreted by the magi as a warning against undertaking the invasion (1.6 ext. 1b).[34] The first of these occasions a reflection on the 'reversal of fortune' theme as Valerius observes that despite his vast army Xerxes was forced to flee Greece like a 'fugitive animal'; the second is used to make a point that the king, in his madness (*in vecordi pectore*) failed to heed warnings to desist from his mission.[35]

With very little embellishment these anecdotes thus call to mind a picture of the king as a stereotypical tyrant, bent on fulfilling his own destructive ambition and impervious to the advice of those around him; later the theme is revisited when Xerxes, in an example of 'arrogance and lack of restraint' (*de superbia et impotentia*) calls upon his advisors only to warn them that their function is not to advise but to obey, and thereby effects a pretence that he sought counsel prior to declaring war on Greece (9.5 ext. 2). We might contrast here Herodotus' detailed account of the process by which Xerxes arrived at the decision to invade Greece (discussed above, pp. 61–3). That such a story might be written up in a very different way, to make an ethical point on a separate issue is apparent, however, from the writing of the younger Seneca (c. 4 BC–AD 65). His moral treatise *De beneficiis* (*On benefits*) has Xerxes appear in an anecdote which might well strike a chord with elite Romans living under an imperial system in the first century AD,[36] and which was apparently designed to point a moral concerning the benefits conferred by telling the truth as opposed to false flattery; along the way he revisits a stereotyped image of Persian tyranny in which the monarch is fawned upon by his subordinates. Here (6.31.1–12) the king is seen being wholeheartedly encouraged in pursuit of the war against Greece by his sycophantic advisors, who urge him on by suggesting that the

---

[34] Although the first portent is related by Herodotus, there is no parallel for the second in extant literature: Wardle (1998), p. 213.

[35] Aelian's later *Varia Historia* (*Historical Miscellany*), a collection of moralizing anecdotes similar to those of Valerius Maximus but written in Greek during the early third century AD, also highlighted several stories relating to Xerxes. He elaborates upon the anecdote recalled by Herodotus in which Xerxes is said to have made offerings to a plane tree, citing this as an example of the king's absurd behaviour (2.14; cf. 9.38) and comments on the luxury and pretension of the king's supply train (12.40); he also records a story relating to Xerxes' violation of the sacred tomb of a Babylonian god (13.3; see p. 130).

[36] M. Griffin (2003) analyses the text's relationship with Roman social conduct.

vast size of his force will guarantee him victory.[37] Only the Spartan Demaratus warns him that the size of his army will ultimately work against him, and that the Spartans at Thermopylae, along with other Greeks, will not falter in their courage and steadfast defence. Seneca's rendering of Demaratus' perspective here apparently owes something to Herodotus' version, and may have been based upon the conversation between the Spartan and the king related by the historian (7.101–5, discussed above, pp. 61–3). Ultimately, Seneca tells us, things turned out as Demaratus had predicted and – in an addition to the story not present in Herodotus' account – the Spartan is rewarded by Xerxes for having been the only person to tell him the truth.[38]

Elsewhere for Valerius, Xerxes is an ideal example to feature in a section on luxury and lust, where he is reported as having published an edict offering a reward to anyone who discovered a new pleasure (9.1. ext. 3). The story is one which had been related earlier by Cicero, for whom Xerxes had also served as a paradigm of greed and excess (*Tusc.* 5.20).[39] We find Xerxes in Valerius' text too in his guise as a bringer of destruction and enslavement, removing from Athens the statues of Harmodius and Aristogeiton[40] – widely thought to be the city's liberators from tyranny (2.10 ext. 1) – and acting as a foil for Leonidas' bravery at Thermopylae (3.2 ext. 3). Here Valerius alludes to Xerxes' attempt to control the sea with chains – an allusion to Xerxes' Hellespont crossing – and to darken the sky with his arrows, a motif which can be traced back to the story told by Herodotus (7.226) of the Spartan Dieneces who, when told that the Persian archers were so numerous that their arrows would block out the sun, replied that therefore the Spartans would fight in the shade. An insight into the way in which such an anecdote might find its way into a moral treatise by another author (although this time with similar brevity to that found in Valerius' collection) is once again offered by the younger Seneca, in whose *De constantia sapientis* (4.2) Xerxes, referred to only as 'that stupid king' (*stolidus ille rex*) is

---

[37] This is reminiscent of the misplaced Persian confidence in the size of Xerxes' army seen in both Aeschylus' and Herodotus' versions of the invasion.

[38] There is also perhaps an echo of the Herodotean Artemisia here; in Herodotus' narrative (8.68), although Xerxes ultimately rejects her advice to avoid a naval engagement at Salamis, she nonetheless earns the king's appreciation for offering her truthful opinion.

[39] Cicero also draws on the theme of Xerxes' reputation for luxurious excess in his *De finibus* (2.111–12). In arguing there that man is made for higher ends than pleasure he imagines how absurd it would be if Xerxes' vast expedition had been launched purely because the king wanted to procure some honey from Hymettus.

[40] Xerxes' removal of the statues is later reported by Pausanias (1.8.5, stating that they were restored to Athens by Antiochus). Valerius (2.10 ext.1) tells us that the statues were returned by Seleucus I; this contradicts the view reported by Arrian that Alexander was responsible for bringing them back (*Anabasis* 3.16.7, 7.19.2; cf. Pliny *NH* 34.70).

adduced as an example of supreme arrogance, showering his arrows to darken the sky and lowering chains into the sea.[41]

Roman Xerxeses

That Xerxes' excesses, his arrogance or his reversal of fortune might furnish those wishing to make universal moral points with a store of appropriate exempla is beyond doubt. Yet the stories preserved by Nepos or Valerius Maximus, while illustrating the ways in which tales from the past might be used to inculcate moral excellence or discourage degenerate living in very general terms, shed little light on how the Xerxes-exemplum might function as a way of casting judgement upon specific contemporary situations or individuals. In the context of the political system of the principate the question of what constituted proper and improper behaviour on the part of a sole ruler was an ever-present one;[42] historical examples of good and bad conduct might therefore prove useful in evaluating the actions of particular emperors. The possibility that a connection might be drawn between a Roman *princeps* and notorious Persian tyrants emerges from a set of examples used by the younger Seneca. Written during the principate of Claudius (AD 41–54) and perhaps directed, at least in part, towards educating this emperor as to how rulers might behave with moderation, his *De ira*, an ethical treatise on anger and the means of alleviating it, considers the damage which can be done when those in a position of power succumb to this extreme emotion.[43] Along the way he considers the actions of such absolute rulers whose examples should be avoided. Here both Darius and Xerxes are featured as demonstrating the ferocity associated with foreign rulers (3.16.3–17.1). Seneca makes the connection between Darius' treatment of Oeobazus' sons, whom the king had killed when their father asked that one of them might be spared from military service, and Xerxes' similar punishment of Pythius by having his son cut in two, with the halves of the corpse placed on either side of the road (cf. Herodotus 4.84 and 7.38–9, discussed above at p. 40).

For Seneca these acts of ferocity and anger can be explained by the fact that these were barbarian kings, 'men untouched by learning or culture of letters'

---

[41] For an earlier Latin reference to the story see Cicero, *Tusc.* 1.101.

[42] See Dunkle (1971) on the development of the figure of the tyrant in Roman rhetoric and historiography in relation to the early emperors.

[43] Harris (2001), pp. 251–3 considers the way in which the text might relate to the politics of the Claudian court. See Cooper and Procopé (1995), pp. 3–16 for a summary of the literary and philosophical context of the work.

(*quos nulla eruditio, nullus litterarum cultus imbuerat*, 3.17.1); yet, he goes on to say, such violent behaviour has been displayed even by cultured figures such as Alexander (3.17.1–4), and Romans too have been susceptible to such irate and savage outbursts. If only such cruelty had remained the province of foreigners and had not become a part of Roman custom too, he reflects (3.18.1), then goes on to condemn the atrocities committed by Sulla and Catiline before cataloguing at length (3.18.3–19.5) the outrageous behaviour – torture and executions – of the recently deceased emperor Gaius Caligula, whose misdemeanours are a recurring feature of this text (cf. 1.20.8, 2.33.3–6).[44] Seneca's catalogue of undesirable and tyrannical behaviour concludes with further examples of barbarian wrath, in this case the irrational actions of Cambyses (3.20.1–4) and Cyrus (3.21.1–4). While here Xerxes appears as only one among several examples of outrageous barbarian behaviour he nonetheless serves for Seneca as a point of comparison for Caligula, that most notorious of Roman emperors whose actions during his principate led to his becoming the 'codified stereotype of the imperial tyrant'[45] in the Roman historiographical tradition.

A more targeted comparison between Caligula and the figure of Xerxes, himself a well-established tyrannical stereotype, finds its way into the literary sources for Caligula's reign in relation to one particular event which was orchestrated by the emperor. Seneca, in his *De brevitate vitae* (*On the shortness of life*), refers to the wasteful extravagance of Caligula who, he says, built bridges of boats and merely 'played' with the resources to which his power gave him access (*ille pontes navibus iungit et viribus imperi ludit*, 18.5) while the rest of the Roman people suffered the threat of famine and devastation. Caligula's actions, says Seneca, were in 'imitation of a raging, foreign, and deplorably proud king' (*furiosi et externi et infeliciter superbi regis imitatio*). The event to which Seneca refers is Caligula's construction of a bridge of boats across the Bay of Naples at Baiae, which formed part of a grandiose spectacle apparently staged in AD 39 shortly before Caligula was to depart on an expedition to Gaul and Germany.[46] Without naming Xerxes, Seneca clearly expected his own readers to recognize the connection which he had drawn between Caligula's bridge and that used by the Persian army to cross the Hellespont in 480 BC. The whole event is narrated in more detail by Cassius Dio (59.17.1–11), whose account describes the bridge's

---

[44] In Seneca's *De beneficiis* (2.12.1–3) Caligula is also criticized as behaving like a Persian monarch by forcing Romans to adopt servile customs when he insisted that a senator whose life he had spared must kiss his golden slipper.

[45] Kleijwegt (1994), p. 652.

[46] See Wardle (2007) on the dating of the event.

elaborate construction and Caligula's actions during his pageant. The emperor is said to have ridden across the bridge upon a horse, wearing a crown of oak leaves, a jewelled purple cloak and a breastplate which he claimed was that of Alexander (on which, see n. 49); on the following day he made the return crossing in a chariot, attended by the praetorian guard and bringing with him a train of 'spoils' and hostages, including a Parthian hostage (son of the Parthian king Artabanus) named Darius. Suetonius provides a similar account (*Caligula* 19), and the bridge is also mentioned briefly by Josephus (*Jewish Antiquities* 19.5–6), who suggests that Caligula considered himself 'master of the sea' and follows it immediately with a reference to Caligula's plundering of works of art from Greek temples (19.7); although Josephus makes no mention of Xerxes, the similarities between his behaviour and that of Caligula might well be noted by an alert reader.[47]

It is in the accounts of Suetonius and Dio where the direct connection between Xerxes and Caligula is made most explicitly. Suetonius asserts that most people considered that the bridge – which was longer than that across the Hellespont – was designed in emulation of Xerxes (*aemulatione Xerxis*, 19.2), and in Dio's account Caligula himself is said to have boasted that he had bridged a wider expanse of sea than either Darius or Xerxes had done (59.17.11).[48] One ruler noted for his tyrannical excess thus becomes assimilated to another whose exercise of absolute power was similarly condemned in the historiographical tradition. In light of the association which was drawn between Parthians and Persians in Roman imperial ideology (see above, pp. 161–2), and the prominent presence of a Parthian hostage who shared a name with several Persian kings, it is possible that Caligula's display was intended by the emperor, at least in part, to demonstrate Roman power to Parthian hostages present in Rome.[49] While Suetonius gives plausible alternatives for Caligula's motivation (that he wished to inspire fear in Germany and Britain, or that he wanted to prove wrong a

[47] Barrett (1989), pp. 211–12 summarizes the sources for Caligula's bridge and their conflicting opinions concerning its purpose.

[48] Here, in an echo of the language used to refer to Xerxes' actions since the descriptions of Aeschylus and Herodotus, Dio also uses the word ζεῦξας to refer to the act of bridging the sea. On Aeschylus' use of the term, see pp. 15–16; for Herodotus, p. 57.

[49] So Balsdon (1934), pp. 53–4. A further layer of possible interpretation is added here by the references in the texts to Caligula's wearing of the breastplate of Alexander. It is conceivable that the emperor styled himself as a new Alexander, who had also defeated a Darius. Such imitation of Alexander was not unprecedented among Roman generals and emperors: for the literary references see Baynham (1998), p. 10, with n. 37. Hannestad (1993) looks at examples of Alexander-*imitatio* in Roman art. The use of Alexander as an exemplum was not in itself uncomplicated, however; Valerius Maximus includes him in both positive and negative categories (including, for example, his bravery, leadership qualities and loyalty as well as his arrogance, cruelty and murderous rage). See Baynham (1998), p. 26, with n. 40, and Baynham (2009), p. 290.

prediction that he 'would no more be emperor than drive his horses across the bay of Baiae'), that the association between Caligula and Xerxes was deemed to be worthy of note by the emperor's biographers is indicative of the way in which implicit moral judgements might be formed on the basis of such comparisons.

This use of the spectre of Xerxes to cast aspersions upon the morality of a powerful individual was not without precedent. Velleius Paterculus, in his history of the Republican period (2.33), tells of the rivalry of Pompey and Lucullus over which of them should assume command in the Mithridatic War during the 60s BC. Pompey, in accusing Lucullus of extravagance, and on the basis of the elaborate feats of marine engineering by which Lucullus had built out into the sea and dug through mountains, is said to have referred to his opponent as *Xerxes togatus*, 'Xerxes in a toga' (2.33.4).[50] The insult played upon the notion that Lucullus' ostentatious building projects aligned him with the figure of the eastern tyrant; his alteration of nature itself might suggest that Lucullus was overstepping the boundaries which should be observed by a decent Roman.[51] The same association with Xerxes' excess and extravagance, manifested in an individual's large-scale building activities, also found its way into the traditions relating to Julius Caesar; Lucan's *De bello civili*, which lambasts Caesar's megalomania, drew an elaborate comparison between his siege-works at Brundisium and Xerxes' Hellespont bridge and Athos canal (2.670–9), a familiar pairing which was by now a well-established paradigm of arrogance.[52]

Josephus: an alternative perspective

The Roman appropriation of the Xerxes-tradition also finds its way into a text originally written in Aramaic, later translated into Greek, and offering a perspective which differs considerably from those of our Latin sources: that text is the *Jewish War* (thought to have been published in AD 75–79) of the Jewish historian Josephus who was born in AD 37/8 and lived through the turbulent events of the first century AD, when Judaea revolted from

---

[50] Pliny (*NH* 9.170) also refers to Pompey's use of this insult. In Plutarch's later Greek version of Lucullus' life (*Lucullus* 39.2–3) it is said to have been Tubero the Stoic who used the expression.

[51] Edwards (1993), pp. 143–9 looks at this story in relation to attacks in Roman moralizing texts upon those who had undertaken such elaborate building projects. See also Purcell (1987), pp. 190–4 for historical examples of grand rulers associated with large-scale projects for altering the landscape. Note also Hardie (2007), p. 133: 'the jibe may have added point when the target is someone with ambitions to continue a career of Roman conquest against eastern enemies'. Jolivet (1987) discusses Lucullus' building activities in detail.

[52] Fantham (2002), p. 212.

Roman control.[53] In his attempt to dissuade the Jews from taking up arms against Roman domination in AD 66, the Roman general Agrippa is quoted as adducing examples of other peoples who have succumbed to the power of Rome. Even the Athenians, he says, are now slaves to Rome, 'the Athenians who, for the sake of the freedom of Greece, gave up their city to the flames, and pursued the haughty Xerxes, who sailed through land and marched over sea, whom the sea could not contain and who brought an army bigger than Europe; they pursued him like a fugitive in a single ship' (*Jewish War* 2.358). The words given to Agrippa by Josephus here appropriate the reversal of fortune motif seen elsewhere in Latin literature, yet this arrogant boast of Rome's irresistible power might also carry an ironic subtext; Roman domination of the Jews could well elicit a comparison with Persian aggression against Greece.

This traditional image of Xerxes is not, however, borne out elsewhere in Josephus' work. Published in AD 93/4, his twenty-book *Jewish Antiquities*, a history of the Jews from the Creation to just before the outbreak of the revolt from Rome, includes an account of Jewish history under Persian rule. While Josephus places the story of the biblical book of Esther during the reign of Artaxerxes (in accordance with the Greek version of Esther; see above, pp. 141–8), he records another series of events, relating to the characters of Ezra and Nehemiah, as having taken place when Xerxes was on the Persian throne. From the outset this Xerxes is a very different type of king from that seen in the dominant Greek and Latin traditions:

> When Darius died, his son Xerxes took over the kingship and also inherited his piety and honour towards God (τὴν πρὸς τὸν θεὸν εὐσέβειαν τε καὶ τιμήν). For concerning religious ritual he followed his father in all things, and was exceedingly generous towards the Jews (πρὸς τοὺς Ἰουδαίους ἔσχε φιλοτιμότατα). (*Jewish Antiquities* 11.120)

The king's piety and benevolence are borne out in the story which follows of his friendship with Ezra, chief priest in Babylon: he grants permission for Ezra and any Jews wishing to accompany him to go to Jerusalem, providing them with a letter of introduction to take to the satrap of Syria. In a detail which may surprise readers more accustomed to seeing Xerxes removing treasures

---

[53] Josephus himself attempted without success to persuade his countrymen to desist from their rebellion; he was then captured in the course of the revolt, later claiming that he was spared when he prophesied to the then military commander Vespasian that he would become emperor. After the war he settled in Rome and was given Roman citizenship. Chapman (2009), pp. 319–25 provides an overview of Josephus' life and works.

from temples in order to augment his own wealth, here he instead allows Ezra to take with him the gold and silver dedicated to God in Babylon, along with expenses from the royal treasury for further dedications (11.124–5, cf. 11.136); Xerxes himself makes an offering of wheat to God and exempts Ezra and his companions from the payment of tribute (11.127–8). Ezra and his Jewish companions are overjoyed by Xerxes' 'piety towards God and goodwill towards Ezra' (τὴν πρὸς τὸν θεὸν εὐσέβειαν καὶ τὴν πρὸς Ἔσδραν εὔνοιαν, 11.132) and are able to return safely to Jerusalem.[54] This picture of piety, munificence, tolerance and respect for a culture other than his own is wholly at odds with the image of Xerxes which prevails in the Greek-derived traditions; it is one which is reinforced too by Josephus' account of Nehemiah's story (11.159–83), in which the king's cupbearer, saddened by news of troubles in Jerusalem, asks to be allowed to go there in order to help rebuild the city walls and to complete the building of the temple there. The pattern here is similar to that in the story of Ezra: Xerxes gives Nehemiah letters instructing the local satraps to pay him respect and to give him the supplies he requires (11.166) so that he is able to carry out the building work necessary when he arrives.

The two episodes related by Josephus have been the cause of chronological confusion, not least as the Old Testament versions of the stories of Ezra and Nehemiah assign them to Artaxerxes' reign rather than to that of Xerxes.[55] Yet that Josephus was content to give the credit for benevolence and religious tolerance to Xerxes suggests that his perspective, as a Jew, was decidedly different from that of the Greek and Latin sources whose views were shaped by the story of Xerxes' invasion of Greece; it provides us with a thought-provoking alternative to the mainstream tradition.[56] Elsewhere Josephus even goes so far as to claim that some Jews fought on the side of Xerxes in the invasion of Greece (*Against Apion* 1.172–4). He cites verses from the poetry of Choerilus of Samos as proof of this assertion, basing his conclusion upon the fact that Choerilus refers to a people from the 'Solymian mountains', which he identifies with Hierosolyma (Jerusalem). Although the connection between the two is thought

---

[54] Cf. *Jewish War* 2.86 in which Josephus corroborates this version of the return to Jerusalem as having taken place during Xerxes' reign.

[55] Rajak (1974, Vol. 2), pp. 118–23 offers a lucid analysis of the relationship of Josephus' text to his source material, suggesting that chronological difficulties may have arisen because he used as the basis for his Ezra narrative *I Esdras*, the substantially altered and chronologically problematic Greek version of the Hebrew *Ezra*.

[56] The good press which is given to the Achaemenids in much of the Jewish tradition is perhaps due in part to the fact that it was under Cyrus that the exiled Jewish community was allowed to return to Jerusalem from Babylon: see Briant (2002), pp. 46–8.

to be wholly erroneous[57] it is nonetheless telling that Josephus was prepared to use this claim as part of his proud assertion of the antiquity of the Jewish people, which contrasts markedly with the stain of medism which haunted Greek states for centuries after the invasion.[58]

A not-so-distant memory? Xerxes reconsidered by subject Greeks

Even when Hellenic independence had become a centuries-old memory and the Greeks were subject to a powerful foreign empire – that of Rome – the story of the Persian Wars, as the archetypal narrative of the ancient Hellenic struggle for freedom against a foreign power, did not cease to maintain its significance as a source of national pride for subject Greeks. Just as writers of Latin texts incorporated this period of history into their repertoire, so too works written by those whose language of expression – and cultural identity – was Greek demonstrate that this element of their homeland's past would continue to occupy a place in their psyche. Even those for whom Roman history was the focus of their endeavours found their work influenced by the memories of the most famous period of Greek history. For Polybius (c. 200–c. 118 BC), writing in the second century BC a history of Rome's rise to domination, Xerxes' expedition to Greece could be used as a means of relative dating, a way in which he could locate key events of Roman history within a historical framework familiar to his Greek audience (3.22.2, 6.11.1).[59] His catalogue of the major events in Greek history prior to the defeat of the Achaean League by Rome (147–6 BC) begins with the crossing of Xerxes to Europe (38.2),[60] which he describes as having been the greatest source of fear ever for the Greeks and as having been brought on by τύχη (fortune). Yet despite the prominent role which he assigned in his history

---

[57] Momigliano (1975), p. 77; Stern (1984), p. 5–6.
[58] Consider, for example, the significance attached by Pausanias to the medism of Greek states (see below, p. 179, with n. 76).
[59] Feeney (2007), pp. 7–67 provides a detailed study of the use of synchronism in Roman historical writing. See Millar (1987), pp. 12–13 on the way in which Polybius uses Greek history as a means of dating events in Roman history. A similar technique was later used by Dionysius of Halicarnassus as a means of conceptualizing Roman history for the benefit of Greek readers (*Roman Antiquities* 9.1.1). Dionysius' familiarity with the traditions relating to Xerxes is clear too from his *On Demosthenes*, in which (41) he converts into Attic Greek the speech given by Herodotus' Xerxes (Hdt. 7.8) explaining his decision to invade Greece.
[60] Clarke (1999), pp. 99–100 notes that, although the crossing of Xerxes is not often explicitly mentioned, similar crossings of natural boundaries form a recurrent motif in attempts at conquest described by Polybius (for example, Hannibal's crossing of the Rhône at 3.44.1–2, or his crossing of the Po using a bridge of boats at 3.66.5–6).

to *Tyche*/fortune[61] Polybius – by contrast with Herodotus, for whom Xerxes' story offered a paradigm in the mutability of human fortune[62] – saw no need to explore further Xerxes' motives and actions, even where he might have used him as an exemplum in relation to his discussion of the progression of Roman imperialism.[63]

On one particular occasion in the course of the history which Polybius narrates, however, we are reminded of the significance of the spectre of Xerxes in the Greek consciousness. In recording the events of the First Macedonian War, after the Romans had allied with the Aetolian League in opposition to Philip V of Macedon and his Greek allies,[64] Polybius relates that embassies were sent (in 210 BC) to Sparta both from the Aetolian League and from Acarnania, an ally of Philip. In urging the Spartans to ally with the Achaeans and Macedonians against Roman aggression, the Acarnanian envoy is said to have reminded them of their forebears' struggle for the freedom of the Greeks (9.38.1–2). He recalls how those ancestors dealt with an envoy sent by Xerxes to demand earth and water as tokens of their submission; they threw him into a well and told him to report back to the king that he had been given what he asked for. In Herodotus' version of the story (7.133.1) envoys thrown into a well by the Spartans came from Darius, and as a result Xerxes refrained from sending to Sparta any further requests for submission. The assimilation of the story to Xerxes' reign in Polybius' text suggests that it was his name, not that of his father, which continued to exercise the most profound resonances for the Greeks in relation to the Persian invasion of their territory. That Polybius has one of his speakers drawing attention to the comparison between Roman and Persian aggression at a point in history when Rome had recently begun to penetrate the Greek east is also a reminder that allusions to Xerxes' invasion might carry subversive undertones.[65] This might be seen to foreshadow Plutarch's concerns about the potentially subversive use of the Persian Wars tradition (see below, pp. 182–7).

Later Greek writers too bear witness to the way in which Xerxes' invasion continued to occupy a place in the collective consciousness.[66] For Strabo (born

---

[61] See Walbank (1957), pp. 16–26.

[62] As discussed above, pp. 64–6.

[63] Consider, for example, 1.2, where Polybius briefly compares the Roman empire, characterized as a more successful and resilient empire than any other in the past, with that of Persia, whose attempts to overstep the boundaries of Asia ended in failure. This also has a parallel in Dionysius' work (1.2.2).

[64] The historical background to the First Macedonian War is provided by Errington (1989), pp. 94–106.

[65] Millar (1987), p. 17.

[66] We might consider here too the work of Diodorus, who resided at Rome during the first century BC, and whose work on the Persian Wars period relied heavily upon the lost fourth-century version of Ephorus. His account of the Xerxes-traditions is discussed in detail above (pp. 135–41).

c. 64 BC and originally from Amasia in Pontus), one of several educated Greeks
who migrated to Rome in the latter part of the first century BC after the turbu-
lence of the civil war had subsided, Xerxes' expedition serves as a useful point of
reference in his descriptions of geographical features. The world now dominated
by Rome was still in many ways defined by the events in Greek history and
this is reflected in his geographical work written – along with Strabo's now lost
History – for the education of statesmen and public alike.[67] His selection of
material where Xerxes is concerned is very much determined by his overarching
literary project, and features at points where it may enhance the reader's understanding of the significance of particular geographical features.[68] Thus Acanthus
is 'on the coast near Xerxes' canal' (fr. 7.33, cf. fr. 7.35) and Doriscus is where
he counted his army (fr. 7.47); the Hellespont bridge is mentioned too (13.1.22,
fr. 7.55). A reference to the Melas river reminds Strabo of Herodotus' claim that
this was insufficient to supply the king's army (7.51); Cape Sepias is said to have
been celebrated in tragedies and song because it was there that Xerxes' fleet was
destroyed by a storm (9.5.22); and Salamis is famed both for its association with
Ajax and for the naval battle after which Xerxes, defeated by the Greeks, fled
for his homeland (9.1.9, 9.1.13). Other references find Xerxes redistributing
territory (for example, in his gifts to Themistocles of three Asian cities, 14.1.10,
cf. 13.1.12)[69] or looting and destroying sanctuaries, including the temples in
the territory of the Branchidae (14.1.5)[70] and the tomb of Belus at Babylon
(16.1.5).[71] Thus Strabo, although making no explicit moral judgements, extracts
brief snapshots from the pre-existing Greek traditions which relate to the image
of Xerxes as sacrilegious destroyer, whose incursion into Greek territory left

---

[67] *Geography* 1.1.22. Strabo also suggests that a knowledge of geography is particularly useful for
military men; examples of military success and failure based on such an understanding include the
wrecks which resulted from errors made by Xerxes' commanders, and Ephialtes' knowledge of the
pass at Thermopylae which enabled the Persians to defeat Leonidas there (1.1.17).

[68] Clarke (1999), p. 300 remarks upon the prominence of the Persian invasions in Strabo's historical
references, offering the following explanation: 'A successful Persian invasion would have had serious
implications for the way the world looked in all senses – political, urban, and ethnic.' Roman
domination too had had similar effects upon the geography of the known world; Nicolet (1991, pp.
95–123 in particular) examines the Roman concern for measuring and controlling geographical
space.

[69] Note that Strabo adopts the version of Themistocles' story transmitted by Diodorus, in which the
exiled Greek came to the court of Xerxes, rather than that seen in Thucydides' account in which he
came before Artaxerxes. See above, p. 137, with n. 40.

[70] Cf. 11.11.4, where the Branchidae are said to have accompanied Xerxes after handing over to him
the riches of the temple at Didyma; at 17.1.43 they are also said to have 'persized' in the time of
Xerxes (ἐπὶ Ξέρξου περσισάντων).

[71] On the problematic tradition of Xerxes' destruction of the sanctuary at Babylon see Kuhrt and
Sherwin-White (1987), discussed above, pp. 91–2.

an impression upon the landscape he described as well as in the minds of its inhabitants.

That moral judgements and parallels with more recent events might still be derived from the stories relating to Xerxes is apparent, however, from a much later geographical work by a Greek living under the Roman empire. For Pausanias, the preoccupation with the past seen in other literary works of the so-called 'Second Sophistic'[72] took on a particular significance as he travelled through mainland Greece in the third quarter of the second century AD and described the locations and monuments which he encountered, often expanding upon these descriptions by providing explanatory historical detail. His ten-book *Guide to Greece* (*Periegēsis Hellados*), a text which demonstrates a concern with fostering a sense of Hellenic identity through its exploration of the relationship between the topography and culture of his native land and the Greek past,[73] shows a particular concern for the Persian Wars period, during which that identity was under threat from invasion by barbarian outsiders. At a time when Greece had become subject to rule by an outside power – that of the Roman empire – the repulse of Xerxes' invasion could still be seen as a defining moment in Greek history.[74] For Pausanias this manifests itself in his descriptions of the still-visible reminders of the Greek resistance to Persia – in particular the monuments and trophies associated with the wars, and even at Athens what was thought to be a replica of Xerxes' tent[75] – as well as in his concern, well over 600 years after the event, to point out on which side Greek states chose to fight.[76] While memories of all of the major battles of the Persian Wars (Marathon, Thermopylae, Salamis and Plataea) are evoked throughout the narrative, and on the Greek side key protagonists (Leonidas, Miltiades, Pausanias and Themistocles) are referred to at relevant points, Xerxes is the Persian king who receives the most attention; Darius is barely mentioned in connection with any

---

[72] On the use of historical themes – particularly in the work of Philostratus – during the Second Sophistic see pp. 151–2, with bibliographic references at nn. 82–4. E. L. Bowie (1996), p. 229 notes the similarity between Pausanias' historical interests and those of the sophists and novelists of his day.

[73] Elsner (1992). On the archaizing tendencies of Pausanias' work see E. L. Bowie (1974), pp. 188–9.

[74] Alcock (1991), pp. 250–9 explores Pausanias' use of the Persian Wars as a way of maintaining Greek identity under Roman subjugation, giving examples of the relevant monuments which feature in his description.

[75] 1.20.4. M. C. Miller (1997), pp. 223–4 identifies the building to which Pausanias refers here as the Odeion of Pericles and suggests that Pausanias' (possibly erroneous) association of this with Xerxes' tent was based on a tradition of unknown origin. Broneer (1944), argued that the tent of Xerxes, taken after Plataea, had been used as the *skēnē* for the Athenian theatre.

[76] Habicht (1985), pp. 107–8 n. 41 lists the occasions on which Pausanias records whether individual states medized or were loyal to Greece; see also Alcock (1994), p. 254.

of the events of the wars.[77] By Pausanias' time it was Xerxes' name which had become synonymous with the Persian threat; where Darius had orchestrated the Marathon campaign from afar, the memory of Xerxes' presence in Greece at the head of his own invasion had ensured that it was him to whom lasting notoriety attached itself.[78] Thus, for Pausanias, the Xerxes whom Leonidas marches out to meet at Thermopylae is 'the proudest (παρασχομένῳ μέγιστον φρόνημα)[79] of all who reigned over the Medes or the Persians who came after them, the one who carried out such renowned feats (ἀποδειξαμένῳ λαμπρὰ οὕτω)' (3.4.8).

As in the case of Strabo's geographical text, for Pausanias too certain locations take on significance as a result of their association with Xerxes' invasion.[80] In keeping with his interest in sanctuaries and their monuments he pays most attention to the effects of Xerxes' acts of theft and vandalism, which had left visible scars upon the sites which Pausanias visited. Thus the king's removal of the statues of Harmodius and Aristogeiton from Athens is noted (1.5.8, where Pausanias attributes the restoration of these to the city by Antiochus),[81] as is his theft of a bronze Apollo from the Branchidae (1.16.3) and an image of Artemis from Brauron (8.46.3).[82] Elsewhere the statues of Athena at Athens are said to be in a fragile state in Pausanias' day because they caught fire during Xerxes' sack of the city (1.27.6); the writer also refers to other cities and sanctuaries which were burned in the course of Xerxes' invasion of Greece (10.3.2, 10.33.8, 10.35.2).[83] That such actions were immoral and often sacrilegious was no more open to question in Pausanias' day than when Herodotus

---

[77] Darius I's name is mentioned in passing in connection with his demands for submission from the Greeks (3.4.2, 3.12.7), the Ionian revolt is said to have taken place during his reign (7.10.1) and at one point Xerxes is described as 'son of Darius' (8.46.3).

[78] On this point in relation to earlier Greek texts see p. 60 (Herodotus) and p. 108 (Isocrates).

[79] Note the relationship of the Greek phrasing here, however, to the concept of *megalophrosunē*, which does not always carry a wholly negative connotation; see above, pp. 56–7.

[80] Thus the defeat of Xerxes' forces on Psyttaleia after Salamis is noted (1.36.2); the Hellenium in Sparta was where the Greeks debated how to resist Xerxes (3.12.6); the mountainous part of Thrace breeds lions which attacked the king's army and camel-train (6.5.4); Mount Pelion is where the diver Scyllias and his daughter Hydne aided in the destruction of Xerxes' fleet by removing the ships' anchors during a storm (10.19.1–1, cf. Herodotus 8.8.1). At 8.42.8 Xerxes' invasion is also used to place the reign of Hieron of Syracuse in its chronological context.

[81] See p. 169, with n. 40, on the variant traditions relating to the eventual restoration of these statues to Athens.

[82] In a tradition not recorded elsewhere another theft of cultural significance is attributed to Xerxes by the second-century Latin author Aulus Gellius, who alleges in his *Noctes Atticae* (7.17.1) that the king removed all books from the public library in Athens in order to take them to Persia. The reference to a public library in Athens is anachronistic, however, and it is likely that the story is a late addition to the Xerxes-tradition.

[83] After Xerxes' departure from Greece the army he left behind with Mardonius is also said to have continued with acts of sacrilege. At 9.25.9 Pausanias relates a story in which some of the men, in an act of contempt for the gods, entered the sanctuary of the Cabeiri in Boeotia; immediately they were struck with madness and flung themselves into the sea to their deaths.

composed his histories; yet for Pausanias and his readers these models of bad behaviour might also take on a wider significance in the context of other incursions into Greek territory. The Gallic invasion of Greece which took place in the third century BC seems, as another threat posed to Greek freedom by outsiders, to have suggested itself as a potential parallel for Xerxes' invasion,[84] but in more recent times it was the Romans who had been responsible for acts of plunder which might be compared with the destruction visited upon Greece by Xerxes and his army.[85] In some cases an explicit connection might be made between the removal of works of art from Greece by Romans and the thefts committed during Xerxes' invasion. For example, in recalling Augustus' removal of the cult statue of Athena Alea from the sanctuary at Tegea after his defeat of Antony and his Arcadian allies (8.46) Pausanias notes that the emperor was not the first to do such a thing when sacking a defeated city, but that precedents had been set by Greeks at Troy, and by the Persians who had stolen artefacts from Greece; the Persian examples given are Xerxes' removal of the image of Artemis at Brauron and a bronze Apollo from the Branchidae. Despite the presence of Greek precedents for these actions the connection between Augustus' theft and those committed by Xerxes is a reminder here that the Romans' domination of Greece had brought with it leaders whose actions at times might also be morally questionable.[86]

Later, when discussing the pillaging of the sanctuary of Delphi, Pausanias again hints that Xerxes might serve as a negative paradigm for a badly behaved emperor (10.7.1): he lists as culprits here the Phlegyans, Pyrrhus, son of Achilles, part of Xerxes' force, the Phocian chieftains and the Gallic army, and concludes with the violation of the sanctuary by the emperor Nero, who is said to have stolen 500 statues from Apollo.[87] Elsewhere, however, Pausanias uses the precedent set by Xerxes as a means of pointing up a contrast between the Persian king and a Roman emperor of whose actions he approves. He compares

---

[84] Alcock (1996), pp. 256–8 examines the occasions where Pausanias' narrative links the Persian invasion with the Gallic threat. Polybius too had drawn a connection between Xerxes' invasion and the Gallic attack on Delphi of 279 BC (2.35.7–8).

[85] Note here Habicht (1985), p. 122, with nn. 19 and 20, giving examples of Roman thefts of Greek works of art.

[86] Arafat (1996), pp. 127–9 discusses Pausanias' treatment of Augustus in relation to this episode and suggests that here examples from the past are used to justify Augustus' actions. I would contend, however, that the mention of Xerxes' thefts – universally condemned in the traditions relating to his invasion – raises the question of whether such acts can ever be deemed to be acceptable.

[87] Comparison between Nero and Xerxes can also be found in Philostratus' *Life of Apollonius* (5.7) and in a text entitled *Nero, or on the digging of the Isthmus* transmitted as part of the Lucianic corpus; there Nero is said to have compared his actions to those of Darius (in bridging the Bosporus) and Xerxes. See Whitmarsh (1999).

the respect shown by the Romans to the sanctuary at Abae and the god of Apollo with the burning of the sanctuary by Xerxes' army (10.35); this comment may well be reflective of the general respect shown by Pausanias for Hadrian (cf. 1.3.2, 1.5.5, 1.20.7 where he is seen as a benefactor of Athens in particular), who declared the people of Abae free and built a temple there.[88] The negative paradigm of Xerxes' acts of sacrilege might therefore be used as a standard by which the actions of later Roman leaders – for good or for bad – could be judged.[89]

Plutarch's problematic Persian

At first glance Plutarch's treatment of Xerxes bears strong similarities to the way in which the king is portrayed in other Greek texts written in a period when the Hellenic world was subject to Roman rule.[90] Within the extensive corpus of the work of Plutarch (c. AD 50–after AD 120) Xerxes' Hellespont crossing and Athos canal might be used to illustrate a moral point about the fragility of human fortune (*Consolation to Apollonius* 110d), as an example of irrationality and ill temper (*On Control of Anger* 455d–e) or as a sign of great folly (*On the Fortune or Virtue of Alexander the Great* 329d–f, where Alexander's joining of Persians with Greeks and Macedonians in marriage is praised as a more appropriate and joyful way of uniting two continents). Elsewhere the now-familiar episode concerning his callous treatment of Pythius' son reappears (*Virtues of Women* 263a–b; see above, p. 40, on Herodotus' version of the story), and in the collection of *Apophthegmata* attributed by some to Plutarch (173b–c) several examples of his conduct are cited in brief, including those illustrating his anger (which he is said to have vented upon the Babylonians who revolted from his rule by preventing them from bearing arms in future and by forcing

[88] Arafat (1996), p. 188 and Bowie (1996), p. 219. On the range of attitudes to different emperors shown by Pausanias – often according to their behaviour towards Greece – see Elsner (1992), p. 18. Habicht (1985), pp. 117–40 considers the broader question of Pausanias' attitude to Roman domination of Greece, suggesting that while he does not demonstrate an openly hostile attitude Pausanias' work nonetheless bears the traces of resentment that Greece should be ruled by outsiders (p. 120).

[89] Xerxes is used on one occasion too as a moral paradigm by which to judge the standards of a Greek commander (9.32.9): in condemning the actions of the Spartan Lysander who refused burial to the Athenians killed at Aegospotami (405 BC) Pausanias notes that even the Persians who fell at Marathon were given a proper burial by the Athenians, and even Xerxes buried the Spartans who died at Thermopylae (this latter is a detail not recorded by Herodotus and which may be a later invention).

[90] For a detailed exploration of the role of barbarians in general in Plutarch's work see Schmidt (1999); an overview of the topic is also given by Schmidt (2002).

upon them trivial activities such as flute-playing and brothel-keeping)[91] and his expansionist ambition (he is said to have refused to eat Attic figs until he acquired for himself the land which produced them).[92] Not all examples are reflective, however, of a wholly negative verdict upon Xerxes. In the same section of the *Apophthegmata* there is also a reference to Xerxes' benevolent treatment of his brother Ariamenes, who, despite his fraternal rivalry for the kingship, remained loyal to Xerxes; the story is one which is also given more detailed treatment in Plutarch's treatise *On Brotherly Love* (488d–f).[93] Finally the text of the *Apophthegmata* also refers to an occasion on which Xerxes found Greek spies in his camp, but rather than do them harm he released them, having told them to observe his army at their leisure;[94] the story has echoes of that in which Bulis and Sperchias – sent as compensation for the Spartans' killing of Persian heralds – are spared by Xerxes (*Apophthegmata Laconica* 235f–236b; cf. Herodotus 7.136, discussed above, pp. 50–1).

Given the familiarity of Plutarch with the traditions relating to Xerxes, and in particular with the work of Herodotus,[95] it is perhaps surprising that even in those of his works which engage directly with the Persian Wars period (the *Lives* of Themistocles and Aristides, and *On the Malice of Herodotus*), Xerxes is at no point afforded a detailed treatment, appearing only intermittently when the needs of the narrative require it. In this respect Plutarch's biographical works in particular – constructed with the aim of educating his readers with examples of virtue[96] – bear similarities to those of Nepos (see pp. 163–4). Plutarch's *Life of Themistocles* uses snapshots of the image of Xerxes familiar since Herodotus'

---

[91] This is the punishment which Herodotus (1.156) claims was inflicted upon the Lydians by Cyrus; there it is described as a way of ensuring that the miscreants will act more like women than men in future. This is perhaps illustrative of the way in which such anecdotes tended to become attached to the figure of the best-known Persian king.

[92] Cf. Athenaeus, *Deipnosophists* 14.652b–c.

[93] The adaptation of the story in another text is illustrative of the way in which the *Apophthegmata* might relate to the Plutarchan corpus as a whole. They do not comprise a completed work in themselves, but appear to be extracts from longer works, possibly from notes taken as part of Plutarch's research, which could then be written up in different ways (although some dispute that they belong to the Plutarchan corpus). On this aspect of Plutarch's methodology see Pelling (2002), pp. 65–71.

[94] The story is in Herodotus' account (7.146–7) where Xerxes' motivation is given as his desire to inspire fear in the Greeks at the size of his army, in the hope that he might conquer them without a fight.

[95] On the different ways in which Plutarch uses Herodotus see Pelling (2007), pp. 153–62, describing the Herodotean account of the Persian Wars as presenting the later writer with a 'repertoire of possibilities' (p. 155, p. 162).

[96] Pelling (2002), pp. 237–51 considers the nature of the political and moral guidance offered by the *Lives*, suggesting that although Plutarch uses examples from the past these highlight issues about the human character which can have timeless relevance. Duff (2010) considers the moralizing purpose of the texts with specific focus on the paired *Lives* of Themistocles and Camillus.

account of Salamis; the king is seen with his vast army (12.2, and 14.1, where
Plutarch also cites the numbers of Persian ships given by Aeschylus) and
observes his forces from a golden stool[97] while his secretaries stand ready to
record the action (13.1). For Plutarch too Xerxes is lured into battle when
Themistocles dupes him into believing that the Greeks are about to flee (12, cf.
the Themistocles *Apophthegmata* 185b–c). The unwitting king, on hearing this
message, is described as being delighted (ἥσθη, 12.5); this is 'the sort of deluded
delight that so often typifies Herodotus' tyrants'.[98] By contrast we later see his
fury, another hallmark of a stereotypical tyrant, after the defeat at Salamis (he is
described as θυμομαχῶν at 16.1) and – in a direct contradiction of Herodotus'
account (8.97) – his attempt to build moles out into the sea in a plan to lead his
army across to the island.

When – in a variation on the earlier traditions relating to Themistocles'
actions after the battle of Salamis[99] – the Athenian commander is seen proposing
to sail to the Hellespont and break up Xerxes' bridge in order to 'capture Asia
in Europe' (τὴν Ἀσίαν ἐν τῇ Εὐρώπῃ λάβωμεν, 16.1, cf. *Aristides* 9.3),[100] he is
dissuaded by Aristides, whose response neatly encapsulates key elements of the
Xerxes-image. Aristides points out that if the Greeks do force Xerxes to remain
in Greece with his vast force, he will no longer 'sit under a golden parasol and
view the battle at his leisure', but will in future risk participation in person and
take better counsel in order to rectify his earlier mistakes (16.2). The image
of the king's idle leisure and luxury is combined here with a suggestion that
Xerxes' failure was a result of bad judgement; that suggestion is one which
was developed in the account of Herodotus (as discussed above, pp. 66–7),
with which Plutarch was clearly familiar. As in Nepos' account the episode is
used to enhance this author's characterization of a shrewd Themistocles, who
subsequently warns the king that the Greeks are planning to destroy his route
home; Xerxes, 'in great fear' (περίφοβος, 16.5, cf. *Aristides* 10.1) hastily begins
his retreat. In his account of Themistocles' later adventures at the Persian court
(26–30) Plutarch is unable to say with certainty whether it was with Xerxes or
Artaxerxes that the Athenian took refuge; as a result he refers only to 'the king'
throughout this part of the *Life*, in which, despite Themistocles' adoption of
Persian customs and language, the Athenian refugee is redeemed as the ultimate

---

[97] Note Frost (1980), *ad loc.*, pointing out that the δίφρος to which Plutarch refers here is a stool, not
(as it has often been mistranslated) a throne.

[98] Pelling (2007), p. 154, with specific Herodotean examples at n. 34.

[99] See pp. 137–9, 152–4 and 163–4.

[100] On the potential resonances of this phrasing in the *Life* of Cato (which is paired with that of
Aristides) see Pelling (2007), p. 152.

patriot and hero for his suicide, by means of which he averts another Persian attack on Greece.[101]

The portrayal of Xerxes' character in the *Life* of Themistocles is limited, then, to very brief descriptions (often conveyed in a only single word in the Greek text) of his most typical emotions – pleasure, anger or fear. This, for Plutarch, is the extent of his characterization of Xerxes; nowhere else in his extant work does he expand further upon the image.[102] The absence of any more detailed examination of some of the key aspects of Xerxes' character might begin to seem puzzling when we consider that elsewhere in his *Lives* Plutarch demonstrated an interest in using the kingly opponents of his protagonists in order to suggest points of comparison or contrast with his principal subjects. This is particularly apparent in the *Life* of the Roman general Aemilius Paullus, much of which is concerned with Aemilius' campaign against Perseus of Macedon (168 BC), among whose defining characteristics we find avarice and parsimony (12.3–12) as well as cowardice (19.4, 34.3–4). By contrast Aemilius' victory is attributed to his own courage and strategic skills (12.2).[103] Plutarch's *Alexander* also devotes some space to the characterization of Alexander's Persian opponent, Darius; here the insights which we are given into the Persian king's response to Alexander's compassionate treatment of his mother, wife and daughters after their capture are used by Plutarch to offer a commentary on Alexander's restraint and humanity at this point in the *Life* (30, 43.3–4).[104]

Plutarch also chose to give one Persian king a *Life* of his own; the *Life of Artaxerxes*, one of the few unpaired *Lives*, gives a vivid account of the luxury and cruelty of the Persian court under Artaxerxes II (405–359 BC), although – like the work of Ctesias and other more 'novelistic' approaches discussed in Chapter 5 – focusing more upon the court surroundings than upon the character of the king himself.[105] Given the presence of so many comparably interesting traditions

---

[101] On the various literary traditions relating to Themistocles' exile in Persia see also above, p. 137, with n. 40.

[102] His *De malignitate Herodoti* (*On the malice of Herodotus*), although it deals with portions of Herodotus' text which relate to the Persian Wars, is more concerned with its criticism of Herodotus than with characterization of the protagonists. One incident in the text which does relate to the figure of Xerxes is the story of the night-attack on the Persian camp at Thermopylae (866a), which is used by Plutarch as an example of the bravery of Leonidas' men. Xerxes, as the target of their assassination attempt, proves elusive. See above, pp. 139–41, for a discussion of Diodorus' earlier account of this tradition.

[103] Swain (1989), p. 325 argues that the contrast between the two adversaries is sustained throughout the *Life*, and is demonstrated particularly in relation to the way in which each responds to adverse fortune. A further example of this comparative technique can be seen in Plutarch's treatment of the character of Hannibal in relation to those of his adversaries in the *Lives* of Fabius Maximus, Marcellus and Flamininus.

[104] See pp. 121–4 on the changes which Alexander's character undergoes later in the course of the *Life*.

[105] Mossman (2010).

surrounding the figure of Xerxes we might well ask why Plutarch devoted so little time to the character or actions of our archetypal barbarian king. The answer may lie in part with the familiarity of Plutarch's audience with the subject matter and the writer's wish to avoid covering old ground, although this did not prevent him from re-examining, for example, the story of Themistocles. It is possible too, however, that his unwillingness to dwell for too long upon the would-be world conqueror may relate to his sensitivity regarding the contemporary political situation. By the time Plutarch was writing, centuries of Greek literary tradition had cemented the symbolic link between Xerxes and the threat to Greek liberty; here was the commander of a mighty foreign power intent on taking over the Greek world and making her inhabitants his subjects. At a time when Greece was subject to a powerful foreign government, however, Plutarch may have thought it prudent to exercise caution in discoursing upon that great moment of the past.

Plutarch's writings show an acute awareness of the limits placed by Roman rule upon Greek freedom in his own day. The theme is one which recurs throughout his paired *Lives* of Philopoemen and Flamininus, which give us an insight into the very beginnings of Roman domination of Greece by delineating the lives of the 'last of the Greeks' (*Philopoemen* 1.7) to stand up for Greek freedom[106] and the Roman who paradoxically declared Greece's liberty from Macedonian rule at the Isthmian Games of 196 BC (*Flamininus* 10.4–7).[107] Nowhere is Plutarch's sensitivity to the extent of Greek freedom more apparent, however, than in his *Political Precepts*, addressed to Menemachus, a Hellenized Lydian seemingly contemplating a career in local politics. Here Plutarch advises his friend that while the holder of a local office might rule over Greek citizens, he himself would nonetheless remain subject to the control of Caesar's proconsuls (813d–e). Plutarch later writes that the Greeks have as great a share of liberty as their rulers grant them (824c); resistance to Roman rule might well lead to the restriction of that liberty. It is in this same text that we also gain an illuminating insight into Plutarch's thoughts on the use of the Persian Wars paradigm by his contemporaries. In advising his reader as to the appropriate use of examples from the past, he cautions statesmen against the use of paradigmatic stories which might inflame public sentiment and excite potentially dangerous

---

[106] Philopoemen's actions at Mantinea at the head of the Achaean confederacy against Sparta also earned him a comparison with the ancestors who had fought against Persia (11.2); at the Nemean Games of 205 BC he was applauded as the opening verse of Timotheus' *Persians* was recited (for a discussion of this text see pp. 37–43).

[107] For a lucid discussion of the paired *Philopoemen* and *Flamininus* in relation to the question of Greek freedom in Plutarch's day see Pelling (2002), pp. 243–7.

responses from an impressionable audience: 'Marathon, the Eurymedon, Plataea and all the other examples which make the masses vainly swell with pride should be left in the schools of the sophists' (814b–c).[108] The possibility of a parallelism between Xerxes and another imperialist conqueror had also been explored by Plutarch in his *Alexander* (see pp. 121–4), and he was well aware that similarly unflattering comparisons might be drawn between the Persian king and individual Roman statesmen; his *Lucullus* (39.2–3) refers to the tradition by which this general's profligacy earned him the derogatory moniker *Xerxes togatus*. As our exploration of the Latin texts showed (see pp. 170–3), the leap to making subversive equations between Xerxes and the Roman emperor himself was not a large one.[109]

The dangers of stirring up such sentiment might go some way to explaining Plutarch's reluctance to explore Xerxes' character in any depth.[110] The viewpoint from which he was writing differed from that of the Latin writers whose texts echoed the Romans' hijacking of the triumphalist Greek rhetoric in serving the purposes of imperial propaganda. While he shared didactic or moralizing intentions with those who sought to appropriate the Xerxes-paradigm as a means of occasioning reflection on ethical questions his more guarded approach acts as a reminder that the story of the king's invasion and the threat which it posed to Greek freedom could, despite the centuries which had passed since that momentous event, continue to stir up an emotional response. His perspective on the Persian king was thus one which recognized both the enduring appeal of the image of Xerxes as a subject for literary exploration and the weight of centuries-old traditions carried by any writer who chose to tackle that theme.

Juvenal, 'lying Greece' and the Xerxes-traditions

It is to a Roman poet writing in Latin that we turn for our final ancient insight into the Xerxes-traditions. Juvenal, whose satirical poetry was composed in

---

[108] Marincola (2010) examines the way in which Plutarch himself uses the Persian Wars paradigm, concluding that, far from dwelling on the battles or espousing nationalistic sentiment, he looks more closely at the role of harmonious co-operation between Greek leaders and their people.

[109] Note also Swain (1996), p. 176, suggesting that in describing the administration of the Roman empire Greek writers – Plutarch included – tended to use the terms which classical authors had used to describe the Persian empire. This meant that the emperor might be described as the 'Great King', on which see also Jones (1986), p. 56, with n. 51.

[110] The perils of drawing attention to exempla which might stir up ill feeling towards an emperor had been experienced by several Roman dramatists under the principate. Champlin (2003), pp. 306–8 has shown that in particular the mythical exemplum of Atreus, which might be used as a paradigm for anti-tyrannical discourse, might touch a nerve for emperors.

the early part of the second century AD, looks to Xerxes in his tenth satire – on the theme of destructive human ambition – as one of a series of illustrative examples of military leaders whose ambitions led to their downfall (10.173–87):

> People believe
> that ships once sailed over Athos, and all the lies that Greece
> has the nerve to tell in her histories: that the sea was covered with boats,
> and the ocean provided a solid surface for wheels. We believe
> deep rivers failed, that streams were all drunk dry by the Persians
> at lunch, and whatever Sostratus sings with his soaking pinions.
> Yet in what state did the king return on leaving Salamis –
> the one who would vent his savage rage on Corus and Eurus
> with whips, an outrage never endured in Aeolus' cave,
> the one who bound the earth-shaking god himself with fetters
> (that, indeed, was somewhat mild; why, he even considered
> he deserved a branding! What god would be slave to a man like that?) –
> yet in what state did he return? In a solitary warship, slowly
> pushing its way through the bloody waves which were thick with corpses.
> Such is the price so often claimed by our coveted glory.[111]

Writing around 600 years after the events to which he refers here, Juvenal saw no need to provide a name for the king to whose actions he alludes, so sure was he of his audience's familiarity with the theme. Described only as *barbarus* (181 – translated here as 'savage'), Xerxes is identified by the motifs which had by now come to serve as shorthand for his invasion. Here are the Hellespont bridge and the Athos canal, the vast armies drinking dry the rivers on their march to Greece, and a king venting his wrath on the elements by whipping and branding the sea.[112] For Juvenal the contrast between this audacious behaviour and the humiliating return of the king, his force reduced by rhetorical exaggeration to a single ship, is striking.[113] By using the Persian king as a moral paradigm – in this case to highlight the subject of the destruction which ensues when men become too ambitious – his take on Xerxes, which neatly captures key elements of the king's image, follows on from the traditions established by his Latin literary predecessors. In Juvenal's text Xerxes sits alongside other well-known examples – Hannibal and Alexander the Great – which demonstrate that the higher one climbs, the further one has to fall.[114]

---

[111] The translation is that of Rudd (1991).
[112] The image is one first seen in Herodotus' account (7.35; 8.109.3); see p. 57.
[113] See p. 166, with n. 29, and p. 174 for other examples of the occurrence of this motif.
[114] Hardie (2007), p. 135 refers to Hannibal, Alexander and Xerxes as 'mirrors of (perverted) Roman ambition'.

It is in his scathing reference to the Greeks' construction of the image of Xerxes, however, that Juvenal divulges his own literary perspective on these tales. In dismissing them as falsehoods (the force of the assertion in the Latin text is stronger than in the translation given here: at line 174 Juvenal refers to *Graecia mendax*, 'lying Greece') the satirist reveals an understanding of the way in which the stories surrounding Xerxes' invasion of Greece had been repeatedly reinvented, embellished and exaggerated until it had become impossible to distinguish historical truth from literary fiction. His reference to Sostratus' dramatic re-enactment of Xerxes' exploits highlights the continuing popularity of the theme as a subject for the declamatory exertions of sophists or poets[115] and acts as a reminder that these ancient stories were still crowd pleasers in Juvenal's own day. In a mere 15 lines of Latin text Juvenal's *exemplum* thus encapsulates around 600 years of literary tradition, combining a reference to the histrionic enactment of Xerxes' character which still bears the traces of Aeschylus' theatrical Xerxes[116] with a Herodotean-inspired vision in which the king – by turns terrifying and pathetic – personifies the transient nature of fortune, as transmitted via the abridged versions of the fourth-century orators and a whole swathe of subsequent Greek and Latin literary retellings. Juvenal's critique offers a fitting reminder that after centuries of literary reinvention the historical Xerxes who crossed the Hellespont in 480 BC had become indistinguishable from the imagined Xerxes of the traditions which developed in his wake.

---

[115] See above, p. 152, on Xerxes as a theme for sophistic oratory. The identity and dates of the Sostratus mentioned here are uncertain; he may have been a poet (as the scholiast suggests) or an orator. See Courtney (1980), p. 472. The Latin text of Juvenal's poem which is translated as 'with soaking pinions' is *madidis ... alis* (178); the scholiast here suggests that this refers to the sweating armpits of an energetic speaker. See Ferguson (1979), p. 266 for a summary of alternative interpretations.

[116] For an exploration of the theatrical aspect of sophistic declamations see Schmitz (1999); on the relationship between rhetoric and drama at Rome see also Batstone (2009).

8. *A Xerxes for the twenty-first century*. Based on the depiction of Xerxes in Zack Snyder's movie *300* (2007)

Epilogue: Re-imagining Xerxes

The Xerxes of Zack Snyder's 2007 Hollywood movie *300* and its 2014 follow-up *300: Rise of an Empire* (see Plate 8) is perhaps our own generation's most widely known response to antiquity's most notorious Persian king. These recent cinematic re-interpretations of his character stand at the end of a long line of reinventions of Xerxes as arch-villain; the range of literary responses inspired by the Xerxes-traditions in the ancient world foreshadowed the Persian king's enduring presence in the cultural repertoire of the post-classical era, during which the lasting appeal of the Persian Wars narratives has given rise to their treatment in diverse forms of written and artistic media.[1] Representations of Xerxes have thus found their way into a staggering array of literary genres, creative media and cultural settings up to the present day, as this archetypal figure and the motifs associated with his story have been revisited time and again, and then assimilated into new historical and artistic settings. Although detailed examination of these later perspectives on Xerxes falls beyond the scope of the present volume, even a brief selection of examples demonstrates that the range of Xerxes-images seen in the post-classical era mimics the breadth of those seen in our survey of the ancient sources.

Dramatic adaptations have drawn upon Aeschylus' *Persians* in contexts as diverse as the nineteenth-century Greek War of Independence or the 1993 Gulf War as a means of making comparisons between Xerxes' rule and more recent oppressive regimes;[2] poetic retellings have taken as their focus memorable images from the Herodotean account of Xerxes' invasion of Greece such as the Hellespont bridge (used famously by Milton as a model for Satan's bridge from heaven to hell in *Paradise Lost*, 10.306–11) or – in the less well-known but far

---

[1]   Bridges, Hall and Rhodes (2007, eds) present discussions of a wide range of case studies.
[2]   Hall (2007) provides a detailed survey of the reception of Aeschylus' *Persians*.

more recent *House of Xerxes* by Paul Violi (2002) – the catalogue of Xerxes' many forces;[3] an image of Persian courtly decadence has served as the backdrop for an opera (Handel's 1738 *Serse*) with Xerxes as its eponymous character[4] and as the setting for a movie which revisits the story of Esther (the 1961 *Esther and the King*).[5]

Meanwhile depictions of Xerxes produced by painters and illustrators recreate the king's imagined appearance in visual media; these pictorial realizations of the Xerxes-image have no parallel in any surviving ancient source originating outside Persia itself[6] yet draw upon the vivid descriptive elements of the ancient dramatic and narrative traditions. Adrien Guignet's 1846 *Xerxès au bord de l'Hellespont*, for example, envisages the king, enthroned and surrounded by attendants at the start of the expedition to Greece; the plain which stretches out beneath him is filled with his army, and ruined columns in the foreground of the image allude to the destruction which is to come. The scene is one which calls to mind Herodotus' account of Xerxes' viewing of his troops at Abydus (7.44; see pp. 64–6 above). Wilhelm von Kaulbach's 1868 *Die Seeschlacht bei Salamis* takes as its cue the actual battle-narrative, again depicting Xerxes seated on his throne, slaves prostrating themselves before him, as he watches the fray of the sea battle beneath him; this image carries echoes of Aeschylus' messenger speech (*Persians* 465–70, with pp. 21–5). Not all images were on such a grand scale as these paintings, however: Edward Lear sketched a series of absurd Xerxes-figures to represent the letter 'X' in his nonsense alphabets[7] and elsewhere lithographs featuring episodes from the story of Xerxes' invasion adorned the pages of illustrated histories.[8] It is perhaps fitting too that the present volume itself makes its own contribution to the body of artistic re-imaginings of Xerxes – while several of the chapter frontispieces are adaptations of earlier illustrations, the artist Asa Taulbut created his own imaginative construction of

[3] To be discussed in Bridges (forthcoming).
[4] Kimbell (2007) analyses Handel's use of the Xerxes-theme.
[5] Llewellyn-Jones (2002), pp. 19–20. See pp. 141–8 for a discussion of the biblical book of Esther. The story is one which, since Racine's 1689 tragedy *Esther* (on which Handel later based his *Esther* oratorio), has enjoyed an extensive afterlife of its own, having inspired works of art including Michelangelo's Sistine Chapel paintings as well as novels (for example, J. Francis Hudson's *Hadassah*, published in 1996, and Debra Spark's 2009 *Good for the Jews*) and more recent movies (*One Night with the King* in 2006 and *Book of Esther* in 2013).
[6] See pp. 133–5 on Greek artistic sources which may have been influenced by the Xerxes-theme. On stylized Persian artistic depictions of the Persian king see also pp. 83–7 above.
[7] See Lateiner (2008) for a discussion.
[8] See, for example, Abbott (1878). The Bridgeman database (http://www.bridgemanart.com/) also features several examples: see, for example, image numbers LLM454247 (Xerxes rebuking the sea, from a nineteenth-century Spanish work), STC416108 (Xerxes crossing the Hellespont, also from the nineteenth century but from an English volume) and LAL278454 (Xerxes watching the battle of Salamis, a colour illustration from a 1971 edition of the children's series *World of Wonder*).

the Persian king in the drawings accompanying the Introduction (*Xerxes' army crosses the Hellespont*) and Chapter 3 (*Xerxes contemplates the brevity of human existence*).

While artworks such as these envisage snapshots of the Xerxes-narrative and transpose them into individual images, it is in the contemporary medium of the cinema – a mode of cultural expression and a use of technology which could not be anticipated by the ancients – that such visual impact is combined with a narrative approach to the events surrounding Xerxes' invasion.[9] Although Greek history on the whole has been ill-served by the movie industry, the Persian attack on Greece has in recent years caught Hollywood's attention.[10] With the 2007 release of *300*, directed by Zack Snyder, the movie-watching public was introduced to a twenty-first-century re-imagining of Xerxes, played by Rodrigo Santoro. As this volume was in the final stages of preparation a 2014 follow-up, *300: Rise of an Empire*, directed by Noam Murro and with Snyder as a producer, revisited Hollywood's vision of the Persian king, focusing this time on the battles of Artemisium and Salamis in 480 BC but also incorporating events of the first Persian invasion of 490 BC. The cinematic treatment of Thermopylae seen in the first *300* film was not without precedent;[11] in 1962 Rudolph Maté's *The 300 Spartans* (with Xerxes played by David Farrar) brought the Spartans' famous fight for freedom in the face of the Persian advance before an audience for whom the 'few versus many' theme was one familiar from Western-genre films.[12] *300*, however, took as its immediate inspiration Frank Miller's 1999 graphic novel of the same name; the 2007 movie adaptation used computer-generated imagery to preserve many of the visually stylized elements of the illustrated work.[13]

In its portrayal of Xerxes the 2007 *300* drew upon elements of the tradition familiar to us from the ancient texts; this king is a cruel dictator, accompanied by a vast servile army which marches under the lash and in fear of the threat of violent reprisals – mutilation and execution – for disobedience. The huge

---

[9] Xerxes also features in another contemporary art form which combines graphics with narrative; he is a character in Sid Meier's *Civilization*, a series of strategy video games.

[10] For wide-ranging discussions of Hollywood's treatment of the ancient world see Solomon (2001) and Paul (2013). On Greece in particular in popular culture see Nisbet (2008), whose revised second edition includes an additional chapter which examines the range of responses to *300*.

[11] Note too that the Thermopylae tradition was the inspiration for a swathe of earlier artistic retellings of the story of the sacrifice made by Leonidas and the three hundred Spartans. For a survey see Cartledge (2006), pp. 175–96.

[12] See Levene (2007) for a discussion of parallels between *The 300 Spartans* and *The Alamo*. Clough (2004), pp. 374–8 considers the political context in which the 1962 film was produced.

[13] On the relationship between the film adaptation and the graphic novel see Murray (2007) and Kovacs (2013).

and ostentatious golden throne upon which he sits as his army marches into battle is emblematic of his position of power and wealth here; it is carried by a cohort of slaves – some of whom prostrate themselves so that he may walk upon their bodies as an extension of the throne's stepped platform – in an image which might almost be a parody of the Persepolis reliefs depicting the king's dais held aloft by figures representing his imperial subjects.[14] This Xerxes, like his counterpart in the earlier Greek traditions, expects that his threats will bring about the immediate submission of the Greeks, and in the movie it is Leonidas (played by Gerard Butler) who, brought face-to-face with the king in a dramatic addition to the ancient narrative, refuses to kneel before him and thus makes his stand for Spartan (and, by extension, Greek) freedom.[15] The opening sequence of the 2014 follow-up has an axe-wielding Xerxes personally carry out the beheading of Leonidas' corpse; this is a graphic reworking of Herodotus' account in which the king vents his anger by ordering the mutilation of the dead Spartan hero's body after Thermopylae (7.238; see also p. 48). Alongside the images of the king's brutality, elsewhere in *300* we also catch a glimpse of the exotic sensuality associated with Xerxes' court as inside his gold-bedecked tent semi-naked women, some deformed or facially disfigured, writhe provocatively for the king's entertainment or inhale unidentified substances; the women are primed to seduce the traitor Ephialtes (depicted here as a deformed Spartan outcast rather than as the resident of Malis with a local's knowledge of Thermopylae described by Herodotus at 7.213.1) as he betrays his countrymen to Xerxes.

The graphic visualization of the king seen in the 2007 film also incorporated new elements drawn not from any ancient description but instead from an imaginative vision which was to prove controversial for many cultural and political commentators. This cinematic Xerxes, described by the actor who played him as 'not human … a creature … an entity',[16] is an androgynous character, heavily made up and dripping with gold jewellery, much of which is attached to his face and body by an extraordinary array of piercings. His towering height, standing as he does head and shoulders above Leonidas, and the depth of his voice (Santoro's natural speaking voice was digitally altered to create this effect) seem to be at odds with the effeminized image of a fully depilated and gold-manicured figure. The overall effect, to the disquiet of

---

[14] See p. 79 and pp. 84–2 with fig. 1.
[15] Cf. Herodotus 7.136.1 in which it is the Spartans Bulis and Sperchias who refuse to do obeisance to Xerxes (discussed above, pp. 50–1).
[16] G. Miller (2007), p. 2.

some critics, is part drag-queen, part outlandish monster, and it is one which is explored in more detail in the movie's sequel, which offers us an insight into the imagined process by which Xerxes is said to have taken on this appearance and to have become a 'god-king'. By bringing Xerxes face-to-face with Leonidas the director also brought into stark focus the contrast between the Persian and his Spartan adversary; the hirsute Leonidas, like the other members of his band of Spartan warriors, is a paradigm of rugged masculinity, unafraid to dirty his hands with the bloodshed in close combat and more than willing to die in the name of the freedom which he and his compatriots strive to uphold in the face of the Persian threat.[17]

300 also goes beyond even anything stated explicitly in our ancient sources in its emphasis upon the divinity of Xerxes. Frequently referred to throughout the film by both Spartans and Persians as the 'god-king', Xerxes himself boasts to Leonidas of his own godhead: 'It is not the lash they [his Persian subjects] fear, it is my divine power. But I'm a generous god; I can make you rich beyond all measure.' Snyder's use of the imagined notion of Xerxes as a god-king, based on a misrepresentation of the Persians as believing in the divinity of their ruler whose origins can be traced as far back as Aeschylus' *Persians* (see above, pp. 16–17), demonstrates that for a twenty-first-century audience too this motif can be used as a means of projecting a vision of Persian flamboyance and foreignness as well as of reinforcing the impression of Xerxes as a tyrannical megalomaniac. This exoticism – presented here as being both fascinating and terrifying – is seen too in the film's depiction of Xerxes' army. As in ancient versions of the story, the Persian horde outnumbers the Spartan force many times over, with the cinematic medium being used to full effect to convey the impression of the mass of troops (in the 2014 follow-up we are also given a striking image of the bridge of boats by which Xerxes' army was conveyed across the Hellespont); Snyder's retelling, however, exercises the prerogative of a Hollywood fantasy by going further than this in order to incorporate into Xerxes' army elements of the monstrous, the fantastical and the sinister. Creatures more akin to mythical beasts than humans appear among the king's troops and the Immortals (described in the film as the king's 'personal guard') are a faceless band of

---

[17] On issues relating to gender in *300* see Turner (2009).

clone-like figures who resemble the imperial Stormtroopers from George Lucas' *Star Wars* movies.[18] Thus does history shade into myth.[19]

A box office success which acquired something of a cult following in North America and Europe, *300* also inspired a range of offshoots, including a video game entitled *300: March to Glory* (2007) and a poorly made (and equally poorly received) movie spoof, *Meet the Spartans* (2008). Xerxes' character later received his own parody in an episode of the cult animated sitcom *South Park* which, in an apparent play upon the indeterminate sexuality of the king in *300*, portrayed a character named Xerxes as a lesbian who attempts to masquerade as a man.[20] In 2010 US rapper King Gordy released an album entitled *Xerxes the God-King*, whose cover, based on artwork from the film, cast the performer in the role of Xerxes. Alongside these commercially driven responses to the film, however, *300* provoked a more politically charged series of reactions which were largely concerned with the way in which Xerxes and his Persian army had been portrayed by the filmmakers. For some Iranians in particular the movie's depiction of the ancient inhabitants of their country was an outrage: President Mahmoud Ahmadinejad and his cultural advisors condemned the film as an attack on Iranian culture and filed a formal complaint against it through the United Nations,[21] while the Iranian press described the film's insulting treatment of the ancient Persians as a declaration of war by Hollywood upon the Iranian people.[22] Some American commentators too denounced it as 'race-baiting fantasy' akin to Nazi propaganda films,[23] suggesting that the theme was too close for comfort in light of contemporary world politics.[24] One critic, himself a Persian immigrant to the US, offered a sardonic summary of the movie which highlighted the potential for drawing parallels between the Spartans' fight against Xerxes and American military policy in the Middle East, suggesting that the portrayal of the Persian king and his army was an intrinsic part of the film's alleged propagandistic and prejudicial agenda (Daryaee 2007):

> What do you get when you take all the 'misfits' that inhabit the collective psyche of the white American establishment and put them together in the form of a

---

[18] The appearance of the Immortals is faithful to the images of Frank Miller's graphic novel; the film goes further than the book, however, in incorporating monstrous semi-mythical figures into Xerxes' army.

[19] On the film's portrayal of the Spartans themselves as mythical characters – 'super-heroes' – see Holland (2007), pp. 177–9.

[20] The *South Park* episode was entitled *D-Yikes!* and was first aired in the United States on 11 April 2007.

[21] Boucher (2010); see also http://news.bbc.co.uk/1/hi/6446183.stm

[22] Moaveni (2007).

[23] Stevens (2007).

[24] Holland (2007) provides an analysis of the political backlash.

cartoonish invading army from the East coming to take your freedom away? Then add a horde of black people, deformed humans who are the quintessential opposite of the fashion journal images, a bunch of veiled towel-heads who remind us of Iraqi insurgents, a group of black cloaked Ninja-esque warriors who look like Taliban trainees, and men and women with body and facial piercings who are either angry, irrational, or sexually deviant. All this headed by a homosexual king (Xerxes) who leads this motley but vast group of 'slaves' known as the Persian army against the 300 handsomely sculpted men of Sparta who appear to have been going to LA (or Montreal) gyms devotedly, who fight for freedom and their way of life, and who at times look like the Marine Corps advertisements on TV? You get the movie '300'.

Filmmakers would counter heated reactions like this one by denying that the movie carried any such subtext and declaring unapologetically that it was conceived merely as entertainment and devoid of any political motivation.[25] Meanwhile the response of some reviewers would be to argue that the Iranian reaction to the film was born out of failure to understand that that the US state exercised no control over Hollywood's output and that *300* was 'less an act of psychological warfare than an act of capitalism',[26] or that suggestions relating to the existence of parallels between the film's content and contemporary politics simply did not stand up to detailed scrutiny.[27]

Irrespective of the political backlash in some quarters, the decision to create a follow-up for release seven years later was no doubt largely a result of the commercial success of the 2007 movie. *300: Rise of an Empire* (2014), in combining the stories of the battles of Artemisium and Salamis (480 BC) with flashbacks to the first Persian invasion of 490 BC, acts as both a prequel and a sequel to the events depicted in *300*. The 2014 film takes the vision of Xerxes – as gold-bedecked god-king with a violent streak – from its predecessor and creates for him a freshly invented backstory designed to explain his actions and appearance as the result of events at Marathon. In a striking departure from the historical tradition the writers have their Xerxes witness the fatal wounding of his father at Marathon; the deadly arrow is fired by Themistocles (played by Sullivan Stapleton). While the placing of both Xerxes and Darius at the battle of Marathon is one of the film's many glaring historical inaccuracies[28] the extraor-

---

[25] Weiland (2007).

[26] Denby (2007); cf. Cartledge (2007).

[27] Queenan (2007). Note, however, Basu, Champion and Lasch-Quinn (2007), highlighting the problematic nature of a film which 'avoids any kind of indication of moral truth in the devastation it describes' and which therefore 'becomes pure entertainment and technique rather than art'.

[28] See Cartledge (2014) and von Tunzelmann (2014).

dinary distortion of the ancient source material here nonetheless bears traces of a theme which dates back to the earliest retellings of the story of Xerxes; that of the relationship between this king and his father, and the extent to which this may have influenced Xerxes' decision to invade Greece.[29]

For the makers of *300: Rise of an Empire* the invented story of Themistocles' assassination of Darius gives rise not merely to the unsubtle suggestion that the second invasion of Greece was motivated by Xerxes' desire for vengeance but it is also used to provide an explanation both for the king's belief in his own divinity and for his remarkable appearance. Manipulated by the ruthless Artemisia (played by Eva Green) – who later, again in a departure from the historical tradition, becomes the brutal commander-in-chief of the Persian navy and thus acts as a driving-force for much of the film's action[30] – Xerxes interprets Darius' death-bed words, 'only the gods could defeat the Greeks', not as an admission of defeat but as a personal challenge. After a journey through the desert the new king, at first bearded, long-haired and fully clothed, bathes in a vat of molten gold and emerges transformed into the depilated, bejewelled and bare-skinned god-king familiar to us from the earlier movie. Appearing before his amassed Persian subjects upon his return, with Artemisia looking over his shoulder, he declares his intention to go to war on Greece. In this way the twenty-first-century filmmakers, through the character of Xerxes, update the ancient theme of the Persian royal household as a setting for outlandish behaviour and the machinations of manipulative female characters; meanwhile the king's 'god complex' and desire to invade Greece are given a pseudo-psychological explanation as having been driven at least in part by the trauma of his father's death.

This modern-day fictional construction of Xerxes illustrates both the enduring fascination exercised by the king and the far-reaching influence of the story of his invasion of Greece. Created two and a half millennia after the events on which the films are based, the cinematic treatments of the Persian king demonstrate the continuing power of the figure of Xerxes to inspire writers, to entertain fresh audiences and to elicit emotionally and politically charged responses. The range of reactions to the 2007 film in particular illustrates the

---

[29] On the father/son theme see pp. 26–30 (Aeschylus' *Persians*) and pp. 58–63 (Herodotus).
[30] Herodotus (7.99) records that Artemisia brought with her five ships from Halicarnassus. See also 8.68–9 (Artemisia advises Xerxes) and 8.87–8 (her role at Salamis). It is tempting to see the film's development of the character of Artemisia as rooted in Xerxes' comment on seeing her performance at Salamis, reported by Herodotus at 8.88.3, that 'my men have become women, my women men', yet it is perhaps more likely that the filmmakers incorporated a strong female lead in order to broaden the demographic of the film's potential audience.

power of his character to invite comment and controversy in the twenty-first century, long after Aeschylus staged his version of Xerxes for the entertainment of his fifth-century Athenian spectators, or Herodotus sought to examine the story of his invasion of Greece as a means of reflecting both upon current political issues and upon wider questions concerning the human condition. Far removed in time and space from the real historical prototype, these contemporary interpretations of, and responses to, his character suggest that the imagined Xerxes holds an enduring place in the cultural encyclopaedia of the western world.

Bibliography

Abbott, J. (1878), *History of Xerxes the Great*. New York: Harper.

Abdi, K. (2010), 'The passing of the throne from Xerxes to Artaxerxes I, or how an archaeological observation can be a potential contribution to Achaemenid historiography', in J. Curtis and St.-J. Simpson (eds), *The World of Achaemenid Persia: History, Art and Society in Iran and the Ancient Near East*. London and New York: I. B. Tauris, pp. 275–84.

Alcock, S. E. (1993), *Graecia Capta: the Landscapes of Roman Greece*. Cambridge: Cambridge University Press.

—(1996), 'Landscapes of memory and the authority of Pausanias', in Bingen (ed.), pp. 241–76.

Alexanderson, B. (1967), 'Darius in the *Persians*', *Eranos* 65, 1–11.

Alexiou, M. (1974), *The Ritual Lament in Greek Tradition*. Cambridge: Cambridge University Press.

Allen, L. (2005), 'Le roi imaginaire: an audience with the Achaemenid king', in O. Hekster and R. Fowler (eds), *Imaginary Kings: Royal Images in the Ancient Near East, Greece and Rome*. Stuttgart: Franz Steiner Verlag, pp. 39–61.

Anderson, G. (1984), *Ancient Fiction: the Novel in the Graeco-Roman World*. London and Sydney: Croom Helm.

—(1986), *Philostratus: Biography and Belles Lettres in the Third Century A.D.* London and Sydney: Croom Helm.

—(1993), *The Second Sophistic: A Cultural Phenomenon in the Roman Empire*. London and New York: Routledge.

Anderson, M. (1972), 'The imagery of *The Persians*', *Greece and Rome* 19, 166–74.

Andrewes, A. (1992), 'The Spartan resurgence', in D. M. Lewis, J. Boardman, J. K. Davies and M. Ostwald (eds), *The Cambridge Ancient History Vol. V²: the Fifth Century BC*. Cambridge: Cambridge University Press, pp. 464–98.

Anti, C. (1952), 'Il vaso di Dario e i Persiani di Frinico', *Archaeologica Classica* 4, 23–45.

Arafat, K. W. (1996), *Pausanias' Greece: Ancient Artists and Roman Rulers*. Cambridge: Cambridge University Press.

Armayor, O. K. (1978), 'Herodotus' catalogues of the Persian empire in the light of the monuments and the Greek literary tradition', *Transactions of the American Philological Association* 108, 1–9.

Avery, H. C. (1972), 'Herodotus' picture of Cyrus', *American Journal of Philology* 93, 529–46.

Bakewell, G. W. (1998), '*Persae* 374–83: Persians, Greeks and ΠΕΙΘΑΡΧΩΙ ΦΡΕΝΙ', *Classical Philology* 93, 232–6.

Bakker, E. J., I. J. F. de Jong and H. van Wees (eds) (2002), *Brill's Companion to Herodotus*. Leiden: Brill.

Balcer, J. M. (1977), 'The Athenian Episkopos and the Achaemenid "King's Eye"', *American Journal of Philology* 98, 252–63.

—(1978), 'Alexander's burning of Persepolis', *Iranica Antiqua* 13, 119–33.

—(1987), *Herodotus and Bisitun: Problems in Ancient Persian Historiography*. Stuttgart: Franz Steiner Verlag.

Baldwin, J. G. (1984), *Esther: An Introduction and Commentary*. Leicester: Inter-Varsity Press.

Balsdon, J. P. V. D. (1934), *The Emperor Gaius (Caligula)*. Oxford: Oxford University Press.

Baragwanath, E. (2008), *Motivation and Narrative in Herodotus*. Oxford and New York: Oxford University Press.

Barchiesi, A. (2009), 'Exemplarity: between practice and text', in Y. Maes, J. Papy and W. Verbaal (eds), *Latinitas Perennis Volume II: Appropriation and Latin Literature*. Leiden: Brill, pp. 41–62.

Barrett, A. A. (1989), *Caligula: The Corruption of Power*. London: Batsford.

Baslez, M.-F. (1992), 'De l'histoire au roman: la Perse de Chariton', in M.-F. Baslez, P. Hoffmann and M. Trédé (eds), *Le Monde du Roman Grec*. Paris: Presses de l'École normale supérieure, pp. 199–211.

Basu, S., C. Champion and E. Lasch-Quinn (2007), '"300": the use and abuse of Greek history', *Spiked*, 3 October 2007 (http://www.spiked- online.com/newsite/article/3918#.U1pAdsIU8cA).

Batstone, W. (2009), 'The drama of rhetoric at Rome', in Gunderson (ed.), pp. 212–27.

Baynham, E. (1998), *Alexander the Great: the Unique History of Quintus Curtius*. Ann Arbor: University of Michigan Press.

—(2003), 'The ancient evidence for Alexander the Great', in Roisman (ed.), pp. 3–29.

—(2009), 'Barbarians I: Quintus Curtius' and other Roman historians' reception of Alexander', in Feldherr (ed.), pp. 288–300.

Behr, C. A. (1986), *P. Aelius Aristides: The Complete Works. Orations I–XVI*, vol. I. Leiden: Brill.

Bell, S. (2008), 'Role models in the Roman world', in S. Bell and I. L. Hansen (eds), *Role Models in the Roman World: Identity and Assimilation* (*Memoirs of the American Academy in Rome*, Supplementary Volume 7). Ann Arbor: University of Michigan Press, pp. 1–39.

di Benedetto, V. (1978), *L'Ideologia del Potere e la Tragedia Greca: Ricerche su Eschilo*. Turin: Giulio Einaudi.

Berg, S. B. (1979), *The Book of Esther: Motifs, Themes and Structure*. Missoula: Scholars Press.

Bevan, E. (1927), *A History of Egypt Under the Ptolemaic Dynasty*. London: Methuen.

Bickerman, E. (1967), *Four Strange Books of the Bible*. New York: Schocken.

Bigwood, J. M. (1978), 'Ctesias as historian of the Persian Wars', *Phoenix* 32, 19–41.

—(1980), 'Diodorus and Ctesias', *Phoenix* 34, 195–207.

Bingen, J. (ed.) (1996), *Pausanias Historien* (*Fondation Hardt, Entretiens sur l'Antiquité Classique* 41). Vandoeuvres-Geneva: Fondation Hardt.

Bischoff, H. (1932), 'Der Warner bei Herodot' (Unpublished dissertation, University of Marburg).

Blösel, W. (2001), 'The Herodotean picture of Themistocles: a mirror of fifth-century Athens', in N. Luraghi (ed.), *The Historian's Craft in the Age of Herodotus*. Oxford: Oxford University Press, pp. 179–97.

Bloomer, W. M. (1992), *Valerius Maximus and the Rhetoric of the New Nobility*. Chapel Hill and London: University of North Carolina Press.

Boardman, J. (1989), *Athenian Red Figure Vases: The Classical Period*. London: Thames & Hudson.

—(2000), *Persia and the West: An Archaeological Investigation of the Genesis of Achaemenid Persian Art*. London: Thames & Hudson.

Boedeker, D. (1987), 'The two faces of Demaratus', *Arethusa* 20: 185–201.

—(1988), 'Protesilaos and the end of Herodotus' *Histories*', *Classical Antiquity* 7: 30–48.

Bonner, S. F. (1977), *Education in Ancient Rome: From the Elder Cato to the Younger Pliny*. London: Methuen.

Bornitz, H-F. (1968), *Herodot-Studien: Beiträge zum Verständnis der Einheit des Geschichtswerks*. Berlin: W. de Gruyter.

Bosworth, A. B. (1988), *From Arrian to Alexander: Studies in Historical Interpretation*. Oxford: Oxford University Press.

—(2003), 'Plus ça change…. Ancient historians and their sources', *Classical Antiquity* 22: 167–98.

Bosworth, A. B. and E. J. Baynham (eds) (2000), *Alexander the Great in Fact and Fiction*. Oxford: Oxford University Press.

Boucher, G. (2010), 'Frank Miller returns to the "300" battlefield with "Xerxes": "I make no apologies whatsoever"', *Los Angeles Times* online edition, 1 June 2010 (http://herocomplex.latimes.com/movies/xerxes-300-frank-miller-300-zack-snyder-300/).

Bovon, A. (1963), 'La représentation des guerriers Perses et la notion de barbare dans la 1re moitié du Ve siècle', *Bulletin de Correspondance Hellénique* 87: 579–602.

Bowersock, G. (1965), *Augustus and the Greek World*. Oxford: Oxford University Press.

—(1969), *Greek Sophists in the Roman Empire*. Oxford: Oxford University Press.

—(1984), 'Augustus and the East: the problem of the succession', in F. Millar and E. Segal (eds), *Caesar Augustus: Seven Aspects*. Oxford: Oxford University Press, pp. 169–88.

—(1994), *Fiction as History: Nero to Julian*. Berkeley: University of California Press.

Bowie, A. M. (2007), *Herodotus, Histories Book VIII*. Cambridge: Cambridge University Press.

Bowie, E. L. (1974), 'Greeks and their past in the Second Sophistic', in M. I. Finley (ed.), *Studies in Ancient Society*. London: Routledge, pp. 166–209.

—(1991), 'Hellenes and Hellenism in writers of the early Second Sophistic', in S. Saïd (ed.), ʹΕΛΛΗΝΙΣΜΟΣ: *Quelques jalons pour une histoire de l'identité grecque*. Leiden: Brill, pp. 183–204.

—(1996), 'Past and present in Pausanias', in Bingen (ed.), pp. 207–39.

—(2009), 'Philostratus: the life of a sophist' in Bowie and Elsner (eds), pp. 19–32.

Bowie, E. L. and J. Elsner (eds) (2009), *Philostratus*. Cambridge: Cambridge University Press.

Boyce, M. (1984), 'Persian religion in the Achaemenid age', in W. D. Davies and L. Finkelstein (eds), *The Cambridge History of Judaism Volume I*. Cambridge: Cambridge University Press, pp. 279–307.

Brady, C. (2007), ' "300" by Zack Snyder: review', *History Ireland* 15.3: 48–9.

Braun, T. (2004), 'Xenophon's dangerous liaisons', in Lane Fox (ed.), pp. 97–130.

Braund, D. and C. Gill (eds) (2003), *Myth, History and Culture in Republican Rome: Studies in Honour of T. P. Wiseman*. Exeter: University of Exeter Press.

Briant, P. (1989), 'Histoire et idéologie: les Grecs et la "décadence perse" ', in M.-M. Mactoux and E. Geny (eds), *Mélanges Pierre Lévêque 2*. Besançon: Université de Besançon, pp. 33–47.

—(2001), 'Gaumāta', *Encyclopaedia Iranica* 10.3, 333–5 (http://www.iranicaonline.org/articles/gaumata-).

—(2002), *From Cyrus to Alexander: A History of the Persian Empire*, P. T. Daniels (trans.). Winona Lake, Indiana: Eisenbrauns.

Bridges, E. (forthcoming), ' "The greatest runway show in history": Paul Violi's *House of Xerxes* and the Herodotean spectacle of war', in A. Bakogianni and V. Hope (eds), *War as Spectacle: Ancient and Modern Displays of Armed Conflict*. London: Bloomsbury.

Bridges, E., E. Hall and P. J. Rhodes (eds) (2007), *Cultural Responses to the Persian Wars: Antiquity to the Third Millennium*. Oxford: Oxford University Press.

Broadhead, H. D. (1960), *The Persae of Aeschylus*. Cambridge: Cambridge University Press.

Brock, R. (2013), *Greek Political Imagery from Homer to Aristotle*. London: Bloomsbury.

Brockington, L. H. (1969), *Ezra, Nehemiah and Esther*. London: Nelson.

Broneer, O. (1944), 'The tent of Xerxes and the Greek theater', *University of California Publications in Classical Archaeology* 1.12: 305–12.

Brosius, M. (1996), *Women in Ancient Persia 559-331 BC*. Oxford: Oxford University Press.

—(2000), *The Persian Empire from Cyrus II to Artaxerxes I*. London: London Association of Classical Teachers.

—(2003), 'Alexander and the Persians', in Roisman (ed.), pp. 169–93.

—(2006), *The Persians: An Introduction*. London and New York: Routledge.

—(2010), 'The royal audience scene reconsidered', in J. Curtis and St.-J. Simpson (eds), *The World of Achaemenid Persia: History, Art and Society in Iran and the Ancient Near East.* London and New York: I. B. Tauris, pp. 141–52.

—(2011), 'Keeping up with the Persians: between cultural identity and Persianization in the Achaemenid period', in Gruen (ed.), pp. 135–49.

Burn, A. R. (1984, rev. edn.), *Persia and the Greeks: The Defence of the West, c. 546-478 B.C.* London: Duckworth.

Byl, S. (2001), 'Aristophane et les guerres médiques', *L'Antiquité Classique* 70: 35–47.

Cahill, N. (1985), 'The treasury at Persepolis: gift-giving at the city of the Persians', *American Journal of Archaeology* 89: 373–89.

Cameron, G. G. (1948), *Persepolis Treasury Tablets.* Chicago: University of Chicago Press.

Campbell, A. Y. (1924), *Horace: A New Interpretation.* London: Methuen.

Campbell, D. A. (1993), *Greek Lyric: Volume V.* Cambridge, MA. and London: Harvard University Press.

Carlsen, J., B. Due, O. S. Due and B. Poulsen (eds) (1993), *Alexander the Great: Reality and Myth* (*Analecta Romana Instituti Danici* suppl. 20). Rome: Academia di Danimarca.

Carroll, K. K. (1982), *The Parthenon Inscription* (*Greek, Roman and Byzantine Monographs* 9). Durham, NC: Duke University.

Cartledge, P. (1987), *Agesilaos and the Crisis of Sparta.* London: Duckworth.

—(1993), 'Xenophon's women: a touch of the other', in H. D. Jocelyn (ed.), *Tria Lustra: Essays and Notes Presented to John Pinsent.* Liverpool: Liverpool Classical Monthly, pp. 5–14.

—(2002, 2nd edn.), *The Greeks: A Portrait of Self and Others.* Oxford and New York: Oxford University Press.

—(2006), *Thermopylae: the Battle that Changed the World.* London: Macmillan.

—(2007), 'Another view', *Guardian*, 2 April 2007 (http://www.theguardian.com/ film/2007/apr/02/features.arts).

—(2013), *After Thermopylae: the Oath of Plataea and the End of the Graeco-Persian Wars.* Oxford and New York: Oxford University Press.

—(2014), ' "300": five historical errors in the new film', *BBC News Magazine*, 8 March 2014 (http://www.bbc.co.uk/news/blogs-magazine-monitor-26484784).

Castriota, D. (1992), *Myth, Ethos and Actuality: Official Art in Fifth-Century B.C. Athens.* Wisconsin: University of Wisconsin Press.

—(2000), 'Justice, kingship and imperialism: rhetoric and reality in fifth-century B.C. representations following the Persian Wars', in B. Cohen (ed.), *Not the Classical Ideal: Athens and the Construction of the Other in Greek Art.* Leiden: Brill, pp. 443–79.

Cawkwell, G. (2004), 'When, how and why did Xenophon write the *Anabasis*?', in Lane Fox (ed.), pp. 47–67.

Champlin, E. (2003), 'Agamemnon at Rome: Roman dynasts and Greek heroes', in Braund and Gill (eds), pp. 295–319.

Chaplin, J. D. (2000), *Livy's Exemplary History*. Oxford: Oxford University Press.

Chapman, H. (2009), 'Josephus', in Feldherr (ed.), pp. 319–31.

Christ, M. R. (1994), 'Herodotean kings and historical enquiry', *Classical Antiquity* 13: 167–202.

Clarke, K. (1999), *Between Geography and History: Hellenistic Constructions of the Roman World*. Oxford: Oxford University Press.

Clines, D. J. A. (1984), 'The Esther Scroll: the Story of the Story', *Journal for the Study of the Old Testament* suppl. 30.

Clough, E. (2003), *In Search of Xerxes: Images of the Persian King* (Ph.D. thesis, University of Durham).

—(2004), 'Loyalty and liberty: Thermopylae in the western imagination', in T. J. Figueira (ed.), *Spartan Society*. Swansea: Classical Press of Wales, pp. 363–84.

Coleman, K. M. (1993), 'Launching into history: aquatic displays in the early empire', *Journal of Roman Studies* 83, 48–74.

Connors, C. (2008), 'Politics and spectacles', in Whitmarsh (ed.), pp. 162–81.

Cooper, J. M. and J. F. Procopé (1995), *Seneca: Moral and Political Essays*. Cambridge: Cambridge University Press.

Couch, H. (1931), 'Proskynesis and abasement in Aeschylus', *Classical Philology* 26, 316–18.

Courtney, E. (1980), *A Commentary on the Satires of Juvenal*. London: Athlone.

Csapo, E. (2004), 'The politics of the new music', in P. Murray and P. Wilson (eds), *Music and the Muses: the Culture of Mousike in the Classical Athenian City*. Oxford: Oxford University Press, pp. 207–48.

D'Angour, A. (2011), *The Greeks and the New: Novelty in Ancient Greek Imagination and Experience*. Cambridge: Cambridge University Press.

Danzig, G. (2007), 'Xenophon's wicked Persian, or, What's wrong with Tissaphernes? Xenophon's views on lying and breaking oaths', in C. Tuplin (ed.), *Persian Responses*. Swansea: Classical Press of Wales, pp. 27–50.

Daryaee, T. (2007), 'Go tell the Spartans: how "300" misrepresents Persians in history', *Iranian.com*, 14 March 2007 (http://iranian.com/Daryaee/2007/March/300/index.html).

Dauge, Y. (1981), *Le Barbare. Recherches sur la conception romaine de la barbarie et de la civilisation* (Collection Latomus, 176). Brussels: Latomus.

Daumas, M. (1985), 'Aristophane et les Perses', *Revue des Études Anciennes* 87, 289–305.

Day, L. (1995), *Three Faces of a Queen: Characterization in the Books of Esther*. Sheffield: Sheffield Academic Press.

de Jong, I. (2001), 'The anachronical structure of Herodotus' *Histories*', in S. J. Harrison (ed.), *Texts, Ideas and the Classics: Scholarship, Theory and Classical Literature*. Oxford: Oxford University Press, pp. 93–116.

de Troyer, C. (1995), 'An oriental beauty parlour: An analysis of Esther 2.8–18 in the Hebrew, Septuagint, and second Greek text', in A. Brenner (ed.), *A Feminist*

Companion to Esther, Judith and Susanna. Sheffield: Sheffield Academic Press, pp. 47–70.

Denby, D. (2007), 'Men gone wild', *The New Yorker* online edition, 2 April 2007 (http://www.newyorker.com/arts/critics/cinema/2007/04/02/070402crci_cinema_denby).

Desmond, W. (2004), 'Punishments and the conclusion of Herodotus' *Histories*', *Greek, Roman and Byzantine Studies*, 44: 19–40.

Devereux, G. (1976), *Dreams in Greek Tragedy: An Ethno-Psycho-Analytical Study*. Berkeley and Los Angeles: University of California Press.

Dewald, C. (1990), 'Review of *The Mirror of Herodotus: The Representation of the Other in the Writing of History* by François Hartog', *Classical Philology* 85, 217–24.

—(2003), 'Form and content: the question of tyranny in Herodotus', in K. Morgan (ed.), *Popular Tyranny*. Austin, Texas: University of Texas Press, pp. 25–58.

—(2006), 'Humour and danger in Herodotus', in Dewald and Marincola (eds), pp. 145–64.

Dewald, C. and J. Marincola (eds) (2006), *The Cambridge Companion to Herodotus*. Cambridge: Cambridge University Press.

Dillery, J. (2009), 'Roman historians and the Greeks: audiences and models', in Feldherr (ed.), pp. 77–107.

Dionisotti, A. C. (1988), 'Nepos and the generals', *Journal of Roman Studies* 78: 35–49.

Dmitriev, S. (2011), *The Greek Slogan of Freedom and Early Roman Politics in Greece*. Oxford: Oxford University Press.

Doenges, N. A. (1981), *The Letters of Themistokles*. New York: Arno.

Dominick, Y. H. (2007), 'Acting other: Atossa and instability in Herodotus', *Classical Quarterly* 57: 432–44.

Drews, R. (1962), 'Diodorus and his sources', *American Journal of Philology* 83, 383–92.

—(1973), *The Greek Accounts of Eastern History*. Washington, DC: Center for Hellenic Studies.

Dubel, S. (2009), 'Colour in Philostratus' *Imagines*', in Bowie and Elsner (eds), pp. 309–21.

Due, B. (1989), *The Cyropaedia: Xenophon's Aims and Methods*. Aarhus: Aarhus University Press.

Duff, T. E. (1999), *Plutarch's Lives: Exploring Virtue and Vice*. Oxford: Oxford University Press.

—(2010), 'Plutarch's *Themistocles* and *Camillus*', in Humble (ed.), pp. 45–86.

Dunkle, J. R. (1971), 'The rhetorical tyrant in Roman historiography: Sallust, Livy and Tacitus', *Classical World* 65: 12–20.

Easterling, P. (1984), 'Kings in Greek tragedy', *Estudios sobre los géneros literarios, II*, Salamanca: Universidad de Salamanca, pp. 33–45.

Edmonds, J. M. (1957), *The Fragments of Attic Comedy Vol. I: Old Comedy*. Leiden: Brill.

Edmondson, J., S. Mason and J. Rives (eds) (2005), *Flavius Josephus and Flavian Rome*. Oxford: Oxford University Press.

Edwards, C. (1993), *The Politics of Immorality in Ancient Rome*. Cambridge: Cambridge University Press.

Elsner, J. (1992), 'Pausanias: a Greek pilgrim in the Roman world', *Past and Present* 135: 3–29.

Errington, R. M. (1989), 'Rome and Greece to 205 B.C.', in A. E. Astin, F. W. Walbank, M. W. Frederiksen and R. M. Ogilvie (eds), *The Cambridge Ancient History Vol. 8²*. Cambridge: Cambridge University Press, pp. 81–106.

Euben, J. P. (ed.) (1986), *Greek Tragedy and Political Theory*. Berkeley, Los Angeles and London: University of California Press.

Evans, J. A. S. (1969), 'The dream of Xerxes and the "nomoi" of the Persians', *Classical Journal* 57: 109–11.

—(1979), 'Herodotus' publication date', *Athenaeum*, 57: 145–9.

—(1991), *Herodotus, Explorer of the Past*. Princeton: Princeton University Press.
Fairweather, J. (1981), *Seneca the Elder*. Cambridge: Cambridge University Press.

Fantham, E. (1992), *Lucan: De Bello Civili Book II*. Cambridge: Cambridge University Press.

Faraguna, M. (2003), 'Alexander and the Greeks', in Roisman (ed.), pp. 99–130.

Favorini, A. (2003), 'History, collective memory and Aeschylus' *The Persians*', *Theatre Journal* 55: 99–111.

Feeney, D. (2007), *Caesar's Calendar: Ancient Time and the Beginnings of History*. Berkeley and London: University of California Press.

Feldherr, A. (ed.) (2009), *The Cambridge Companion to the Roman Historians*. Cambridge: Cambridge University Press.

Ferguson, J. (1979), *Juvenal: The Satires*. New York: Macmillan.

Ferrary, J.-L. (1988), *Philhellénisme et Impérialisme*. Rome: École Française de Rome.

Finkel, I. (ed.) (2013), *The Cyrus Cylinder*. London and New York: I. B. Tauris.

Fisher, N. R. E. (1992), *Hybris: A Study in the Values of Honour and Shame in Ancient Greece*. Warminster: Aris and Phillips.

—(2002), 'Popular morality in Herodotus', in E. J. Bakker, I. J. F. de Jong and H. van Wees (eds), pp. 199–224.

Flory, S. (1978), 'Laughter, tears and wisdom in Herodotus', *American Journal of Philology* 99: 145–53.

—(1980), 'Who read Herodotus' *Histories*?', *American Journal of Philology* 101: 12–28.

Flower, H. I. (2000), 'The tradition of the *spolia opima*: M. Claudius Marcellus and Augustus', *Classical Antiquity* 19: 34–64.

Flower, M. A. (1998), 'Simonides, Ephorus, and Herodotus on the battle of Thermopylae', *Classical Quarterly* 48: 365–79.

—(2000a), 'Alexander the Great and Panhellenism', in A. B. Bosworth and E. J. Baynham (eds), pp. 96–135.

—(2000b), 'From Simonides to Isocrates: the fifth-century origins of fourth-century panhellenism', *Classical Antiquity* 19: 65–101.

—(2006), 'Herodotus and Persia', in Dewald and Marincola (eds), pp. 274–89.

—(2012), *Xenophon's Anabasis, or The Expedition of Cyrus*. Oxford: Oxford University Press.

Flower, M. A. and J. Marincola (eds) (2002), *Herodotus: Histories Book IX*. Cambridge: Cambridge University Press.

Flower, M. A. and M. Toher (eds) (1991), *Georgica: Greek Studies in Honour of George Cawkwell*. London: Institute of Classical Studies.

Foley, H. P. (1993), 'The politics of tragic lamentation', in A. H. Sommerstein, S. Halliwell, J. Henderson and B. Zimmerman (eds), *Tragedy, Comedy and the Polis*. Bari: Levante, pp. 101–43.

Fornara, C. W. (1971), *Herodotus: An Interpretative Essay*. Oxford: Oxford University Press.

Forsdyke, S. (2009), 'The uses and abuses of tyranny', in R. K. Balot (ed.), *A Companion to Greek and Roman Political Thought*. Oxford: Blackwell, pp. 231–46.

Fox, M. V. (2001, 2nd edn.), *Character and Ideology in the Book of Esther*. Michigan and Cambridge: William B. Eeerdmans.

Francis, E. D. (1990), *Image and Idea in Fifth-Century Greece: Art and Literature After the Persian Wars*. London and New York: Routledge.

Fredricksmeyer, E. (2000), 'Alexander the Great and the kingship of Asia', in A. B. Bosworth and E. J. Baynham (eds), pp. 136–66.

Freese, J. H. (1920), *The Library of Photius*. London and New York: Society for Promoting Christian Knowledge.

Frost, F. J. (1980), *Plutarch's Themistocles: A Historical Commentary*. Princeton: Princeton University Press.

Frye, R. N. (1972), 'Gestures of deference to royalty in ancient Iran', *Iranica Antiqua* 9: 102–7.

Gagarin, M. (1976), *Aeschylean Drama*. Berkeley and Los Angeles: University of California Press.

Gagné, R. (2013), *Ancestral Fault in Ancient Greece*. Cambridge: Cambridge University Press.

Gantz, T. (1982), 'Inherited guilt in Aischylos', *Classical Journal* 78: 1–23.

Garvie, A. F. (1978), 'Aeschylus' simple plots', in R. D. Dawe, J. Diggle and P. E. Easterling (eds), *Dionysiaca: Nine Studies in Greek Poetry*. Cambridge: Cambridge University Library, pp. 63–86.

—(2009), *Aeschylus: Persae*. Oxford and New York: Oxford University Press.

Gehman, H. S. (1924), 'Notes on the Persian words in the Book of Esther', *Journal of Biblical Literature* 43: 321–8.

Gehrke, H-J. (1987), 'Die Griechen und die Rache: ein Versuch in historischer Psychologie', *Saeculum* 38: 121–49.

Georges, P. (1994), *Barbarian Asia and the Greek Experience*. Baltimore and London: Johns Hopkins University Press.

Gera, D. (1993), *Xenophon's Cyropaedia: Style, Genre and Literary Technique*. Oxford: Oxford University Press.

—(2007), 'Themistocles' Persian tapestry', *Classical Quarterly* 57: 445–57.

Gharib, B. (1968), 'A newly found Old Persian inscription', *Iranica Antiqua* 8: 54–69.

Gill, C. (1983), 'The question of character-development: Plutarch and Tacitus', *Classical Quarterly* 33: 469–87.

—(1990), 'The character-personality distinction', in Pelling (ed.), pp. 1–31.

—(1996), *Personality in Greek Epic, Tragedy and Philosophy*. Oxford: Oxford University Press.

Goff, B. (ed.) (1995), *History, Tragedy, Theory: Dialogues on Athenian Drama*. Austin: University of Texas Press.

Goldhill, S. (1987), 'The Great Dionysia and civic ideology', *Journal of Hellenic Studies* 107: 58–76.

—(1988), 'Battle narrative and politics in Aeschylus' *Persae*', *Journal of Hellenic Studies* 108: 189–93.

—(2000), 'Civic ideology and the problem of difference: the politics of Aeschylean tragedy, once again', *Journal of Hellenic Studies* 120: 34–56.

Gordis, R. (1976), 'Studies in the Esther narrative', *Journal of Biblical Literature* 95: 43–58.

Gorman, V. (2001), *Miletos, the Ornament of Ionia: A History of the City to 400 B.C.E.* Ann Arbor: University of Michigan Press.

Gow, A. S. F. (1928), 'Notes on the *Persae* of Aeschylus', *Journal of Hellenic Studies* 48, 133–58.

Gowing, A. M. (2009), 'The Roman *exempla* tradition in imperial Greek historiography: the case of Camillus', in Feldherr (ed.), pp. 332–47.

Gray, V. J. (2000), 'Xenophon and Isocrates', in C. Rowe and M. Schofield (eds), *The Cambridge History of Greek and Roman Political Thought*. Cambridge: Cambridge University Press, pp. 142–54.

—(2002), 'Short stories in Herodotus', in E. J. Bakker, I. J. F. de Jong and H. van Wees (eds), pp. 291–317.

Green, P. (2006), *Diodorus Siculus, Books 11-12.37.1*. Austin, Texas: University of Texas Press.

Grethlein, J. (2009), 'How not to do history: Xerxes in Herodotus' *Histories*', *American Journal of Philology* 130: 195–218.

Griffin, J. (1998), 'The social function of Attic tragedy', *Classical Quarterly* N.S. 48: 39–61.

Griffin, M. (2003), '*De beneficiis* and Roman society', *Journal of Roman Studies* 93: 92–113.

—(1995), 'Brilliant dynasts: power and politics in Aeschylus' *Oresteia*', *Classical Antiquity*, 14: 62–129.

—(1998), 'The king and eye: the rule of the father in Greek tragedy', *Proceedings of the Cambridge Philological Society* 44: 20–84.

—(2007), 'The king and eye: the rule of the father in Aischylos' *Persians*', in Lloyd (ed.), pp. 93–140.

Griffith, R. D. (2011), 'An offer you can't retract: Xerxes' nod and Masistes' wife (Herodotus 9.111.1)', *Classical Quarterly* 61: 310–12.

Griffiths, A. (1989), 'Was Cambyses mad?', in A. Powell (ed.), *Classical Sparta: Techniques behind her Success.* London: Routledge, pp. 51–78.

Gruen, E. S. (1984), *The Hellenistic World and the Coming of Rome (Vol. 1).* Berkeley, Los Angeles and London: University of California Press.

—(1992), *Culture and National Identity in Republican Rome.* Ithaca and New York: Cornell University Press.

—(2002), *Diaspora: Jews Amidst Greeks and Romans.* Cambridge, MA and London: Harvard University Press.

—(2004), 'Rome and the Greek world', in H. Flower (ed.), *The Cambridge Companion to the Roman Republic.* Cambridge: Cambridge University Press, pp. 242–68.

—(ed.) (2011), *Cultural Identity in the Ancient Mediterranean.* Los Angeles: Getty Research Institute.

Gunderson, E. (ed.) (2009), *The Cambridge Companion to Ancient Rhetoric.* Cambridge: Cambridge University Press.

Habicht, C. (1961), 'Falsche Urkunden zur Geschichte Athens im Zeitalter der Perserkriege', *Hermes* 89: 1–35.

—(1985), *Pausanias' Guide to Ancient Greece.* Berkeley, Los Angeles and London: University of California Press.

Hägg, T. (1983), *The Novel in Antiquity.* Oxford: Blackwell.

Hall, E. (1989), *Inventing the Barbarian: Greek Self-Definition through Tragedy.* Oxford: Oxford University Press.

—(1993), 'Asia unmanned: images of victory in classical Athens', in J. Rich and G. Shipley (eds), *War and Society in the Greek World.* London: Routledge, pp. 107–33.

—(1994), 'Drowning by nomes: the Greeks, swimming, and Timotheus' *Persians*', in H. A. Khan (ed.), 'The Birth of the European Identity: The Europe-Asia Contrast in Greek Thought 490-322 BC', *Nottingham Classical Literature Studies Vol. 2.* Nottingham: University of Nottingham, pp. 44–89.

—(1996), *Aeschylus: Persians.* Warminster: Aris and Phillips.

—(1999), 'Actor's song in tragedy', in S. Goldhill and R. Osborne (eds), *Performance Culture and Athenian Democracy.* Cambridge: Cambridge University Press, pp. 96–122.

—(2002), 'The singing actors of antiquity', in P. Easterling and E. Hall (eds), *Greek and Roman Actors: Aspects of an Ancient Profession.* Cambridge: Cambridge University Press, pp. 3–38.

—(2006), *The Theatrical Cast of Athens: Interactions Between Ancient Greek Drama and Society.* Oxford: Oxford University Press.

—(2007), 'Aeschylus' *Persians* via the Ottoman Empire to Saddam Hussein', in Bridges, Hall and Rhodes (eds), pp. 167–99.

Halliwell, S. (1990), 'Traditional Greek conceptions of character', in Pelling (ed.), pp. 32–59.

Hammond, N. G. L. (1983), *Three Historians of Alexander the Great: The So-called Vulgate Authors Diodorus, Justin and Curtius*. Cambridge: Cambridge University Press.

—(1993), *Sources for Alexander the Great: An Analysis of Plutarch's Life and Arrian's Anabasis Alexandrou*. Cambridge: Cambridge University Press.

Hannestad, N. (1986), *Roman Art and Imperial Policy*. Aarhus: Aarhus University Press.

—(1993), '*Imitatio Alexandri* in Roman art', in Carlsen, Due, Due and Poulsen (eds), pp. 61–9.

Hansen, O. (1984), 'On the date and place of the first performance of Timotheus' *Persae*', *Philologus* 128: 135–8.

Hardie, P. (2007), 'Images of the Persian Wars in Rome', in Bridges, Hall and Rhodes (eds), pp. 127–43.

Hardwick, L. and S. Harrison (eds) (2013), *Classics in the Modern World: A Democratic Turn?* Oxford: Oxford University Press.

Harris, W. V. (2001), *Restraining Rage: The Ideology of Anger Control in Classical Antiquity*. Cambridge, Mass.: Harvard University Press.

Harrison, T. (1998), 'Aeschylus, Atossa and Athens', *Electrum* 2: 69–86.

—(2000), *The Emptiness of Asia: Aeschylus' Persians and the History of the Fifth Century*. London: Duckworth.

—(2002), 'The Persian invasions', in E. J. Bakker, I. J. F. de Jong and H. van Wees (eds), pp. 553–78.

—(2011), *Writing Ancient Persia*. Bristol: Bristol Classical Press.

Hartmann, H. (1937), 'Zur neuen Inschrift des Xerxes von Persepolis', *Orientalische Lieteraturzeitung* 40, cols. 145–60.

Hartog, F. (1988), *The Mirror of Herodotus: The Representation of the Other in the Writing of History*, J. Lloyd (trans.) (original French version 1980). Berkeley: University of California Press.

Haubold, J. (2007), 'Xerxes' Homer', in Bridges, Hall and Rhodes (eds), pp. 47–63.

Henderson, M. M. (1975), 'Plato's *Menexenus* and the distortion of history', *Acta Classica* 18: 25–46.

Henkelman, W. F. M. (2008), *Achaemenid History XIV. The Other Gods Who Are: Studies in Elamite-Iranian Acculturation Based on the Persepolis Fortification Texts*. Leiden: Nederlands Instituut voor het Nabije Oosten.

Herington, J. (1985), *Poetry into Drama: Early Tragedy and the Greek Poetic Tradition*. Berkeley and Los Angeles: University of California Press.

Herrenschmidt, C. and J. Kellens (1993), 'Daiva', *Encyclopaedia Iranica* 6.6, pp. 599–602 (http://www.iranicaonline.org/articles/daiva-old-iranian-noun).

Herzfeld, E. E. (1932), *A New Inscription of Xerxes from Persepolis*. Chicago: University of Chicago Press.

Hirsch, S. W. (1985a), '1001 Iranian nights: history and fiction in Xenophon's *Cyropaedia*', in M. H. Jameson (ed.), *The Greek Historians: Literature and History. Papers Presented to A. E. Raubitschek*. California: Anma Libri, pp. 65–85.

—(1985b), *The Friendship of the Barbarians: Xenophon and the Persian Empire*. Hanover and London: University Press of New England.

Holland, T. (2005), *Persian Fire: the First World Empire and the Battle for the West*. London: Little, Brown.

—(2007), 'Mirage in the movie house', *Arion* third series 15.1: 173–82.

Holland, T. and P. Cartledge (2013), *Herodotus: the Histories*. London: Penguin.

Hordern, J. H. (1999), 'Some observations on the *Persae* of Timotheus', *Classical Quarterly* N.S. 49: 433–8.

—(2002), *The Fragments of Timotheus of Miletus*. Oxford: Oxford University Press.

Hornblower, S. (1994) (ed.), *Greek Historiography*. Oxford: Oxford University Press.

—(2004), 'Persia', in D. M. Lewis, J. Boardman, S. Hornblower and M. Ostwald (eds), *The Cambridge Ancient History Vol. VI²: the Fourth Century BC*. Cambridge: Cambridge University Press, pp. 45–96.

Hose, M. (1994), 'Response to Hall', in H. A. Khan (ed.), *The Birth of the European Identity: The Europe-Asia Contrast in Greek Thought 490-322 BC, Nottingham Classical Literature Studies Vol. 2*, Nottingham: University of Nottingham, pp. 81–9.

How, W. W. and J. Wells (1912), *A Commentary on Herodotus* (2 vols). Oxford: Oxford University Press.

Hudson, J. F. (1996), *Hadassah: a Novel of Ancient Persia*. Oxford: Lion.

Humble, N. (ed.) (2010), *Plutarch's Lives: Parallelism and Purpose*. Swansea: Classical Press of Wales.

Immerwahr, H. R. (1954), 'Historical action in Herodotus', *Transactions of the American Philological Association* 85: 16–45.

—(1966), *Form and Thought in Herodotus*. Cleveland, Ohio: Press of Western Reserve University.

Isaac, B. (2004), *The Invention of Racism in Classical Antiquity*. Princeton: Princeton University Press.

Jacoby, F. (1958), *Die Fragmente der griechischen Historiker, III*. Leiden: Brill.

Janssen, T. H. (1984), *Timotheus Persae: A Commentary*. Amsterdam: A. M. Hakkert.

Jenkinson, E. M. (1973), '*Genus scripturae leve*: Cornelius Nepos and the early history of biography at Rome', *Aufstieg und Niedergang der Römischen Welt* 1.3: 703–19.

Jolivet, V. (1987), '*Xerxes togatus*: Lucullus en Campanie', *Mélanges de l'École Française de Rome: Antiquité*: 857–904.

Jones, C. P. (1971), *Plutarch and Rome*. Oxford: Oxford University Press.

—(1978), 'Three foreigners in Attica', *Phoenix* 32: 222–34.

—(1986), *Culture and Society in Lucian*. Cambridge, Mass. and London: Harvard University Press.

Kantzios, I. (2004), 'The politics of fear in Aeschylus' *Persians*', *The Classical World* 98: 3–19.

Keaveney, A. (2003), *The Life and Journey of the Athenian Statesman Themistocles (524-460 B.C.?) as a Refugee in Persia*. New York: Edwin Mellen Press.

Kent, R. G. (1937), 'The daiva-inscription of Xerxes', *Language* 13: 292–305.

—(1943), 'Old Persian texts', *Journal of Near Eastern Studies* 2: 302–6.

—(1953), *Old Persian: Grammar, Texts, Lexicon*. New Haven: American Oriental Society.

Ketterer, R. C. (1991), 'Lamachus and Xerxes in the exodos of *Acharnians*', *Greek, Roman and Byzantine Studies* 32: 51–60.

Kierdorf, W. (1966), *Erlebnis und Darstellung der Perserkriege: Studien zu Simonides, Pindar, Aischylos und den attischen Rednern*. Göttingen: Vandenhoeck and Ruprecht.

Kimbell, D. (2007), 'Operatic variations on an episode at the Hellespont', in Bridges, Hall and Rhodes (eds), pp. 201–30.

Kleijwegt, M. (1994), 'Caligula's "triumph" at Baiae', *Mnemosyne* 47: 652–71.

Konstan, D. (1987), 'Persians, Greeks and empire', *Arethusa* 20: 59–73.

Kovacs, G. A. (2013), 'Truth, justice and the Spartan way: Freedom and Democracy in Frank Miller's *300*', in Hardwick and Harrison (eds), pp. 381–92.

Kraus, C. S. (2005), 'From *exempla* to *exemplar*? Writing History Around the Emperor in Imperial Rome', in Edmondson, Mason and Rives (eds), pp. 181–200.

Kuhrt, A. (1983), 'The Cyrus Cylinder and Achaemenid imperial policy', *Journal for the Study of the Old Testament* 25: 83–97.

—(2007), *The Persian Empire: A Corpus of Sources from the Achaemenid Period*. London and New York: Routledge.

—(2009), 'Sancisi-Weerdenburg, Heleen', *Encyclopaedia Iranica* (online edition: http://www.iranicaonline.org/articles/sancisi-weerdenburg-heleen).

—(2010), 'Xerxes and the Babylonian temples: a restatement of the case', in J. Curtis and St.-J. Simpson (eds), *The World of Achaemenid Persia: History, Art and Society in Iran and the Ancient Near East*. London and New York: I. B. Tauris, pp. 491–4.

Kuhrt, A. and H. Sancisi-Weerdenburg (1987), 'Introduction', in Sancisi-Weerdenburg and Kuhrt (eds), pp. ix–xiii.

Kuhrt, A. and S. Sherwin-White (1987), 'Xerxes' destruction of Babylonian temples', in Sancisi-Weerdenburg and Kuhrt (eds), pp. 69–78.

Kurke, L. (1999), *Coins, Bodies, Games and Gold: the Politics of Meaning in Archaic Greece*. Princeton: Princeton University Press.

Lane Fox, R. (1973), *Alexander the Great*. London: Allen Lane.

—(ed.) (2004), *The Long March: Xenophon and the Ten Thousand*. New Haven and London: Yale University Press.

—(2007), 'Alexander the Great: 'Last of the Achaemenids'?' in Tuplin (ed.), pp. 267–311.

Larmour, D. H. J. (1991), 'Making parallels: *synkrisis* and Plutarch's "Themistocles and Camillus"', *Aufstieg und Niedergang der Römischen Welt* 2.33.6: 4154–200.

Lateiner, D. (1977), 'No laughing matter: a literary tactic in Herodotus', *Transactions of the American Philological Association* 107: 173–82.

—(1985), 'Limit, propriety and transgression in the *Histories* of Herodotus', in M. H. Jameson (ed.), *The Greek Historians: Literature and History. Papers Presented to A. E. Raubitschek*. California: Anma Libri, pp. 87–100.

—(1987), 'Nonverbal communication in the *Histories* of Herodotus', *Arethusa* 20: 83–117.

—(1989), *The Historical Method of Herodotus*. Toronto: University of Toronto Press.

—(2008), 'Review of *Herodotus, Explorer of the Past* by J. A. S. Evans', *Bryn Mawr Classical Review* (http://bmcr.brynmawr.edu/1991/02.05.08.html).

Lattimore, R. (1939), 'The wise adviser in Herodotus', *Classical Philology* 34, 24–35.

Lazenby, J. F. (1988), 'Aischylos and Salamis', *Hermes* 116: 168–85.

Lecoq, P. (1997), *Les inscriptions de la Perse achéménide*. Paris: Gallimard.

Lenardon, R. J. (1959), 'The chronology of Themistokles' ostracism and exile', *Historia* 8: 23–48.

—(1978), *The Saga of Themistocles*. London: Thames & Hudson.

Lenfant, D. (1996), 'Ctésias et Hérodote', *Revue des Études Grecques* 109: 348–80.

—(2000), 'Nicolas de Damas et le corpus des fragments de Ctésias. Du fragment comme adaptation', *Ancient Society* 30: 293–318.

—(2004), *Ctésias de Cnide: La Perse, L'Inde, autres fragments*. Paris: Les Belles Lettres.

—(2012), 'Ctesias and his eunuchs', *Histos* 6: 257–97.

Levene, D. S. (2007), 'Xerxes goes to Hollywood', in Bridges, Hall and Rhodes (eds), pp. 383–403.

Levenson, J. D. (1997), *Esther*. London: SCM Press.

Lévy, I. (1939), 'L'inscription triomphale de Xerxès', *Revue Historique* 185: 105–122.

Lewis, D. M. (1977), *Sparta and Persia*. Leiden: Brill.

—(1989), 'Persian gold in Greek international relations', *Revue des Études Anciennes* 91: 227–34.

Llewellyn-Jones, L. (2002), 'Eunuchs and the royal harem in Achaemenid Persia (559-331 BC)', in S. Tougher (ed.), *Eunuchs in Antiquity and Beyond*. London: Classical Press of Wales and Duckworth, pp. 19–49.

—(2012), 'The Great Kings of the fourth century and the Greek memory of the Persian past', in J. Marincola, L. Llewellyn-Jones and C. Maciver (eds), *Greek Notions of the Past in the Archaic and Classical Eras*. Edinburgh: Edinburgh University Press, pp. 317–46.

Llewellyn-Jones, L. and J. Robson (2010), *Ctesias' History of Persia: Tales of the Orient*. London and New York: Routledge.

Lloyd, A. B. (1988), 'Herodotus on Cambyses. Some thoughts on recent work', in A. Kuhrt and H. Sancisi-Weerdenburg (eds), *Achaemenid History III: Method and Theory*. Leiden: Nederlands Instituut voor het Nabije Oosten, pp. 55–66.

Lloyd, M. (ed.) (2007), *Aeschylus*. Oxford: Oxford University Press.

Lobur, J. A. (2008), *Consensus, Concordia and the Formation of Roman Imperial Ideology*. London and New York: Routledge.

Long, T. (1986), *Barbarians in Greek Comedy*. Carbondale and Edwardsville: Southern Illinois University Press.

Loraux, N. (1986), *The Invention of Athens: the Funeral Oration in the Classical City*, A. Sheridan (trans.) (original French version 1981). Cambridge, Mass. and London: Harvard University Press.

Macan, R. W. (1908), *Herodotus, the Seventh, Eighth and Ninth Books with Introduction and Commentary*. London: Macmillan.

Mallock, S. J. V. (2001), 'Gaius' bridge at Baiae and Alexander-*imitatio*', *Classical Quarterly* 51: 206–17.

Marincola, J. (1997), *Authority and Tradition in Ancient Historiography*. Cambridge: Cambridge University Press.

—(2007a), 'The Persian Wars in fourth-century oratory and historiography', in Bridges, Hall and Rhodes (eds), pp. 105–25.

—(ed.) (2007b), *A Companion to Greek and Roman Historiography Vol. I*. Malden and Oxford: Blackwell.

—(2010), 'Plutarch, "parallelism" and the Persian-War *Lives*', in Humble (ed.), pp. 121–43.

Marr, J. (1995), 'The death of Themistocles', *Greece and Rome* 42: 159–67.

McClure, L. (1999), *Spoken Like a Woman: Speech and Gender in Athenian Drama*. Princeton: Princeton University Press.

McClure, L. (2006), 'Maternal authority and heroic disgrace in Aeschylus's *Persae*', *Transactions of the American Philological Association* 136: 71–97.

Michelini, A. M. (1982), *Tradition and Dramatic Form in the Persians of Aeschylus*. Leiden: Brill.

Mikalson, J. D. (2002), 'Religion in Herodotus', in Bakker, de Jong and van Wees (eds), pp. 187–98.

Millar, F. G. B. (1987), 'Polybius between Greece and Rome', in J. T. A. Koumoulides (ed.), *Greek Connections: Essays on Culture and Diplomacy*. Notre Dame, Indiana: University of Notre Dame Press, pp. 1–19.

Millard, A. R. (1977), 'The Persian names in Esther and the reliability of the Hebrew text', *Journal of Biblical Literature* 96: 481–8.

Miller, F. (1999), *300*. Milwaukie, Oregon: Dark Horse Comics.

Miller, G. (2007), 'Inside "300"' (http://entertainment.howstuffworks.com/inside-300.htm).

Miller, M. C. (1988), 'Midas as the Great King in fifth-century Attic vase-painting', *Antike Kunst* 31, 79–89.

—(1997), *Athens and Persia in the Fifth Century B.C.: A Study in Cultural Receptivity*. Cambridge: Cambridge University Press.

—(2003), 'Art, myth and reality: Xenophantos' lekythos re-examined', in E. Csapo and M. Miller (eds), *Poetry, Theory, Praxis: The Social Life of Myth, Word and Image in Ancient Greece*. Oxford: Oxbow, pp. 19–47.

—(2010), 'I am Eurymedon: tensions and ambiguities in Athenian war imagery', in D. M. Pritchard (ed.), *War, Democracy and Culture in Classical Athens*. Cambridge: Cambridge University Press, pp. 304–38.

Mitchell, L. (2007), *Panhellenism and the Barbarian in Archaic and Classical Greece*. Swansea: Classical Press of Wales.

Moaveni, A. (2007), '"300" sparks an outcry in Iran', *Time* online edition, 13 March 2007 (http://content.time.com/time/world/article/0,8599,1598886,00.html).

Moles, J. (1996), 'Herodotus warns the Athenians', *Papers of the Leeds International Latin Seminar* 9, 259–84.

—(2002), 'Herodotus and Athens', in Bakker, de Jong and van Wees (eds), pp. 32–52.

Momigliano, A. (1975), *Alien Wisdom: the Limits of Hellenization*. Cambridge: Cambridge University Press.

—(1993), *The Development of Greek Biography*. Cambridge, MA.: Harvard University Press.

Moore, C. A. (1971), *Esther*. New York: Doubleday.

Morgan, J. R. and R. Stoneman (1994, eds), *Greek Fiction: the Greek Novel in Context*. London and New York: Routledge.

Mossman, J. (1988), 'Tragedy and epic in Plutarch's *Alexander*', *Journal of Hellenic Studies* 108: 83–93.

—(1991), 'Plutarch's use of statues', in Flower and Toher (eds), pp. 98–119.

—(2010), 'A life unparalleled: *Artaxerxes*', in Humble (ed.), pp. 145–68.

Munson, R. V. (1991), 'The madness of Cambyses', *Arethusa* 24: 43–65.

Murray, G. N. (2007), 'Zack Snyder, Frank Miller and Herodotus: three takes on the 300 Spartans', *Akroterion* 52: 11–35.

Nadon, C. (2001), *Xenophon's Prince: Republic and Empire in the Cyropaedia*. Berkeley and Los Angeles: University of California Press.

Nicolet, C. (1991), *Space, Geography and Politics in the Early Roman Empire*. Ann Arbor: University of Michigan Press.

Nisbet, G. (2008, 2nd edn.), *Ancient Greece in Film and Popular Culture*. Bristol: Bristol Phoenix Press.

Nouhaud, M. (1982), *L'Utilisation de l'histoire par les orateurs Attiques*. Paris: Les Belles Lettres.

Oliver, J. J. (1968), 'The civilizing power: a study of the Panathenaic discourse of Aelius Aristides', *Transactions of the American Philosophical Association* 58: 1.

Olmstead, A. T. (1948), *History of the Persian Empire (Achaemenid Period)*. Chicago: University of Chicago Press.

O'Neill, E. (1942), 'Notes on Phrynichus' *Phoenissae* and Aeschylus' *Persae*', *Classical Philology* 37, 425–7.

Page, D. L. (1950), *Select Papyri: Volume III*. Cambridge, MA.: Harvard University Press.

Papillon, T. (1996), 'Isocrates', in I. Worthington (ed.), *A Companion to Greek Rhetoric*. Oxford: Blackwell, pp. 58–74.

Paton, L. B. (1908), *A Critical and Exegetical Commentary on the Book of Esther*. Edinburgh: T & T Clark.

Paul, J. (2013), *Film and the Classical Epic Tradition*. Oxford: Oxford University Press.

Pearson, L. (1941), 'Historical allusions in the Attic orators', *Classical Philology* 36: 209–29.

Pelling, C. (1988), *Plutarch: Life of Antony*. Cambridge: Cambridge University Press.

—(1989), 'Plutarch: Roman heroes and Greek culture', in M. Griffin and J. Barnes (eds), *Philosophia Togata: Essays on Philosophy and Roman Society*. Oxford: Oxford University Press, pp. 199–232.

—(ed.) (1990), *Characterization and Individuality in Greek Literature*. Oxford: Oxford University Press.

—(1991), 'Thucydides' Archidamus and Herodotus' Artabanus', in Flower and Toher (eds), pp. 120–42.

—(1997), 'East is east and west is west – or are they? National stereotypes in Herodotus', *Histos* 1: 51–66.

—(ed.) (1997), *Greek Tragedy and the Historian*. Oxford: Oxford University Press.

—(2002), *Plutarch and History: Eighteen Studies*. Swansea: Classical Press of Wales and Duckworth.

—(2006), 'Speech and narrative in the *Histories*' in Dewald and Marincola (eds), pp. 103–21.

—(2007), '*De malignitate Plutarchi*: Plutarch, Herodotus, and the Persian Wars', in Bridges, Hall and Rhodes (eds), pp. 145–64.

Pérez Jiménez, A. (2002), '*Exemplum*: the paradigmatic education of the ruler in the *Lives* of Plutarch', in Stadter and van der Stockt (eds), pp. 105–14.

Perlman, S. (1961), 'The historical example, its use and importance as political propaganda in the Attic orators', *Scripta Hierosolymitana* 7, 150–66.

—(1976), 'Panhellenism, the polis and imperialism', *Historia* 25, 1–30.

Perrot, J. (ed.) (2013), *The Palace of Darius at Susa: the Great Royal Residence of Achaemenid Persia*, D. Collon and G. Collon (trans.) (original French version 2010). London: I. B. Tauris.

Pfeiffer, R. H. (1952), *Introduction to the Old Testament*. London: Adam and Charles Black.

Pitcher, L. V. (2007), 'Characterization in ancient historiography' in Marincola (ed.), pp. 102–17.

Podlecki, A. J. (1975), *The Life of Themistocles*. Montreal and London: McGill-Queen's University Press.

—(1986), '*Polis* and monarch in early Attic tragedy', in Euben (ed.), pp. 76–100.

—(1993), 'Κατ' ἀρχῆς γὰρ φιλαίτιος λεώς: the concept of leadership in Aeschylus', in A. H. Sommerstein, S. Halliwell, J. Henderson and B. Zimmerman (eds), *Tragedy, Comedy and the Polis*. Bari: Levante, pp. 55–79.

—(1999, 2nd edn.), *The Political Background of Aeschylean Tragedy*. Bristol: Bristol Classical Press.

Pohlenz, M. (1937), *Herodot: der erste Geschichtsschreiber des Abendlandes*. Stuttgart: B. G. Teubner.

Pownall, F. (2004), *Lessons from the Past: The Moral Use of History in Fourth-Century Prose*. Michigan: Ann Arbor.

Priestley, J. (2014), *Herodotus and Hellenistic Culture: Literary Studies in the Reception of the Histories*. Oxford: Oxford University Press.

Purcell, N. (1987), 'Town in country and country in town', in E. B. MacDougall (ed.), *Ancient Roman Villa Gardens* (*Dumbarton Oaks Colloquium on the History of Landscape Architecture* 10), pp. 185–203.

—(2003), 'Becoming historical: the Roman case', in Braund and Gill (eds), pp. 12–40.

Queenan, J. (2007), 'Briefs encounter', *Guardian*, 17 March 2007 (http://www.theguardian.com/film/2007/mar/17/culture.features).

Raaflaub, K. A. (1987), 'Herodotus, political thought and the meaning of history', *Arethusa* 20, 221–48.

—(2002), 'Philosophy, science, politics: Herodotus and the intellectual trends of his time', in Bakker, de Jong and van Wees (eds), pp. 149–86.

—(2003), 'Stick and glue: the function of tyranny in fifth-century Athenian democracy', in K. A. Morgan (ed.) *Popular Tyranny*. Austin, Texas: University of Texas Press, pp. 59–93.

Raeck, W. (1981), *Zum Barbarenbild in der Kunst Athens im 6. und 5. Jahrhundert v. Chr.* Bonn: Habelt.

Rajak, T. (1974), 'Flavius Josephus: Jewish History and the Greek World' (2 vols) (Unpublished D.Phil thesis, University of Oxford).

—(2001), *The Jewish Dialogue with Greece and Rome: Studies in Cultural and Social Interaction*. Leiden: Brill.

—(2003, 2nd edn.), *Josephus: the Historian and his Society*. London: Duckworth.

Reardon, B. P. (1974), 'The Second Sophistic and the novel', in G. Bowersock (ed.), *Approaches to the Second Sophistic: Papers Presented at the 105th Annual Meeting of the American Philological Association*. Pennsylvania: American Philological Association, pp. 23–9.

—(ed.) (1989), *Collected Ancient Greek Novels*. Berkeley: University of California Press.

Redfield, J. (1985), 'Herodotus the tourist', *Classical Philology* 80: 97–118.

Reinhardt, K. (1960), *Vermächtnis der Antike*. Göttingen: Vandenhoek.

Rex Stem, S. (2012), *The Political Biographies of Cornelius Nepos*. Ann Arbor: University of Michigan Press.

Rhodes, P. J. (1970), 'Thucydides on Pausanias and Themistocles', *Historia* 19, 387–400.

—(2003), 'Nothing to do with democracy: Athenian drama and the polis', *Journal of Hellenic Studies* 123: 104–19.

—(2007), 'The impact of the Persian Wars on classical Greece', in Bridges, Hall and Rhodes (eds), pp. 31–44.

Robertson, N. (1976), 'False documents at Athens: fifth-century history and fourth-century publicists', *Historical Reflections* 3.1: 3–25.

Roisman, J. (1988), 'On Phrynichos' *Sack of Miletus* and *Phoinissai*', *Eranos* 86: 15–23.

—(ed.) (2003), *Brill's Companion to Alexander the Great*. Leiden and Boston: Brill.

Roller, M. (2004), 'Exemplarity in Roman culture: the cases of Horatius Cocles and Cloelia', *Classical Philology* 99: 1–56.

—(2009), 'The exemplary past in Roman historiography and culture', in Feldherr (ed.), pp. 214–30.

Rollinger, R. (2004), 'Herodotus, Human Violence and the Ancient Near East', in V. Karageorghis and I. Taifacos (eds), *The World of Herodotus*. Nicosia: Foundation Anastasios G. Leventis, pp. 121–50.

Romm, J. (1998), *Herodotus*. New Haven and London: Yale University Press.

—(2004), 'Travel', in Whitmarsh (ed.), pp. 109–26.

Rood, T. (2004), 'Panhellenism and self-presentation: Xenophon's speeches', in Lane Fox (ed.), pp. 305–29.

Root, M. C. (1979), *The King and Kingship in Achaemenid Art: Essays on the Creation of an Iconography of Empire*. Leiden: Brill.

—(2011), 'Embracing ambiguity in the world of Athens and Persia', in Gruen (ed.), pp. 86–95.

Rosenbloom, D. (1993), 'Shouting "Fire" in a crowded theater: Phrynichos's *Capture of Miletus* and the politics of fear in early Attic tragedy', *Philologus* 137: 159–96.

—(1995), 'Myth, history, and hegemony in Aeschylus', in Goff (ed.), pp. 91–130.

—(2006), *Aeschylus: Persians*. London: Duckworth.

Rosivach, V. J. (1984), 'The Romans' view of the Persians', *The Classical World* 78: 1–8.

Rowe, C. (2007), 'Plato and the Persian Wars', in Bridges, Hall and Rhodes (eds), pp. 85–104.

Rudd, N. (1991), *Juvenal: The Satires*. Oxford: Oxford University Press.

Rutherford, R. B. (1994), 'Learning from history: categories and case-histories', in R. Osborne and S. Hornblower (eds), *Ritual, Finance, Politics: Athenian Democratic Accounts Presented to David Lewis*. Oxford: Oxford University Press, pp. 53–68.

Sacks, K. S. (1994), 'Diodorus and his sources', in Hornblower (ed.), pp. 213–32.

Saïd, E. (1978), *Orientalism*. London: Routledge.

—(1981), 'Darius et Xerxès dans les *Perses* d'Eschyle', *Ktema* 6: 17–38.

—(2002), 'Herodotus and tragedy', in Bakker, de Jong and van Wees (eds), pp. 117–47.

—(2007), 'Tragedy and reversal: the example of the *Persians*', in Lloyd (ed.), pp. 71–92.

Sancisi-Weerdenburg, H. (1980), 'Yaunā en Persai: Grieken en Perzen in een ander perspectief' (Unublished Ph.D. thesis, University of Leiden).

—(1983), 'Exit Atossa: images of women in Greek historiography on Persia', in A. Cameron and A. Kuhrt (eds), *Images of Women in Antiquity*. London: Croom Helm, pp. 20–33.

—(1987a), 'Decadence in the empire or decadence in the sources? From source to synthesis: Ctesias', in H. Sancisi-Weerdenburg (ed.), *Achaemenid History I: Sources, Structures and Synthesis*. Leiden: Nederlands Instituut voor het Nabije Oosten, pp. 33–45.

—(1987b), 'The fifth oriental monarchy and hellenocentrism: *Cyropaedia* VIII and its influence', in Sancisi-Weerdenburg and Kuhrt (eds), pp. 117–31.

—(1987c), 'Introduction', in H. Sancisi-Weerdenburg (ed.), *Achaemenid History I: Sources, Structures and Synthesis*. Leiden: Nederlands Instituut voor het Nabije Oosten, pp. xi–xiv.

—(1989), 'The personality of Xerxes, King of Kings', in L. de Meyer and E. Haerinck (eds), *Archaeologica Iranica et Orientalis: Miscellanea in Honorem Louis Vanden Berghe Vol. I*. Gent: Peeters, pp. 549–61.

—(1993a), 'Alexander and Persepolis', in Carlsen, Due, Due and Poulsen (eds),
pp. 177–88.

—(1993b), Review of *Inventing the Barbarian* by E. Hall, *Mnemosyne* 46: 126–32.

—(1999), 'The Persian kings and history', in C. S. Kraus (ed.), *The Limits of
Historiography: Genre and Narrative in Ancient Historical Texts*. Leiden: Brill,
pp. 91–112.

Sancisi-Weerdenburg, H. and A. Kuhrt (eds) (1987), *Achaemenid History II: The Greek
Sources*. Leiden: Nederlands Instituut voor het Nabije Oosten.

Schenker, D. (1994), 'The Queen and the Chorus in Aeschylus' *Persae*', *Phoenix* 48:
283–93.

Schmidt, E. F. (1953), *Persepolis I: Structures, Reliefs, Inscriptions*. Chicago: University
of Chicago Press.

Schmidt, T. S. (1999), *Plutarque et les Barbares: la Rhétorique d'une Image*. Namur:
Société des Études Classiques.

—(2002), 'Plutarch's timeless barbarians and the age of Trajan', in Stadter and van der
Stockt (eds), pp. 57–71.

Schmitt, R. (1984), 'Perser und Persisches in der Alten Attischen Komödie', *Acta
Iranica* 9: 459–72.

—(1990), 'Bīsotūn iii. Darius's inscriptions', *Encyclopaedia Iranica* 4.3, 299–305 (http://
www.iranicaonline.org/articles/bisotun-iii).

Schmitz, T. A. (1999), 'Performing history in the Second Sophistic', in
M. Zimmermann (ed.), *Geschichtsschreibung und Politischer Wandel im 3. JH. n.
Chr. (Historia Einzelschriften* 127), pp. 71–92.

Schwartz, S. (2003), 'Rome in the Greek novel? Images and ideas of empire in
Chariton's Persia', *Arethusa* 36: 375–94.

Seager, R. (1994), 'The Corinthian War', in D. M. Lewis, J. Boardman, S. Hornblower
and M. Ostwald (eds), *The Cambridge Ancient History Vol. VI²: the Fourth Century
BC*. Cambridge: Cambridge University Press, pp. 97–119.

Shahbazi, A. S. (1993), 'Darius iii. Darius I the Great', *Encyclopaedia Iranica* 7.1: 41–50
(http://www.iranicaonline.org/articles/darius-iii).

Shapiro, H. A. (2009), 'The invention of Persia in classical Athens', in M. Eliav-
Feldon, B. Isaac and J. Ziegler (eds), *The Origins of Racism in the West*. Cambridge:
Cambridge University Press, pp. 57–87.

Shapiro, S. O. (1994), 'Learning through suffering: human wisdom in Herodotus',
Classical Journal 89, 349–55.

—(1996), 'Herodotus and Solon', *Classical Antiquity* 15, 348–66.

—(2000), 'Proverbial wisdom in Herodotus', *Transactions of the American Philological
Association* 130, 89–18.

Sherk, R. K. (1988), *The Roman Empire: Augustus to Hadrian*. Cambridge: Cambridge
University Press.

Skidmore, C. (1996), *Practical Ethics for Roman Gentlemen: The Work of Valerius
Maximus*. Exeter: University of Exeter Press.

Smith, A. C. (1999), 'Eurymedon and the evolution of political personifications in the early classical period', *Journal of Hellenic Studies* 119: 128–141.

Solmsen, F. (1974), 'Two crucial decisions in Herodotus', *Mededelingen der Koninklijke Nederlandse Akademie van Wetenschappen, Afd. Letterkunde* N.S. 37.6: 3–33.

Solomon, J. (2001), *The Ancient World in the Cinema.* New Haven: Yale University Press.

Sommerstein, A. H. (1980), *Aristophanes: Acharnians.* Warminster: Aris and Phillips.

—(1995), 'Aeschylus' epitaph', *Museum Criticum* 30: 111–17.

—(2010, 2nd edn.), *Aeschylean Tragedy.* London: Duckworth.

Spark, D. (2009), *Good for the Jews.* Ann Arbor: University of Michigan Press.

Sparkes, B. A. (1997), 'Some Greek images of others', in B. L. Molyneaux (ed.), *The Cultural Life of Images.* London and New York: Routledge, pp. 130–58.

Spawforth, A. (1994), 'Symbol of unity? The Persian-Wars tradition in the Roman empire', in Hornblower (ed.), pp. 233–47.

Spencer, D. (2002), *The Roman Alexander: Reading a Cultural Myth.* Exeter: University of Exeter Press.

Stadter, P. A. (1984), 'Searching for Themistocles: a review article' (review of Frost 1980), *Classical Journal* 79: 356–63.

—(1991), 'Fictional narrative in the *Cyropaideia*', *American Journal of Philology* 112: 461–91.

—(2010), 'Parallels in three dimensions', in Humble (ed.), pp. 197–216.

Stadter, P. A. and L. van der Stockt (eds) (2002), *Sage and Emperor: Plutarch, Greek Intellectuals, and Roman Power in the Time of Trajan (98-117 A.D.).* Leuven: Leuven University Press.

Starr, C. G. (1975), 'Greeks and Persians in the fourth century B.C.: a study in cultural contacts before Alexander. Part I: Political, economic and social developments', *Iranica Antiqua* 11: 39–99.

—(1976), 'Greeks and Persians in the fourth century B.C.: a study in cultural contacts before Alexander. Part II: The meeting of two cultures', *Iranica Antiqua* 12: 49–115.

Steiner, D. T. (1994), *The Tyrant's Writ: Myths and Images of Writing in Ancient Greece.* Princeton: Princeton University Press.

Stern, M. (1984), *Greek and Latin Authors on Jews and Judaism* Vol. 3. Jerusalem: Israel Academy of Sciences and Humanities.

Stevens, D. (2007), 'A movie only a Spartan could love: the battle epic "300"', *Slate,* 8 March 2007 (http://www.slate.com/articles/arts/movies/2007/03/a_movie_only_a_ spartan_could_love. html).

Stevenson, R. B. (1997), *Persica. Greek Writing about Persia in the Fourth Century* BC. Edinburgh: Scottish Academic Press.

Stoessl, F. (1952), 'Aeschylus as a political thinker', *American Journal of Philology* 78: 113–39.

Strauss, B. (2004), *The Battle of Salamis: The Naval Encounter that Saved Greece – and Western Civilization.* New York: Simon and Schuster.

Strid, O. (2006), 'Voiceless victims, memorable deaths in Herodotus', *Classical Quarterly* 56: 393–403.

Stronk, J. P. (2007), 'Ctesias of Cnidus, a reappraisal', *Mnemosyne* 60: 25–58.

—(2010), *Ctesias' Persian History* Part I: *Introduction, Text and Translation*. Düsseldorf: Wellem Verlag.

Sussman, L. A. (1978), *The Elder Seneca* (*Mnemosyne supplement* 51). Leiden: Brill.

Swain, S. (1989), 'Plutarch's Aemilius and Timoleon', *Historia* 38: 314–34.

—(1996), *Hellenism and Empire: Language, Classicism and Power in the Greek World AD 50-250*. Oxford: Oxford University Press.

Talmon, S. (1963), ' "Wisdom" in the Book of Esther', *Vetus Testamentum* 13: 419–455.

Taplin, O. (1977), *The Stagecraft of Aeschylus: The Dramatic Use of Exits and Entrances in Greek Tragedy*. Oxford: Clarendon Press.

—(2007), *Pots and Plays: Interactions between Tragedy and Greek Vase-painting of the Fourth Century B.C.* Los Angeles: The J. Paul Getty Museum.

Tatum, J. (1989), *Xenophon's Imperial Fiction: On the Education of Cyrus*. Princeton: Princeton University Press.

—(1994), 'The education of Cyrus', in Morgan and Stoneman (eds), pp. 15–28.

Thalmann, W. G. (1980), 'Xerxes' rags: some problems in Aeschylus' *Persians*', *American Journal of Philology* 101: 260–82.

Thomas, R. (1989), *Oral Tradition and Written Record in Classical Athens*. Cambridge: Cambridge University Press.

—(2000), *Herodotus in Context: Ethnography, Science and the Art of Persuasion*. Cambridge: Cambridge University Press.

Thompson, W. E. (1983), 'Isocrates on the peace treaties', *Classical Quarterly* 33: 75–80.

Todd, S. C. (2007), *A Commentary on Lysias, Speeches 1-11*. Oxford: Oxford University Press.

Trendall, A. D. and T. B. L. Webster (1971), *Illustrations of Greek Drama*. London: Phaidon.

Tuplin, C. (1996), *Achaemenid Studies, Historia Einzelschriften* 99. Stuttgart: Franz Steiner Verlag.

—(2004a), 'Doctoring the Persians: Ctesias of Cnidus, physician and historian', *Klio* 86: 305–47.

—(2004b), 'The Persian Empire', in Lane Fox (ed.), pp. 154–183.

—(2005), 'Darius' accession in (the) Media', in P. Bienkowski, C. Mee and E. Slater (eds), *Writing and Near Eastern Society: Papers in Honour of Alan R. Millard*. New York and London: T&T Clark International, pp. 217–244.

—(ed.) (2007), *Persian Responses*. Swansea: Classical Press of Wales.

—(2011), 'The limits of Persianization: some reflections on cultural links in the Persian empire', in Gruen (ed.), pp. 150–82.

Turner, S. (2009), ' "Only Spartan women give birth to real men": Zack Snyder's "300" and the male nude', in D. Lowe and K. Shahabudin (eds), *Classics for All: Reworking*

Antiquity in Mass Culture. Newcastle upon Tyne: Cambridge Scholars Publishing, pp. 128–49.

Ubsdell, S. (1982), 'Herodotus on Human Nature' (Unpublished D.Phil thesis, University of Oxford).

Usher, S. (1990), *Greek Orators* Volume III: *Isocrates Panegyricus and To Nicocles.* Warminster: Aris and Phillips.

—(1993), 'Isocrates: *paideia*, kingship and the barbarians', in H. A. Khan (ed.), *The Birth of the European Identity: The Europe-Asia Contrast in Greek Thought 490-322 BC. Nottingham Classical Literature Studies Vol. 2.* Nottingham: University of Nottingham, pp. 134–145.

—(1999), *Greek Oratory: Tradition and Originality.* Oxford: Oxford University Press.

van der Blom, H. (2010), *Cicero's Role Models: The Political Strategy of a Newcomer.* Oxford: Oxford University Press.

van Minnen, P. (1997), 'The performance and readership of the *Persai* of Timotheus', *Archiv für Papyrusforschung* 43(2): 246–60.

Vlassopoulos, K. (2013), *Greeks and Barbarians.* Cambridge: Cambridge University Press.

von Tunzelmann, A. (2014), ' "300: Rise of an Empire" doesn't know its Artemisia from its elbow', *Guardian* film blog, 12 March 2014 (http://www.theguardian.com/film/filmblog/2014/mar/12/300-rise-of-empire-reel-history- persians-greeks-salamis).

Walbank, F. W. (1957), *A Historical Commentary on Polybius, Volume I.* Oxford: Oxford University Press.

Wallinga, H. T. (2005), *Xerxes' Greek Adventure: The Naval Perspective* (*Mnemosyne supplement* 264). Leiden: Brill.

Wardle, D. (1998), *Valerius Maximus: Memorable Deeds and Sayings Book I.* Oxford: Oxford University Press.

—(2007), 'Caligula's bridge of boats: AD 39 or 40?', *Historia* 56, 118–20.

Wardman, A. (1976), *Rome's Debt to Greece.* London: P. Elek.

Waters, K. H. (1971), *Herodotus on Tyrants and Despots: A Study in Objectivity. Historia Einzelschriften.* Wiesbaden: F. Steiner.

Webb, R. (2009), *Ekphrasis, Imagination and Persuasion in Ancient Rhetorical Theory and Practice.* Farnham: Ashgate.

Weiland, J. (2007), ' "300" post-game: one-on-one with Zack Snyder', *Comic Book Resources* 14 March 2007 (http://www.comicbookresources.com/?page=article&old=1&id=9982).

West, M. L. (1992), *Ancient Greek Music.* Oxford: Oxford University Press.

Whitmarsh, T. (1999), 'Greek and Roman in dialogue: the pseudo-Lucianic *Nero*', *Journal of Hellenic Studies* 119: 142–60.

—(2001), *Greek Literature and the Roman Empire: The Politics of Imitation.* Oxford: Oxford University Press.

—(2005), *The Second Sophistic.* Greece and Rome New Surveys in the Classics. Oxford: Oxford University Press.

—(ed.) (2008), *The Cambridge Companion to the Greek and Roman Novel*. Cambridge: Cambridge University Press.

—(ed.) (2011), *Narrative and Identity in the Ancient Greek Novel: Returning Romance*. Cambridge: Cambridge University Press.

Wiesehöfer, J. (1978), *Der Aufstand Gaumātas und die Anfänge Dareios I*. Bonn: Habelt.

—(1996), *Ancient Persia*, A. Azodi (trans.). London: I. B. Tauris.

Willett, S. J. (2000), 'Catching Xerxes' tears in English: the styles of Herodotean translation. Review of *The Histories* by Robin Waterfield', *Arion* third series 8.1: 119–43.

Wills, L. M. (1994), 'The Jewish novellas', in Morgan and Stoneman (eds), pp. 223–38.

—(1995), *The Jewish Novel in the Ancient World*. Ithaca and London: Cornell University Press.

Winnington-Ingram, R. P. (1973), 'Zeus in the *Persae*', *Journal of Hellenic Studies* 93: 210–19.

Wiseman, T. P. (1979), *Clio's Cosmetics: Three Studies in Greco-Roman Literature*. Leicester: Leicester University Press.

Wolff, E. (1964), 'Das Weib des Masistes', *Hermes* 92: 51–8.

Worthington, I. (2003), 'Alexander, Philip, and the Macedonian background', in Roisman (ed.), pp. 69–98.

Wright, M. (2008), *Euripides: Orestes*. London: Duckworth.

Yamauchi, E. M. (1990), *Persia and the Bible*. Michigan: Baker Book House.

Zahrnt, M. (1996), 'Alexanders Übergang über den Hellespont', *Chiron* 26: 129–147.

Zanker, P. (1988), *The Power of Images in the Age of Augustus*, A. Shapiro (trans.). Ann Arbor: University of Michigan Press.

Index

A page reference in italics denotes an illustration.